Iron Aviator

ALSO BY CHRISTOPHER C. WEHNER
AND FROM MCFARLAND

*The 11th Wisconsin in the Civil War:
A Regimental History* (2008; softcover 2020)

IRON AVIATOR
*Cal Rodgers and the
First North American
Transcontinental Flight*

CHRISTOPHER C. WEHNER

McFarland & Company, Inc., Publishers
Jefferson, North Carolina

Library of Congress Cataloging-in-Publication Data

Names: Wehner, Christopher, 1969– author.
Title: Iron Aviator : Cal Rodgers and the first North American transcontinental flight / Christopher C. Wehner.
Description: Jefferson, North Carolina : McFarland & Company, Inc., Publishers, 2024 | Includes bibliographical references and index.
Identifiers: LCCN 2024024833 | ISBN 9781476693224 (paperback : acid free paper) ∞
ISBN 9781476651439 (ebook)
Subjects: LCSH: Rodgers, Calbraith Perry. | Vin Fiz (Airplane) | Air pilots—United States—Biography. | Transcontinental flights—United States—History—20th century. | BISAC: TRANSPORTATION / Aviation / History | LCGFT: Biographies.
Classification: LCC TL540.R576 W44 2024 | DDC 629.13092 [B]—dc23/eng/20240716
LC record available at https://lccn.loc.gov/2024024833

British Library cataloguing data are available
ISBN (print) 978-1-4766-9322-4
ISBN (ebook) 978-1-4766-5143-9

© 2024 Christopher C. Wehner. All rights reserved

No part of this book may be reproduced or transmitted in any form or by any means, electronic or mechanical, including photocopying or recording, or by any information storage and retrieval system, without permission in writing from the publisher.

Front cover images: Cal Rodgers, preparing to take off during his transcontinental journey (courtesy of San Diego Air & Space Museum); *top, Vin Fiz* Wright Model EX takes off from Sheepshead Bay, September 17, 1911 (The Wright Brothers Aeroplane Company— A Virtual Museum of Pioneer Aviation)

Printed in the United States of America

McFarland & Company, Inc., Publishers
Box 611, Jefferson, North Carolina 28640
www.mcfarlandpub.com

For Danny and Tori

Flight path of Cal Rodgers's transcontinental journey (author's collection).

Table of Contents

Preface	1
1. "I am a part of all that I have met"	5
2. "Death by scientific suicide"	14
3. "There is nothing in your old, flat world"	24
4. "The Windy City"	35
5. "[The] people below seemed to belong to the past"	46
6. "It was the only one of its kind the Wrights ever built"	56
7. "Carried by Rodgers aeroplane, *Vin Fiz*"	67
8. "I Endure.... I Conquer"	70
9. "Once you have left the ground to fly through the air"	79
10. "I hope I never have any more trouble in the air than I had today"	85
11. "There were five thousand pairs of eyes"	93
12. "The panorama of little villages spread out ahead"	97
13. "I breathed when I sailed over the edge of the cloud"	104
14. "Ambition coupled with energy is the driving force of mankind"	108
15. "For all of his back of steel determination"	114
16. "All the population that could get out of doors gazed"	121
17. "[Cal] is going to master the air and fly to the Pacific coast"	126
18. "[The] American people were melting down old heroes"	135
19. "I will not stop until I have reached the Pacific"	144

20.	"Thrilled as they never were before"	152
21.	"But as long as someone had to establish the long-distance record"	156
22.	"He [Rodgers] remains outwardly unimpressed"	168
23.	"I am proud to have blazed the way to the Pacific"	178
24.	"The spirit of man and his willingness to sacrifice his life"	183

Afterword: "The Iron Aviator"	191
Chapter Notes	195
Bibliography	213
Index	217

Preface

By the end of 1911, kicking off one of the most transformative decades in modern history, one of the top newsmakers in America and perhaps even the world was Calbraith Perry Rodgers and his attempt at aviation history. For three months, his transcontinental journey captured the imagination of the entire country. At a time when less than 2 percent of the nation had even seen an airplane, Cal's journey would draw thousands of people wherever he went. Tens of thousands filled parks and stadiums and lined fields to watch him fly. He was even proclaimed to be the greatest aviator there ever was.

A year earlier, Cal Rodgers was a virtual unknown. Even as he began his quest for aviation history, there were many who thought him ill-suited to be an aviator. Some said he was simply too big. In the early twentieth century, the average height and weight for a man were five feet eight and 150 pounds; Cal Rodgers stood at a massive six-four and weighed two hundred pounds. He had to almost fold himself into the pilot's chair. He was easily the largest aviator in America and perhaps the world. By comparison, the aircraft he would fly during the first ever transcontinental journey weighed about eight hundred pounds and could be easily carried by just a few men—as long as Cal was not in it. Perhaps most importantly, Rodgers lacked experience. He had only flown solo for an astonishing ninety minutes total while receiving his pilot's license just a little over a month before his attempt at aviation history, leaving him enough time to compete in only one aviation meet in Chicago.[1]

Rodgers's instructors noted that he had trouble with equilibrium and often could not keep the aircraft level: "Imagine flying across the country at a tilt!" said one. Others thought Rodgers to be a "mediocre" pilot at best. The Wright brothers privately considered Cal's attempt to be a "crazy" idea because their biplanes were not designed to travel four thousand miles. In fact, Cal's prowess was not in his flying skills at all, but in his incredible ability to light a cigar while in flight and keep it lit. To top it all off, Rodgers suffered from a crucial disability due to a childhood illness that left him almost completely deaf and impaired his senses. In an era when the pilot's senses were crucial because there were no instruments, Rodgers would not always know if his engine was even running properly. As he started his journey in September 1911, the odds seemed stacked against Rodgers even surviving his quest, let alone completing it.[2]

Cal Rodgers preparing to take off during his transcontinental journey (San Diego Air & Space Museum).

But the concerns and predictions about Cal Rodgers turned out to be ill-founded. After months of flying, sixty-nine landings and takeoffs, and sixteen crashes, he was nearing the end of his journey. By November, as he approached Los Angeles during the final leg of what the country and the world described as the most incredible feat in modern aviation, Rodgers had taken on an iconic status. Orville Wright could not help but declare that Cal must have been born with "four horseshoes in his pockets" to have survived such a journey. Those closest to him came to believe he was invincible, while some simply called him "the Iron Aviator." It was understandable, considering Rodgers had survived so many crashes, including several near-death experiences and two hospitalizations.[3]

As the Iron Aviator approached Imperial Junction, California, on November 4, speeding over the Salton Sea at four thousand feet, his worn-out engine exploded. The blast sent shrapnel slicing through the air, shredding Rodgers's leather jacket, and peeling the skin off his arm and shoulder. The plane lurched and almost rolled because of the explosion. His biplane was sent hurtling toward the earth in an unrecoverable dive at over a hundred miles an hour. Miraculously, Cal kept his wounded hand firmly gripping the elevator and warping wire levers as the plane spun out of control. He was nearly thrown from his seat because there was no harness to hold him in. But Rodgers did not fall, and after a few perilous moments, he managed to pull his aircraft back from its dive as smoke poured out of the ten-inch hole in his engine block. Though temporarily in control, he still had to land his dead aircraft somewhere safely, and he was running out of time.

1

"I am a part of all that I have met"

> "I am a part of all that I have met;
> Yet all experience is an arch where through
> Gleams that untravelled world,
> whose margin fades
> Forever and forever when I move."
> —Alfred Tennyson

The first time Charles Wiggin laid eyes on Calbraith Perry Rodgers, he was sure Cal was lost. The lanky, firm-jawed, giant of a man strolled into the hangar at the Wright brothers' flying school in Dayton, Ohio, sometime in June 1911, wearing an expensive suit and a shit-eating grin. Wiggin probably thought him to be another crazy investor, or maybe a salesman, or perhaps even a professional ball player wanting to take a ride in a flying machine—he never would have guessed he was meeting a future history-making aviator.[1]

Wiggin was a skinny sixteen-year-old who, just a year before, was a schoolboy in Atlanta when he first witnessed an airplane in flight while working at an auto speedway. Cal Rodgers would come to call Wiggin affectionately "the Kid" or "Wiggie." Anything that moved fast was the Kid's passion, and nothing moved as fast as a flying machine. He wanted to learn how to fly. Wiggin recalled years later, "I left home with two clean shirts and five dollars." He had headed out in search of the Wright brothers and would not stop until he found them.[2]

Wiggin wasn't much for school, but he was mechanically astute and determined to work on engines. When he learned about the Wright brothers' introductory flying school in Montgomery, Alabama, he left his family behind, hitching and walking the 160 miles. Because it took several days to get there, he missed the Wrights because they had already left to go back to Ohio. So, Wiggin continued on to Ohio and Dayton, where he began asking around about the Wright brothers. Someone told him to head out to Simms Station and that he couldn't miss it. There, he found Orville and Wilbur and begged for a chance to work with them. "I tried to make myself useful," remembered Wiggin, and that he did. He volunteered to do anything and everything. He cleaned up oil spills, picked up after the mechanics, and most importantly, he listened and watched. He slowly learned about airplanes and the engines that powered them. He spent countless hours in the hot sun, clipping the grass field that was the runway. When farmer Huffman's cows wandered out onto the runway, he was the first to shoo them away, often just in the nick of time as an aviator was about to land. Wiggin was "Johnny on the spot," but what he wanted more than anything was to earn his pilot's license.[3]

"You're too young, kid," said the Wrights whenever the Kid asked if he could fly. Still Wiggin begged and pleaded with every aviator that came and went to teach him how to fly, but the answer was always the same: "Sorry, kid." Though disappointed, he was not deterred; at least at first, he was just thrilled to get the chance to be a part of history. And that's how it went for Wiggin, day after day, until that hot June morning. As he was helping Al Welsh (the Wrights' chief instructor) with engine repairs, the silhouette of Calbraith Perry Rodgers broke the morning sunlight spilling onto the floor of the hangar.[4]

Born on January 12, 1879, in Pittsburgh, Pennsylvania, Rodgers was from the stock of American heroes. His forebears were adventurers and warriors. His great-granduncle was Oliver Hazard Perry, the hero of the Battle of Lake Erie during the War of 1812. He famously refused to abandon his crippled ship, the USS *Lawrence*, until it sank, forcing him to move to another vessel to continue the fight. It is not surprising that his ship's battle flag carried the slogan, "Never Give Up." It was in Cal's blood to be a fighter, to never give up. Cal's great-grandfather was none other than Matthew Calbraith Perry, the famous American navy commodore who opened Japan to the Western world in 1854. Not to be outdone, Rodgers's father, also named Calbraith Perry, was an army captain when he died fighting American Indians in the Southwest. Ironically, it wasn't a bullet or arrow that struck down Captain Rodgers, but a lightning strike. Caught with his men in a severe thunderstorm, lightning struck their camp and killed only Perry; no one else was injured. Though he did not die in battle, he was respected and admired for his bravery and character. Captain Perry was only thirty-three years old when he orphaned Cal and left his mother a widow. To read the tribute for him in the *United States Army and Navy Journal*, that he was "brave to recklessness" and "his character was perfect," provokes one to think of his son during his transcontinental journey.[5]

"Before you could get a Perry to abandon his mission," noted one newspaper reporter, "the Devil would have to drag him 'round Good Hope and 'round the Horn and 'round perdition's flames." Calbraith Perry Rodgers, in his quest for greatness, would have the same determination and suffer from the same stubbornness.[6]

Cal's mother, Maria Wrightman, married his father on December 11, 1873, outside of Pittsburgh. Her family were wealthy landowners and extremely religious. The elder Calbraith met Maria while he was in the military, stationed in Pittsburgh. When Captain Rodgers died, they had two children, and she was four months pregnant with Cal. Maria decided to stay in Pittsburgh to be close to her mother, Martha Chambers. His mother and grandmother, two strong and independent women, raised Cal. Maria's sister Elizabeth, interestingly, married Captain Calbraith's younger brother, John. They were brought together during the captain's funeral and married a year later. Cal grew up in Shadyside and lived a comfortable but not extravagant childhood; his mother raised him and his siblings on an army widow's pension. Though not as wealthy as some of the Rodgerses, they never went without.[7]

Shadyside was like much of the growing American suburbia, stuck between Gilded Age industrialization and the Progressive Era of transformation. Cities were filthy and crime ridden; electricity wasn't realized until 1882 and was not widely utilized until the early twentieth century. The airplane and automobile were unknown. But the suburbs were quiet and isolated from the crime and filth of urbanization. Trains and trolleys rumbled out of the cities and through the suburbs consistently, and they always captured Cal's attention.[8]

Cal was an adventurous boy who loved exploring the countryside and the neighborhoods near him. He was also mechanically inclined. His mother noted, "My boy was a mechanical genius," showing an appreciation for all things motorized, especially trains. He even told his mother that one day he was going to be an "engineer on a locomotive train." Cal was described as playful and inquisitive. His mother was confident he could use these traits to succeed in a fashion that would suit the Perry lineage.[9]

On some weekends and holidays, Cal spent time with his cousin John Rodgers, whose parents, John and Elizabeth Rodgers, lived a lavish lifestyle in Havre de Grace. Cal and John became very close, playing on the massive grounds and in the many rooms of the mansion the Rodgers lived in. John was Cal's best friend and very influential in his life. John was the first to introduce airplanes to Cal and traveled with him on his historic journey.[10]

Everything changed for Cal in 1885 when he fell ill with scarlet fever. The highly infectious disease ravaged him. He spiked a high fever, and his body turned red and swollen. Cal's skin literally peeled off, starting around his neck and continuing until nearly his entire body seemed to shed a layer like a snake. The pain was excruciating. Doctors worried that severe complications such as pneumonia or organ failure could materialize. Fortunately, the fever broke, the swelling subsided, and the doctors told his mother he would make a full recovery. But what they did not know yet was that the Eustachian tube in his ears had ruptured, causing irrevocable damage and nearly complete hearing loss.[11]

When Cal fully recovered, he was not the same kid. It took some time for his mother and the family doctor to understand the extent of his deafness. The outgoing, rambunctious, and adventurous boy was now a withdrawn and soft-spoken one. Cal became, as his mother noted, a more "serious boy" than his mates. His speech became low pitched and unclear because of his significant hearing loss. "He talked with great effort and very slowly," it was noted. Cal now struggled to follow conversations and became confused and irritated, and ultimately, withdrawn. A growth spurt churned out a teenager who was bigger than anyone else, which only added to the distress, loneliness, and isolation. Adults regularly confused him for being older and more mature and then were left befuddled by his apparent aloofness and detachment.[12]

Though raised without a father, he did not want for male companionship. As mentioned, his cousin John was a constant in his life and very important to him. Virtually all of Cal's male influences were in the army or navy, which helped to shape his personality, his seriousness, and his confidence, even after his sickness, when he became entrenched in loneliness and isolation. During his teen years, Cal grew apart from his religious mother and grandmother, both of whom were devout Presbyterians. Cal had little interest in the church and instead threw himself into working with his hands, assembling and disassembling anything mechanical he could find. When he was forced to attend Sunday service, he always snuck something in to tinker with. Cal was interested in mechanics—things that moved and were fast. He liked to ride fast horses as a boy, and when he was older, the automobile arrived on the scene. Fast cars and motorcycles drew his attention. He also learned quickly that his size had one important advantage: at a time when a young man in his position could end up on vastly different paths, Cal fortunately found himself engaged in sports and physical adventure.[13]

1. "I am a part of all that I have met"

Because of Cal's disability, he was not an especially good student. His mother meekly stated that he simply "didn't care much for books." Whatever the reason, while Cal's brother, John Perry, attended the prestigious Shady Side Academy, Cal ended up attending the startup Mercersburg Academy. Cal was not a good student there either but instead cared more for "sports and tinkering with things." Cal's mother, Maria, successfully encouraged him to stay in school, where he focused primarily on sports. In 1897, when Cal enrolled, he was seventeen years old and was ready to leave the confines of his mother's residence and her overbearing influence. Not surprisingly, he played football. At six-three and 170 pounds, he was the largest player and helped lead the team to their best season since the school's founding. An 1898 yearbook photo of the team shows the broad-shouldered Cal, obviously bigger than anyone else, right in the middle.[14]

In that same yearbook, Cal Rodgers's class photo included the quote, "I am part of all that I have met." The quote is from British poet and author of *The Charge of the Light Brigade*, Alfred Tennyson:

> "I am a part of all that I have met;
> Yet all experience is an arch where through
> Gleams that untravelled world,
> whose margin fades
> Forever and forever when I move."

Cal's quote is very telling; he was a young man of sensitivity and intelligence, more so than was probably thought of him at the time. No one knew it yet, but his future would belong to an "untravelled world" of flight and history-making adventure. What most likely saved Cal were his athletic career and his adventurous spirit. He threw himself into football like he would with racing and, eventually, flying.

He didn't stay at Mercersburg Academy but instead enrolled at St. Luke's in Bustleton, northeast of Philadelphia. There, he became a football standout. The local newspaper had a writeup on the football team, and Cal was described as "having considerable football experience," having already played a season at Mercersburg. He was described as the largest player on the team by far. The team featured a solid starting unit with a fullback that was highly touted. The newspaper article noted that the "prospects were high" for St. Luke's that season.[15]

Football demanded physical prowess, intelligence to grasp play concepts, and toughness and courage to execute the game plan. Rodgers possessed all those characteristics, but what most likely drew him to the sport was that, once the play started, no communication was required. No other sport fit Rodgers like football. Baseball would have involved too much constant communication that Cal simply would not have been able to do.

The St. Luke's football team struggled, but that didn't stop Rodgers from excelling. The squad opened the season being manhandled by Germantown, twenty-nine to zero; Germantown was bound for the playoffs. The next game against the Bordentown Military Institute went a little better, but St. Luke's was still skunked eleven to nothing. A few weeks later, a rematch saw St. Luke's battle to a tie, zero to zero. Between those two games, St. Luke's was upended by Delancey, twenty-three to zero, with a reporter writing that Delancey had their way with the St. Luke's line "with the exception of right guard Rodgers." St. Luke's finished the season strong, however, with a series of convincing shutout wins. The winning streak proved good enough to help Rodgers make All-Conference. Cal was a first-team selection and described as "the giant guard from St. Luke's."[16]

After finishing his football and academics at St. Luke's, Cal moved to New York, probably to get further away from his controlling mother. His sister, Martha, lived in New York; she was married and had a room for her brother to rent. His mother, however, now Maria Sweitzer, had remarried and kept a part-time residence in New York as well. Not long after moving, Cal joined the New York Yacht Club, intending to follow the family tradition of naval captains.[17]

The first automobile parade took place on November 4, 1899, in downtown New York. A year later, on November 3, 1900, America's first national automobile show opened in Madison Square Garden. New York was in the midst of the Gilded Age, and the massive industrialization created not just a large horizontal city but an ever-growing vertical one as well. Skyscrapers, automobiles, factories, and the hustle and bustle of city life were no doubt appealing to Cal's adventurous spirit. When he arrived in New York, it was a bustling city on the move, which would have stimulated his curiosity.

Cal's dream of becoming a naval officer did not last long. His cousin John Rodgers had already been accepted to the Naval Academy at Annapolis, and Cal expected to join him, only to learn that his hearing disability excluded him from eligibility. Cal's "deep disappointment" with being unable to follow in the family footsteps and become a "sea fighter" cannot be overstated. Devastated, Cal withdrew again from another social group and found himself right back where he was as a young boy, rejected and isolated.[18]

On September 14, 1901, while attending the Pan-American Exposition in Buffalo, anarchist Leon Czolgosz assassinated President William McKinley. McKinley's bold and charismatic vice president, Teddy

Roosevelt, became the youngest president in United States history. The Progressive, trust-busting Roosevelt was about to reside over a period of great change in the country. That same year, Rodgers's uncle, Admiral Frederick Rodgers, invited him to attend a ceremony in Japan celebrating his ancestor, Commodore Perry. Cal apparently wasn't all that interested and later was uninvited. His embarrassment at not making the Naval Academy was most likely the reason. His mother was disappointed in his lack of interest in the event, and in an effort to get him to do something, she sent him on a railroad trip to the West Coast. This he did enthusiastically, but when he arrived in Los Angeles, he was not impressed. "Although 100,000 souls call it home, they do not do much to show themselves, and the atmosphere is one of a small village," he wrote his mother. "Hollywoodland" and the hustle and bustle of show business had not yet taken place. The movie industry was still largely in New York and New Jersey. Los Angeles, compared to New York, was indeed a small, though growing, city at the time, with a population of just over one hundred thousand. Still, the journey across the country must have been an eye-opening experience for Cal, seeing and experiencing new regions of the country, some of which he would travel through during his transcontinental voyage.[19]

Rodgers's final stop was San Francisco, and the vibe and energy of the town suited him, though mainly he showed more interest in the women, who were "quite friendly." The city was bigger and more to Cal's liking, though it would tragically experience its great earthquake in 1906, devastating the city and killing over one thousand of its inhabitants. Apparently, Rodgers never discovered love while continuing to explore the state, returning east a few weeks later. But California never left him—he must have seen his future there.[20]

On December 17, 1903, Wilbur and Orville Wright successfully flew the first airplane at Kitty Hawk. Though the dawn of a new era was approaching, the idea of flying machines carrying someone across more than just a field was still some years away. In early 1904, Rodgers was still pursuing boating as he maintained his membership in the New York Yacht Club and even considered the idea of racing. He also met and mingled with some of the country's wealthiest and most important people, including family members of the Armour Company out of Chicago, which would play a very important role in his aviation career.[21]

His cousin John got Rodgers hooked on motorcycles for a time after he purchased a Harley-Davidson in 1904. Together, they worked on it and entered races, eventually competing in a five-hundred-mile race from New York to Buffalo. About this time, Cal took up his one and only vice, smoking cigars. He could often be seen riding his motorcycle, wearing a leather jacket and a cloth cap. Cal dated and was even seen as a bit of a playboy because of his height and charming looks. But he never found himself in a serious relationship. How much his disability hindered him while dating is unknown.

During the fall of 1905, Cal was a crewmember on a boat participating in a yacht race to Bermuda. Mabel Avis Graves was boarding a different yacht heading for Nassau when she missed a step and fell into the water. Rodgers was nearby, saw her take a spill, jumped into the water, and carried her out. Mabel was immediately smitten with the handsome and tall Calbraith Rodgers, and after a short courtship, the twenty-seven-year-old Cal married the twenty-three-year-old Mabel on May 4, 1906, in New York. But there was one significant issue: Cal's mother, Maria, didn't care for his new wife and may have even pleaded with him not to marry her. By most accounts, it was a rocky relationship between two very strong-willed women.[22]

Cal and Mabel settled into married life and lived uneventfully for the next few years, and this must have greatly annoyed the adventurist Cal. He did continue to sail, race yachts, and drive fast cars. He also continued his motorcycle racing in upstate New York. But it wasn't

Cal and Mabel Rodgers, unknown location, circa 1911 (San Diego Air & Space Museum).

1. "I am a part of all that I have met" 13

enough; he wanted to prove himself in some grand way. Perhaps the final straw that motivated him was when Mabel's father asked Cal to join his real estate company in Bennington. Rodgers declined and took Mabel on a cruise, pondering his future. Mabel was loyal to Cal (perhaps even to a fault) in whatever he wished to do, and she always had his back. He wanted to do more than just celebrate the ancestry he had thus far endured. And most certainly, he wanted to do more than settle down and become, of all things, a salesman. Adventure was calling to him.[23]

Rodgers's quest for greatness started the morning he stepped into the Wrights' hangar and first met the Kid. Wiggin didn't know it yet, but he would join Cal on his journey of a lifetime just a few months later—an experience that would forever affect the young man. Rodgers introduced himself and told Wiggin that he was there to see about some flying lessons and perhaps even purchase a biplane.

2

"Death by scientific suicide"

There was a calmness after the squall of wind as the crowd that gathered twelve miles west of New Orleans in Harahan, Louisiana, stood in stunned silence. They watched in horror as the pilotless monoplane's tail swung up and then plummeted nose first into the soft swampy ground. Just moments before, a gust of wind had thrown the pilot from the plane. He fell one hundred feet headfirst into the ground, his mangled body sticking partially out of the earth as his aircraft crashed just feet away. There would be no airshow tomorrow.[1]

It was December 31, 1910, and the pilot was John B. Moisant of Chicago, considered one of the most experienced and daring pilots in the world. Moisant was preparing for the next day's event in New Orleans. He was confident; some would have said flamboyant, perhaps even to a fault. Recently, after a close call when his plane crashed at Belmont Park and he miraculously walked away unscathed, Moisant proclaimed, "No aeroplane can kill me.... I know it can't kill me." He was a pioneer of sorts in early aviation—one of the first to carry a passenger over the English Channel, to fly over cities, to perform stunts at airshows, and he was also a cofounder of the first flying circus. Moisant took flying lessons at the Blériot School, instructed by none other than the great Louis Blériot. Moisant once said that flying was "nine tenths confidence" and "one tenth luck." Unfortunately, the luck of flying caught up to him, as it did to so many other pioneers of aviation.[2]

Seventeen hundred miles away, perhaps on the very next day, the most beloved aviator (certainly among his peers) in America perished tragically as well. It was during the Los Angeles International Air Meet—the first of its kind to take place in North America. Archibald Hoxsey was getting ready to try to best his own altitude record of 11,474 feet (accomplished just days before) when he heard the news of Moisant's passing. "There's another good man gone," Hoxsey noted, "but he was awfully reckless." Hoxsey had no intention of taking any chances that day and was already considering retirement from the sport. "I want to get enough money to see my mother comfortably fixed," he said, "to get a nest egg for myself, then I will get into something else." Something with a real future, he surmised. Hoxsey smiled and joked with those around him as he readied for takeoff. "The crowd must be entertained," he meekly said, and away he went. After a half hour of flying at about seven thousand feet, his biplane became erratic and then plummeted to the earth, killing him instantly. As with so many other such incidents of the era, the cause of the crash was never fully understood. Some surmise that he succumbed to altitude sickness and lost consciousness after days of high flying.[3]

They called it "scientific suicide." The science of aviation was so new that many considered flying to be suicidal. Newspapers described it as "falling" or "dropping"—a sudden, unexpected dive, lurch, dip, or occasionally a topple and then a rapid plunge as the plane crashed into the earth. The wind could lift and throw these light biplanes and monoplanes without warning. Reports of pilots being blown off course by miles in a matter of minutes were common. By 1910, many had concluded that humans were not meant to fly.[4]

There is no progress without struggle, without sacrifice. Failure is a part of success. Thomas Edison once said, "I have not failed 10,000 times—I've successfully found 10,000 ways that will not work." Edison failed thousands of times while trying to find the right filament for his incandescent lightbulb. With aviation, failure was indeed progress, but it was costly. How many lost souls would it cost to advance the science of aviation, some wondered? Outwardly, aviators were usually cocky and, as some thought, an arrogant bunch. "Give me enough power," boasted Eugene Ely, "and I'll fly a barn door."[5]

It didn't matter that some thought it crazy and suicidal to fly; aviators believed in their profession and believed they were improving it. "If I thought that aviation was only a sensational way of committing suicide," said aviator Walter Brookings, "I would not go up." Pilots knew that some called it scientific suicide and defended their profession with unequivocal faith. "It cannot be called scientific suicide except for the reckless," said another aviator when asked. He continued, "Once a man becomes an aviator he cannot stop," and "it's in his blood." Passion was something most if not all aviators possessed; the majority thrived on it.[6]

Aviator casualty stories in the news were often full of the terrifying, the tragic, and sometimes the strange. Figuring out the direct cause of the fall rarely, if ever, concluded in a consensus among those who witnessed the event. When aviator Ralph Johnstone careened into the ground outside the mile-high city of Denver, Colorado, there were so many contradictory accounts of the crash that no one really knew what had happened. Some witnesses described the wings of his machine folding up or giving way. Others saw him lose control, panic, overcorrect, and crash. One eyewitness even said he thought Johnstone tried to crawl and reach for something. Whatever the cause, it was concluded that

> after the machine toppled over, he lost his seat and the control of the levers, and even after the machine had righted itself on the way down, he was unable to get hold of the levers and continue the balance.[7]

Flying was described as "balancing" in the air like a rider on a bucking horse. Obviously, the airplanes of the era were antiquated by today's standards. These early airplanes, known as biplanes or monoplanes, were flimsy and prone to all kinds of mechanical failures. New technology was always unstable in its infancy. The first steamships a century before sometimes randomly exploded, killing and scalding everyone aboard. The only good thing about early airplanes was that there was usually just one soul aboard when the machines exploded or crashed. There were no cockpits or protective siding of any kind. The pilot was not harnessed with seatbelts. There were no gauges or instruments save for a warping lever and elevator, and just a strip of rag attached to a brace told the pilot if the plane was ascending or descending. That was about it. There were no airports or proper maps; aviators had to follow railroads (known as their *iron compass*) to make their way.[8]

One of the most frightening things pilots encountered was invisible. Only an aviator in the sky knows "how turbulent is the atmosphere even at its most calmest," stated a 1911 flying manual. Air currents and what they called "air pockets" caused the airplanes to lose altitude quickly. These pockets were heated by the sun and surrounded by cooler air in the clouds, producing what we know today as turbulence. Warm air rises, and cold air descends rapidly. These early aviators noted that it was warmer air that became unstable when surrounded by cooler air, thus creating pockets that caused them to drop suddenly. Aviators preferred to fly in the morning or late afternoon, when the air tended to be more stable. Think of the most harrowing modern-day jetliner flight you have ever had, and imagine yourself in a flimsy biplane—terrifying, to be sure. These pockets of unstable air could be deadly, and when combined with crosswinds shooting off hills, tall buildings, or bluffs, the helpless biplane of 1911 was usually thrown into an unrecoverable dive, plummeting down to earth.[9]

Wilbur Wright was known for reminding his pilots regularly that "the more you know about the air, the fewer the chances you are willing to take." Too often, the novice or daredevil without sense did not heed these words or even try to understand the wind, and the results were deadly. Even seasoned and relatively "safe" pilots fell victim to the wind and its perils. After all, as one modern-day observer exaggeratedly noted, these flying pioneers flew on what could be described as essentially two large ironing boards wired together.[10]

On top of turbulence, no matter the season, it is cold at high altitude. To battle the cold, aviators wore cork-lined leather hats, leather jackets, gloves, corduroy pants, and often stuffed newspapers inside their jackets to help stem the cold of altitude weather. They had goggles, and for extreme temperatures, some used facemasks to protect them from the ice-cold wind. The altitude and freezing cold could render the pilot unconscious in moments. It was called "ethereal asphyxia," essentially the reduction of oxygen causing the brain to shut down and the uncontrolled plane to rapidly descend, with pilots sometimes regaining consciousness just in time to realize their fate as the earth rushed up at them. "It lurks in the pockets of the upper air strata," Cal Rodgers said, not completely understanding the science of it. It "creeps irresistibly upon the senses of the aviator," and before the pilot knew it, it was over.[11]

Motor failure was a common problem. The first airplane engines sometimes erupted or simply choked and sputtered to a halt. Without power, early airplanes were left gliding before volplaning and then usually had an emergency crash landing.[12]

Another horrific crash resulted in the following description in *Aeronautics* magazine:

> Testimony is conflicting, but the census of opinion seems to indicate that [the pilot] tried to [re]start his motor. The propellers revolved swiftly a few times, then the engine stopped.... He was headed steeply for the ground and after turning over, the machine plunged head on at a very steep angle for the ground.[13]

How often pilot error was responsible for crashes was debatable. As one can imagine, very few dared to fly. These first airplanes were so unreliable, so limited in their capacity for prolonged flight that they were shipped by railroad to aviation meets. You didn't dare fly them that far. To fly long distances, most believed, was foolhardy; an aircraft would never make the trip in one piece.

Those men and women that did fly were called "birdmen," "skymen," and "aviators." They were often speed junkies and daredevils, so it is no wonder why many thought it suicidal to fly. It was very dangerous, and a large percentage of the first generation of pilots simply did not live long. Life expectancy for aviators was so short that not a single life insurance company in the United States was willing to insure them. A state congressional representative even brought forth a bill prohibiting flight above one thousand feet, because it was considered suicide to fly to such heights and beyond. What the distinguished representative did not understand was that at higher altitude, a pilot had longer with a dead aircraft to volplane down and find a safe landing spot, thus making it safer.[14]

If these aviators felt fear, which they certainly did at some point, they rarely shared that emotion. They knew what they were doing was dangerous; that was obvious. They spoke of luck, or the lack of it, and what they called the "hoodoo" of flying. The allure or challenge of flight—the need to experience the rush of speed and flight—was too tempting for some. The feeling they received—that high they undoubtedly experienced as the endorphins were released—was enough to drive them time and again to go up, to challenge themselves and their machines. Every time they came back down to earth, they were a little bit more fearless and a lot more determined to go back up again. And the stories of near-death escapes they could tell were just as much a part of the thrill.

In 1910, thirty-two American pilots died, while another seventy-seven perished worldwide. One comedian at the time bloviated that aviators "flew like birds and came down like stones." Sadly, there was a lot of truth in that. Philip Parmelee, one of the Wright brothers' exhibition fliers, noted that "fifty per cent" of the aviators flying in 1910 were dead by the summer of 1911. Parmelee himself perished on June 1, 1912, in Yakima, Washington, when his plane fell into an unrecoverable dive during bad weather and plummeted to the ground, most likely the victim of an air pocket.[15]

The list of causes for aviator crashes included "wings snapped off," "motor exploded," "crushed under machine," "fell on rocks with machine," "fell 350 feet with machine," "dropped 500 feet," "killed instantly (by something)," "dropped out of sight," "machine turned over twice" and then dropped. As noted, with no safety measures, the pilot's survival was left to chance—usually no chance at all. Not to mention that the engines were usually mounted behind or next to the pilots and often crushed them to death on impact, which is why it was standard practice for pilots to try to jump from their plane before impacting the ground.[16]

In 1911, in response to the rising death toll, the Aero Club of America placed more stringent rules on receiving a pilot's license and increased the difficulty of the test one had to pass. But still, the casualty list grew. Rodgers had to pass this test when he gained his license, which he did easily in one day.[17]

2. "Death by scientific suicide"

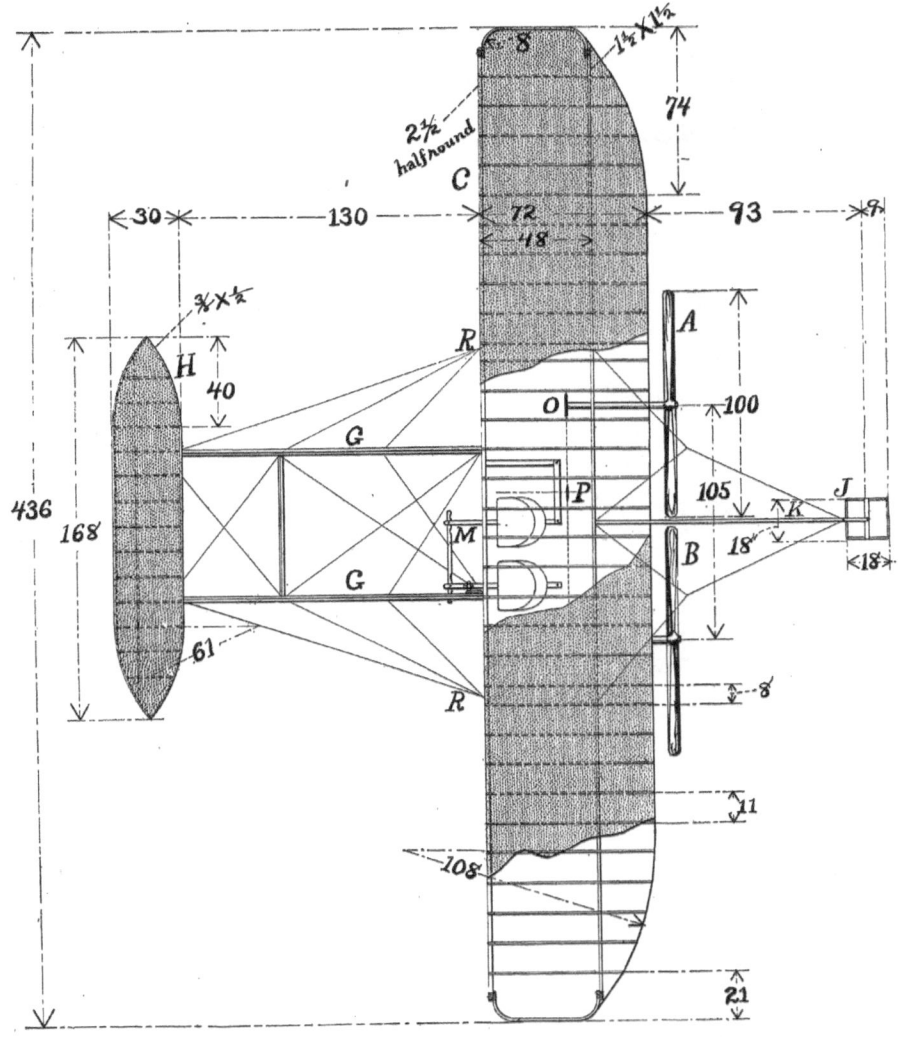

Schematic view looking down on a Wright Biplane (author's collection).

"It is deplorable that such a frightful toll must be paid while the advances in the science [of aviation] are being made," said an editorial in the *New York Times*. There was a price to be paid, as one pilot described it, the "devil's due," and in order for aviation to advance as a science, there was a "toll demanded for advancement and progress." So they continued to fly, defying gravity, and some even wondered if they were perhaps even defying God.[18]

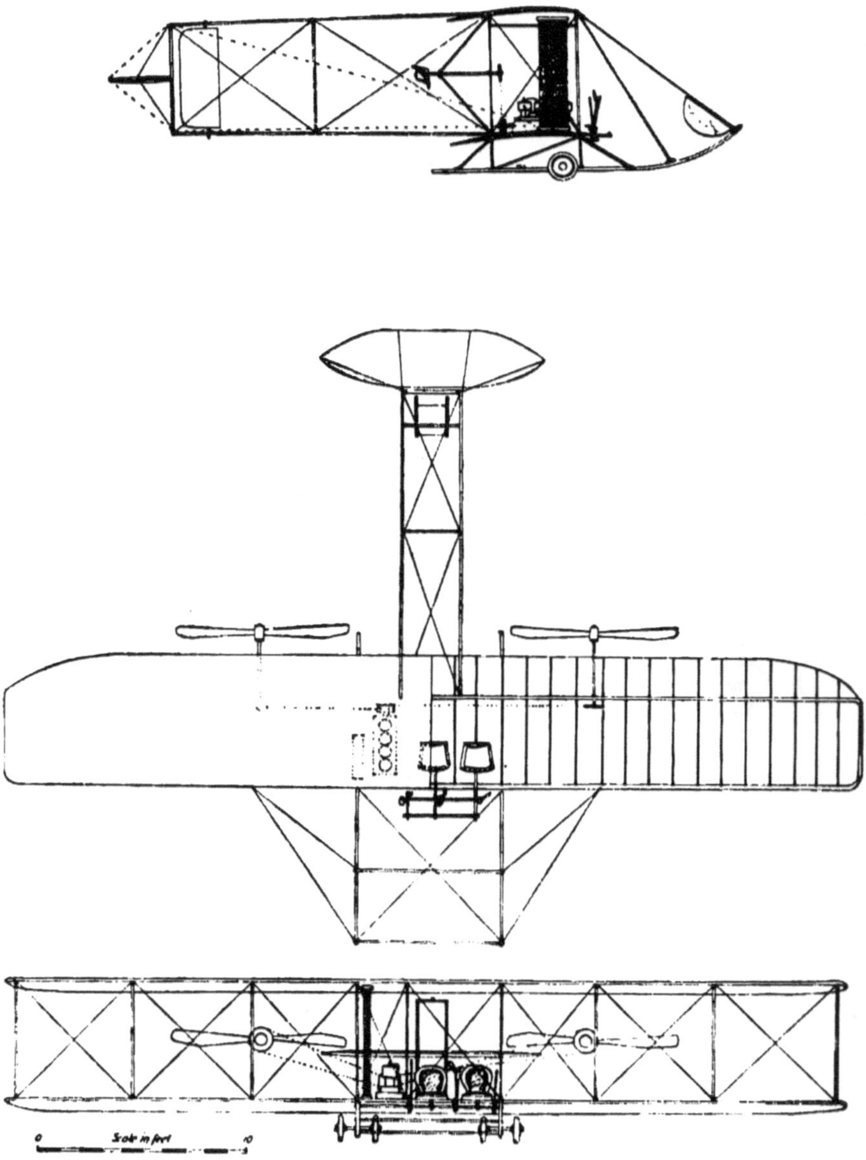

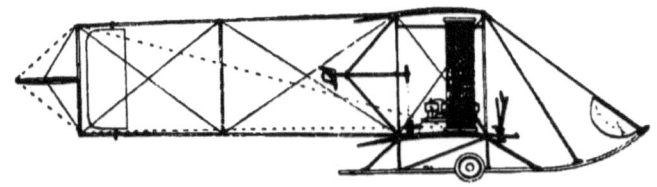

PLAN AND ELEVATION OF THE WRIGHT BIPLANE, MODEL B

Wright Model B Biplane diagram (author's collection).

2. "Death by scientific suicide" 21

Excellent view of how exposed the aviator is in the biplanes of the era. Photograph is of a Wright Model B, pilot unknown (author's collection).

After the deaths of Johnstone and Badger during the Chicago International Aviation Meet, the *New York Times* ran another editorial titled, "Competitive Aviation Reprehensible." The writer stated that the present capabilities of airplanes were "so ill-adapted to the purpose" of safe flying that they should be banned until the science of flying had caught up. Some believed these early pilots only flew for the amusement of the crowds and were ill-suited to helping advance the "art of aviation" anyway. Aviation meets and air shows were simply a spectacle of death and bemusement for the morbid crowds. The editorial went on to note the "appalling" death rate among aviators seeking fortune and fame.[19]

The crowds themselves were often boisterous and vitriolic, and even taunted aviators to take chances. One headline read, "Aviator, Jeered into Air by Crowd, Killed." In Troy, Ohio, on September 22, 1911, as Cal Rodgers was attempting his historic journey, twenty-three-year-old pilot Frank H. Miller had already performed an air show but was scheduled to fly one last time in the afternoon when the wind picked up. He told the crowd that he was done for the day, which was met with hostility. Eventually, the crowd began to chant "coward" over and over. The young pilot could not get out of the crowd; angered, he boarded his aircraft, had his mechanic start the engine, yelled at the crowd, "I'll be glad when this is over," and took off. Shortly after takeoff, he had engine trouble, and the wind picked up the aircraft and slammed it into the field like a ball meeting a bat. It hit with such force that the gas tank exploded, scattering pieces of the biplane "hundreds of feet away," killing Miller instantly.[20]

It was not uncommon for pilots to encounter hostile crowds if they refused to fly or if they performed what the crowd thought was an uninspired demonstration. The crowds demanded excitement, and one observer even commented that what the morbid masses desired the most (perhaps like some of today's NASCAR audiences) was to witness a crash. One of the aerial stunts the crowd wanted the aviator to perform was the *loop to loop*, which required the pilot to fly close to upside down in order to complete the circle—a dangerous maneuver that tested not only the mettle of the pilot but the limited engine power and lift of these early airplanes. Very few pilots even attempted such a stunt.[21]

In early November 1911, aspiring aviator Frank B. Elser was about to fly during an event when he witnessed the death of a good friend who lost control and crashed during a loop maneuver. Elser took off his jacket and walked away from the aviation show. He never flew again. He later became a reporter and wrote for the *Saturday Evening Post* about the ills of flying: "The appalling and ever growing death list is making even the daredevils think—they are not laughing the specter off and talking about fatalism as they used to."[22]

The results of aviation meets routinely appeared in newspapers and sometimes on the front page. The exploits of these early fliers were spoken of in an almost reverential tone. Just as Cal Rodgers was starting his historic transcontinental flight, a newspaper story told of yet another "amateur" pilot who "fell" (260 feet) to his death while flying his aircraft during a trial run. It was the fifty-third such death in 1911 alone. By the end of the year, 131 pilots had lost their lives—one every three days. How many aviators worldwide were flying is unknown, but of the known pilots (licensed), one in three met their deaths while flying in 1911.[23]

The percentage of pilot deaths between 1910 and 1912 has been estimated to be as high as 70 percent, a truly staggering number. Precise numbers are hard to ascertain, but a safe estimate is that during these early years, over half died. The Wright brothers' flying team was so decimated by crashes and deaths that it disbanded in November 1911 after a bloody year of traveling airshows. According to one study in 1912, of the one hundred and thirty aviator deaths, twenty-four were attributed to defects in the machine itself. But the vast majority, fifty-four, were directly traceable to pilot error. What pilot error meant was always up

2. "Death by scientific suicide"   23

for interpretation at a time when few truly understood what it took to fly.²⁴

Like most new professions, the field of aviation was at first dismissed. In February 1911, it was admitted that aviation was a "special field of cranks and idlers." Jealousy and fights were not unheard of among aviators and their managers, as well as lawsuits. On top of struggling for recognition as a profession, some pilots weren't even paid well. If you couldn't afford to own your own airplane, you flew for the Wrights, the Curtiss Company, or an owner or manager. They took most of their pilots' winnings from meets and only paid them a pittance. Aviators called out their managers, describing the situation as "starvation wages." At the Chicago Aviation Meet, in conditions described as dangerous, about forty aviators participated under contract, sometimes making only fifty dollars for flying while making their managers thousands of dollars. The Chicago meet was one of the most dangerous to take place, resulting in several deaths and numerous crashes. The Wrights were even accused of being stingy with their pilots under contract.²⁵

In 1912, the former secretary of the Aero Club of America noted the qualities demanded of an aviator to safely pilot an airplane, stating a pilot must "meet new demands on eyesight, hearing, and powers of enduring the cold and fatigue." The pilot must also have a heightened sense of equilibrium and be physically and mentally sound.²⁶

When one considers the qualities required for flight, Cal did not meet the suggested criteria. Hearing and equilibrium were essential for safe and successful flight. "It is the aviator's ear that enables him to distinguish the characteristic sounds of the motor," noted one expert. Though he was severely defective regarding hearing and equilibrium, nothing would stop Rodgers from attempting aviation history.²⁷

3

"There is nothing in your old, flat world"

> "There is nothing in your old, flat world that can prepare you for the experience of this new one."
> —Lieutenant John Rodgers to Cal Rodgers

Cal Rodgers was enduring his life until the fateful afternoon when his cousin John Rodgers informed him of the speed and thrill of flying machines and invited him to come see what it was all about. In March 1911, the United States Congress appropriated $25,000 designated for naval aviation research, which paved the way for Cal's cousin Lieutenant John Rodgers, US Navy, to train at the Wright brothers' facility. He arrived in Dayton, Ohio, on March 29 with a mission to study the "art of aviation" and how the navy could use airplanes. The consensus in military circles was that sharp shooters and snipers could easily take out the exposed pilots, and they weren't wrong. But there were still other uses for reconnaissance and communication that airplanes in their current state could be used for.[1]

Wilbur Wright was in France overseeing the French Wright Company, which was having financial difficulties. Orville met with Lieutenant Rodgers, and it was agreed that the navy would send three pilots, including the lieutenant, to come back in early May to learn how to fly a Wright biplane. After learning to fly, Lieutenant Rodgers reached out to Cal with the exciting news. By this time, Cal had already sailed and raced cars and motorcycles; no doubt, the idea of flying an airplane appealed to him. So, when he heard from his cousin about the speed of flight, he was hooked. John wrote to him, saying, "There's nothing like it [flying]. You're up there. Watching the land glide by, bobbing, dipping as if in a boat but you can see nothing, only feel it. For speed you can't beat flying." After just a few lessons, "you'll be soaring like a hawk." Cal wasted no time and headed out to Ohio and the Wright brothers' flying school.[2]

Cal Rodgers arrived at the Wright Brothers Company in June 1911, where he encountered Wiggin ("the Kid") and was introduced to aviators Walter Brookins, Clifford Turpin, and Arthur "Al" Welsh. All were former Wright students who were now instructors and part of the Wright brothers' exhibition team that traveled the country performing airshows. Welsh was assigned as Rodgers's flight instructor. He was considered one of the Wrights' finest aviators, and though he performed stunts, Welsh was known for being cautious. He respected the aviation profession and bemoaned the risk-takers who trivialized it. Sadly, Welsh perished on June 11, 1912, while flying a Wright Brothers test plane for the army. The biplane plummeted from a thousand feet and crashed, killing him and a passenger instantly.[3]

Orville Wright greeted Cal and took him to his office for paperwork. Rodgers paid $850 to learn how to fly, an enormous sum of money at the time. Consider paying a large amount of money to be taught how to do something incredibly dangerous that might ultimately kill you—priceless, to be sure. When the paperwork was completed, Orville and

Clifford Turpin (*left*) and Lieutenant John Rodgers (*right*) (Library of Congress).

Orville (*left*) and Wilbur Wright (*right*) on the porch of their home at 7 Hawthorne Street in Dayton (Library of Congress).

3. "There is nothing in your old, flat world"   27

Rodgers shook hands. "Don't be nervous," Orville told Cal. "It's just like learning to ride a bicycle." Then he smiled and walked away. Cal Rodgers's arrival in Dayton was so uneventful to Orville Wright that Rodgers did not receive a single entry or note in their log or diary, whereas Lieutenant Rodgers was mentioned numerous times during his visits.[4]

From there, Rodgers was introduced to Charles E. Taylor, the Wrights' chief mechanician. A mechanical expert who had been with the Wrights since Kitty Hawk, Taylor was a gruff man of few words and had grown tired of thrill seekers with money buying their way into the "game." Al Welsh and Taylor would serve as Cal's mentors. Welsh, like Taylor, had little patience for someone like Rodgers. Welsh looked up at Cal, who was six inches taller than he was, and said, "You'll never make a flier ... tall ships never leave the water." And that was how Rodgers was introduced to the world of aviation—with smug dismissiveness, a degree of contempt, and doubt about his abilities. But it wasn't all thorny for Cal; Wiggin "the Kid" took a liking to him and was his supporter and, by the time he started his continental journey, ultimately, his friend.[5]

They took Rodgers into a hangar (really more of a big shed) where a Wright Flyer Model B biplane stood. No doubt, Cal was wide-eyed with wonder as he placed his hands on an airplane for the first time. They spent some time going over every detail of the biplane and how it worked. Rodgers would not just be able to fly by the time he was done, but he would also be able to work on the biplane when it malfunctioned. The seasoned aviators greeted the beginner pilots with "alright ground huggers."

"How long will it take to learn how to fly?" Cal asked.

"Three or four days," Clifford Turpin replied.[6]

Next came what amounted to a very crude flight simulator. It was what they called a "balancing machine," (referred to by some aviators as a "kiwi bird"), which was essentially a Model B Wright without its engine or rear section, mounted on a wooden horse. It had the elevator lever and the warping lever. The simulation did not use the elevator lever; in flight, the pilot pulled the elevator up to elevate and pushed it down to descend. The kiwi bird was the best simulation for flight available and allowed aviators to instinctively learn how to fly, or "balance in air." The main task for balancing, which was how they described the art of flying, was properly working the warping lever, banking the airplane right and left. The top of the warping lever handle was hinged so that it could move the rudder right or left. It was as confusing as it sounds. On the balancing machine, these wires were not hooked up to the wing's planes or rudder but were hooked instead to a pulley with a motor that moved the wooden horse side to side as if banking. This simulation usually took several days or longer to master.[7]

A Wright biplane turns by warping the wings slightly along with the rudder, hence the name *warping lever*. It was, at the time, a complicated device that was mounted right next to the pilot's seat on the side opposite the elevator lever. But as noted, that was the sum of the gauges and devices a pilot had in 1911. The only other thing was the string attached to a brace that told them if they were going up or down in case of thick cloud cover or disorientation. There were two wicker seats, and the warping lever was between them. So, sitting in the right or left seat while learning determined whether you became a right- or left-handed flier, and you never changed once you mastered that hand. Cal was a left-seat pilot, so he used his right hand for warping. The constant adjustment of warping the wings demanded that the pilot "master a hundred things," said Wilbur Wright, and all of them at once. There was a *feel* to flying that pilots had to sense as they attempted to balance. Welsh was blunt with Cal: "He who has imagination without knowledge, has wings but no feet," hence no stability, no balance. There was an art to flying, and the biplane painted the sky with its wings on air. For professionals like Welsh, the skill of flying simply could not be taught. You either had "it" or you didn't. He didn't think Rodgers had it.[8]

For several days, Cal worked on balancing until Taylor and Welsh thought he was ready to move on to actual flight. He was then taken to Simms Station, which had a large hangar. Next to the hangar was the runway, which was really a converted cow pasture that was impeccably mowed by Wiggin. Once there, Rodgers met two other students, both military, Lieutenants Milling and Arnold, who were cold and aloof toward Rodgers. Inside the hangar were two B-model Wright biplanes. The military pilots were condescending and thought Cal spoke funny, which, of course, he did due to his hearing loss. Wright pilot and instructor Cliff Turbin was training the military pilots. Neither of whom thought much of Rodgers; Lieutenant Arnold was only taken by Rodgers's height saying, "You ever see a bean pole that could fly?"

"Yeah, neither have I," replied Milling.[9]

Welsh walked Cal to one of the biplanes and again reviewed the movement of its parts and the nuances of flight—how a good pilot developed senses while flying, understanding air pressure, while a great pilot anticipated when to ascend or descend. Repetition was learning, and for Welsh, you could never be too careful. Rodgers had to really focus on Welsh and listen intently. When it was quiet, he could hear a little, but when in a room full of people, he could not make out what anyone was saying. Welsh told him that before each takeoff, a good pilot always

3. "There is nothing in your old, flat world"

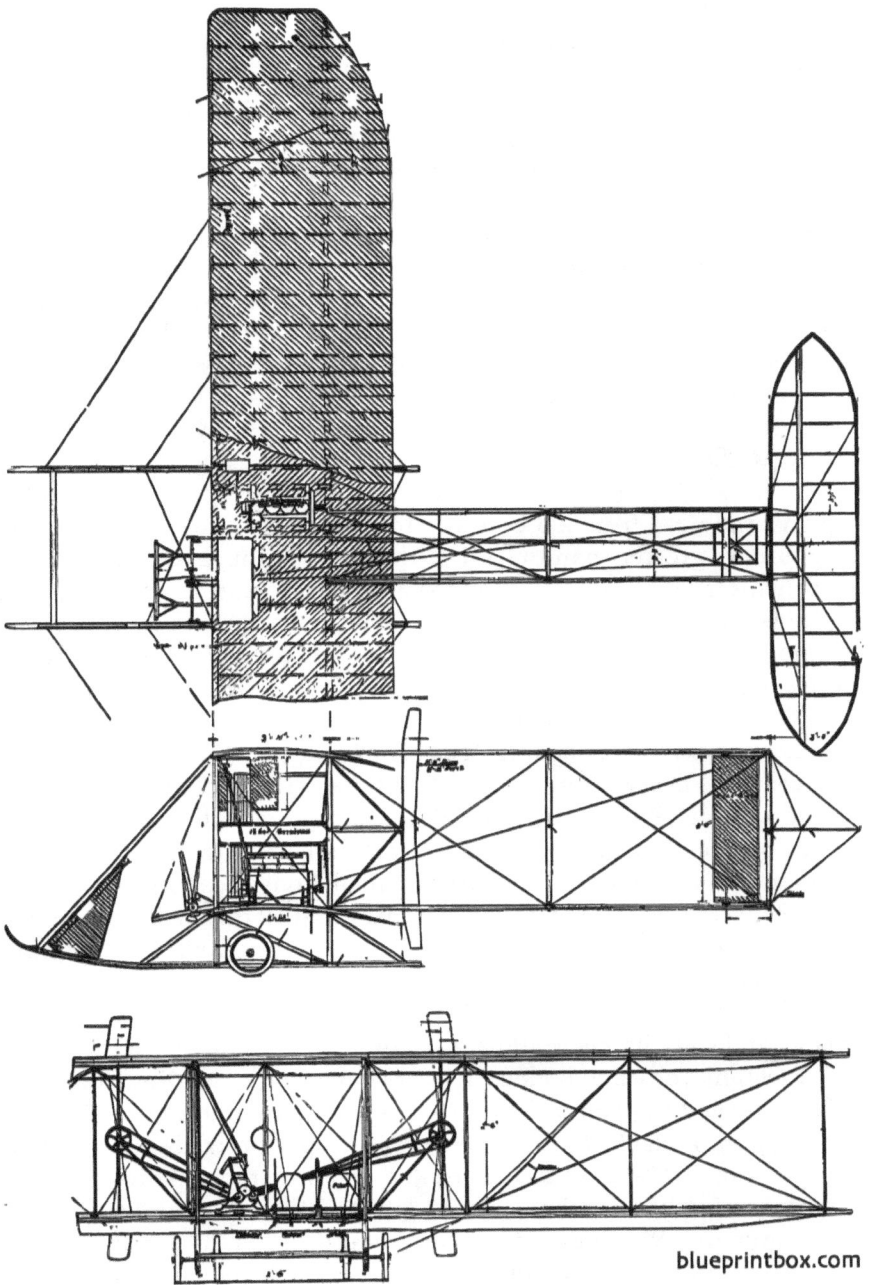

A 1910 diagram of the Wright Model B Biplane (author's collection).

inspects his plane. "An ounce of precaution can save your life, or more important mine," Welsh quipped as he led Cal around the biplane. Rodgers absorbed everything that Welsh was willing to share; he was grateful for it. As a master aviator, Welsh's knowledge and insight were invaluable. They stopped at the two cane-wicker seats that were customary on a Wright biplane, attached to the front section of the lower plane.[10]

Welsh climbed aboard and sat in the right seat, Rodgers in the left. "To change speed, you have the spring-loaded foot treadle, which is pressed down for full speed to take off," said Welsh. He again talked Cal through the elevator and how important it was to know when to ease on the elevator and when to crank it. The warping lever, when combined with the proper elevator technique, allowed for the plane to gracefully ascend and descend. He also instructed Cal that using the wind on take-offs and landings aided for better flight. "Now, did you get all that?" asked Welsh.[11]

The *angle of incidence* is the angle at which the biplane moves against the air. A frontal breeze aids in *lift* for rising, so long as the driving force is greater than the wind. The effect of the *resistance* or *pressure* helps the aircraft ascend. The key is that the wind can't be too great, and the airplane must have sufficient *drive* to get up into the wind. The climbing effect, however, also depends on the angle of takeoff. If the angle of incidence is negative, it *depresses* the airplane, and it can't take off. Once in the air, the wind is a driving force in and of itself. A 1911 publication on flying documented that a Wright or Curtiss biplane was "subjected to every whim in the air" and that if the pilot did not navigate these winds effectively, the "machine will capsize." All of this was part of the balancing act an aviator had to maintain while in flight. They considered this skill to be truly an art and an obvious necessity for flying.[12]

Rodgers was confident that he understood all this. "All right, you're in the catbird seat now," said Welsh. "Don't squirm about; we don't want you to fall off until you've paid all your fees."

But he was not flying solo just yet. First, Welsh would fly the airplane, and Cal's hands would also be on the levers. Welsh switched on the fuel tank valve and nodded at the two mechanics holding the wings. Welsh turned the compression release, and the engine roared to life with a puff of black smoke. "We keep it in spark-retard until it's running smooth," Welsh yelled out to Rodgers, who most assuredly could not hear him. The mechanics then grabbed the wings and waited for the command. Welsh called out for them to "let 'er go" while simultaneously pressing his foot down on the treadle. The biplane lurched forward, and Welsh slowly adjusted the elevator as the biplane took off down the field.[13]

3. "There is nothing in your old, flat world"

Cal was crossing a great divide of sorts; at a time when humanity barely knew of flight, he had traversed into the realm of birds. Rodgers's first flight was short, not very high, and, by his own admission, a transformative one for him. "Your first lesson you will be instructed in making a turn properly," said Welsh.[14]

After just an hour of instruction, Welsh allowed Rodgers to handle the levers by himself. The wind currents immediately surprised Cal. A pilot feels the wind as they rush forward into it, but the crosswinds catch beginners by surprise and require proper use of the warping level—a technique that takes some time and some getting used to. As the plane turns, it tends to start to put its nose down, because the rudder is no longer in a vertical position. Adjustments to the warping level and elevator are constant. "When you have the machine in the proper bank," Welsh said, "pull back on the warping lever to neutral."[15]

The Wright Model B biplane was exhausting to fly—all biplanes of the time were. There was obviously no windshield, so the wind pounded the pilot, especially if it was cold. Holding onto the warping lever and elevator while being bounced around was difficult and tiresome. The constant fight with wind currents and air pockets while avoiding being tossed from your seat was grueling. Luckily for Cal, his size was an advantage. Welsh and Taylor looked at a pilot's physique as if they were horse jockeys—Welsh was the size of a jockey. Cal's size had little to do with the biplane's ability to cut through the wind, as a jockey did on a horse. Size certainly wasn't an indicator of ability, though whether Welsh felt that way is debatable. And if jockeys had to be fearless, aviators had to have ice in their veins.[16]

Much to the surprise of Taylor and Welsh, Rodgers picked up the art of flying quickly. His instructors were blown away by Cal's aptitude for warping and maneuvering the biplane—balancing. Though he occasionally flew at a tilt, they noted that he handled the air masterfully. Banking (turning) was the most difficult maneuver for beginners. It involved all three aspects of the levers: the elevator, the warping, and the rudder. The tendency was to take the biplane out of its bank too early, because one had the feeling that the aircraft was going to turn over and throw the pilot from it—a truly terrifying feeling at hundreds or thousands of feet in the air and a fear that the aviator must work through and overcome. Welsh instructed Cal on maintaining the proper bank to complete turn after turn and how to judge when it was time to pull out of it. After only a day of flight instruction, Welsh allowed Rodgers to fly solo; it was a first for the teacher. Rodgers started solo flying faster than any student Welsh had ever had. Within just a few days, his doubts about Rodgers were gone.[17]

Days passed, and Rodgers did more and more flying with Welsh. During one of their final days of lessons, Turpin was getting ready to take off with someone about Cal's weight. Turpin was not very big, and as the aircraft elevated, it immediately tilted to the weight, but Turpin adjusted the warping and the biplane perfectly leveled as it ascended. Welsh pointed out how difficult it was to make slight adjustments, but that they were crucial to be able to accomplish. The air currents and pockets would toss a biplane around, and the aviator had to be constantly balancing within it.[18]

One of the final lessons still had to be learned. With Cal next to him, Welsh took off and ascended to a couple thousand feet. He smiled at Cal, then reached back and turned off the motor. They were now gliding. He then began what was called "volplaning," a controlled descent in large spirals. The key was to keep the angle of descent at twenty to no more than forty-five degrees in order to avoid a drastic and unrecoverable dive. At those angles, the strength of the gravity pull was no more than seventy miles per hour, a manageable speed. At any greater descent angle, gravity pulls the aircraft at such a high rate of speed that it becomes almost unrecoverable. Welsh brought the biplane down, leveling off toward the runway, pushing and pulling the levers to drop down, bouncing gently over the field until landing.[19]

After landing, they went right back up, and this time, Rodgers had to volplane. The wind was gusting, and as the engine was cut off, Rodgers was in a fight. Warping and elevating the biplane without power into its controlled descent was extremely hard, but he worked it. Welsh watched as Rodgers fought gravity and the wind. Rodgers was not a smooth flier, which made it even more difficult for him, but he was strong and could still control the aircraft and volplane at the proper angle. Slowly, they descended to a hundred feet or so, and Welsh made Cal level off and drop to ten feet above the field before allowing him to land. The feeling of skimming the earth at just ten feet was unnerving, but something every pilot had to experience and learn how to "drop" the aircraft gently down.[20]

After just about a week, Rodgers had perfected landings and takeoffs, proper gliding, banking, skimming, and figure eights—all required to gain a pilot's license. By the end of June, he was flying solo with confidence and displaying ability that was frankly shocking to Welsh. But perhaps most shocking was Cal's insistence on smoking cigars while flying and that he could light them while in flight. Clifford Turpin was Rodgers's mentor for the second half of June as Welsh left for Belmont Park, New York, to establish a Wright flying school there.[21]

On August 7, 1911, at Simms Station in Dayton, Rodgers was

3. "There is nothing in your old, flat world"

certified by the Aero Club of America and received his license. Every new aviator had to perform a flying test with an official of the Aero Club present. Cal received license number forty-nine—making him a member of a small, elite, and, some thought, crazy group. The test consisted of three different flights in which he had to perform a series of maneuvers, including the figure eight. The figure eight circuit was performed by simply flying around two markers five hundred meters apart (547 yards) in the figure of the numeral eight. There were also landing and takeoff tests, as well as dives and altitude flights. In the end, Cal performed wonderfully and, for the first time in his life, achieved something that many could not.[22]

The only thing left was for him to purchase a biplane. The plan was for him and his cousin John Rodgers to split the cost. Cal stayed in Ohio to oversee the construction of a Wright Model B and continue to fine-tune his skills. By overseeing how they constructed a biplane, he also gained key insights into how he could rebuild any part of the airplane, including the engine, which would come in handy during his coast-to-coast expedition.[23]

One morning, Rodgers asked the Kid to help him get the biplane out of the shed and prepped for takeoff, a request that was not unusual. After getting the engine started, Wiggin held the wing, waiting for Rodgers's command. Cal looked at him and motioned for him to jump on; the Kid smiled and climbed aboard. "You want to go flying?" Of course he did, and with that, they roared down the runway and into the sky. Once at altitude, Cal let Wiggin take control and fly the plane out toward Dayton.

On August 2, Rodgers wrote to Harold McCormick, organizer of the Chicago International Aviation Meet, requesting admission to the event pending his successful completion of his aviation license. He proposed that he fly from Dayton to Chicago and land at Grant Park, where the event was being held, and he would do so for a prize of $1,000. McCormick must have been stupefied at the audacity of this complete unknown in the aviation world making such a request, but that was Cal Rodgers. He was bold, confident, and he had his sights set on making a splash in the world of aviation. McCormick ignored Rodgers's letter, but Cal was not deterred. He paid the entry fee, and by August 10, his biplane was ready. He telegraphed Mabel, loaded his Wright Model B onto a train, and headed to Chicago, where she would meet him. Rodgers was on a mission to prove himself there.[24]

Just months before the beginning of Rodgers's historic transcontinental journey, the longest sustained flight was 89.6 miles by Arch Hoxsey. J.A.D. McCurdy beat that record when he reached ninety miles in two hours and eight minutes. It was a new world record for a single sustained flight as well. But perhaps most impressive was McCurdy's flight, which took place entirely over water, traveling from Havana to Key West, Florida. Odds are good that Cal was well aware of Hoxsey and McCurdy, and the thought of a long-distance attempt was already rolling around in the back of his mind.[25]

4.

"The Windy City"

Advertised as the "Greatest Event" in the history of aviation, it lived up to the title: the Chicago International Aviation Meet was the largest of its kind to take place in North America, surpassing the 1910 Los Angeles Meet in attendance. An average of 250,000 people watched the meet daily, with an estimated five hundred thousand on the first day alone. The *Chicago Examiner* wildly estimated that a "half-million" spectators crammed into downtown Chicago to watch the meet open. Unknown quantities of beer, hamburgers, and hotdogs were sold to feed the massive crowd daily. Upward of forty aviators paid the $1,000 entry fee to test their mettle, some even recklessly, all chasing after the $80,000 in purse money—the most prize money ever offered. The meet opened on August 12 and lasted a staggering nine days. It was a picturesque spot for a meet, right alongside Lake Michigan. The lake was filled with boats loaded with spectators daily. The blue water stretched out to the far horizon. The only problem with the location in the Windy City was that it was particularly windy along the large lake. The wind carried out from the massive body of water, pushing off the buildings on Michigan Boulevard and down on the field, hindering landings and takeoffs. It was extremely dangerous at times, and the wind concerned pilots enough that there were days some didn't dare fly, but most did brave the air pockets and unpredictable currents. When all was said and done, some considered the meet a success for the ages. Others thought it a tragic spectacle, because the meet was one of the most dangerous ever put on and cost the lives of two pilots.[1]

The meet was the brainchild of Harold McCormick, a wealthy and influential Chicagoan and industrial tycoon. He was from the American aristocracy—the son-in-law of none other than John D. Rockefeller. James E. Plew, the president of the Aero Club of Illinois, liked McCormick's idea of hosting an air meet, but the club didn't have many members and few influential ones. McCormick was a flying enthusiast;

Chicago hometown favorite "Jimmy" Ward flying above the massive crowd in his Curtiss biplane *Shooting Star* (*Chicago Tribune*, August 12, 1911).

"Birdman's View," photograph of Grant Park during air meet taken by W.H. Durborough (*Chicago Examiner*, August 13, 1911).

he had even funded a failed biplane venture, the McCormick-Romme Company, and badly wanted to be at the center of the aviation community. In an attempt to sway the city's elites into helping fund an air show, McCormick hosted a dinner party at the swanky Blackstone Hotel. In attendance were some of the wealthiest and most influential men the state had to offer. It worked; they raised enough money and interest to make the air meet a spectacle.[2]

The Aero Club of Illinois owned makeshift runways, essentially converted fields, across the state but no airport and no grandstands—no booths and gates either. The club was essentially in its infancy. The first airplane to fly over Chicago wasn't reported until October 1909 and garnered little attention. The location for the meet was the first priority. It had to be grand, and McCormick had ostentatious plans to organize the largest meet ever. He pushed for a downtown location, Grant Park, much to the objection of Plew and others. It would be expensive and dangerous with the lake right there. McCormick would not be deterred and got his way; he gained the support of John Barton Payne, a key South Park board member—the South Park board controlled Grant Park. In May 1911, with the support of the city and enough capital to produce the meet, it was officially announced that it would take place there in August. Though the Aero Club of Illinois would insert itself onto a national stage, by the end of the meet, it was mired in controversy, because it was accused of making a money grab instead of acting in the best interest of its members.[3]

McCormick raised $200,000 in pledges to cover the purse money and expenses so that Grant Park could be modified to host the meet. However, remembering the debacle of the Belmont Park Meet in New York, where fliers were guaranteed money just for showing up and subsequently passed on flying when the weather wasn't just right, their purse wasn't guaranteed. In the Windy City, the flying conditions were rarely just right, so instead, aviators were not guaranteed any money unless they performed, and they knew that offering the largest purse ever would ensure competition, and indeed it did.[4]

Grant Park Stadium (later renamed Soldier Field) had seating for seventy thousand, and the park area itself could hold tens of thousands more. With Michigan Boulevard and the lakefront, hosting hundreds of thousands of spectators was easily feasible. They built three massive hangars to house the airplanes, separate press and judge stands, and a hospital station. The stadium also had five hundred special boxes for the wealthy to watch in privacy. Miles of telegraph and telephone wires had to be run from the relay station to the press box so the results of each event could be announced worldwide. Among his many hats,

McCormick was also president of the Playground Association and saw to it that twenty thousand children gained free access to watch the air meet. Businesses shut down for parts of the week, and many decorated their rooftops with messages for the pilots. The Chicago Board of Trade closed its doors all day Wednesday to attend. Governor Charles S. Deneen and the state legislature shut down as well to attend and host a gala in honor of the aviators. The entire city would watch the meet from whatever vantage point a person could find.[5]

They called it "Aeroplane-itis" because people were crazy with excitement, so Chicago was buzzing as the meet opened. Everyone was watching, hundreds of thousands, wild with anticipation, with "flying fever." Everyone watching the flying machines wanted to fly, to soar with the birds in the heavens. About twenty aviators had attended the banquet at the Chicago Athletic Club the night before the meet opened. They were treated like modern-day rock stars. Women lined up to talk to them. Drinks were bought, and adoring smiles exchanged. There were numerous speeches and proclamations, with McCormick and Plew toasting the aviators and proclaiming the success of the meet before it even opened.[6]

The row of hangars that housed all the airplanes was called "Hangar Avenue" by newspaper reporters, who noted there was no shortage of pride among the cocky aviators. There you found plenty of fliers "proud of their clothes, their animals, their jewels, their ships, and their faces." Aviation was perhaps a wealthy person's sport for some, but not for others like Cal. It was a means to an end. Many aviators were gambling with their lives, pushing the limits of flight to win a large amount of money. They sought financial security and, for some, as in Rodgers's case, to make a name for themselves.[7]

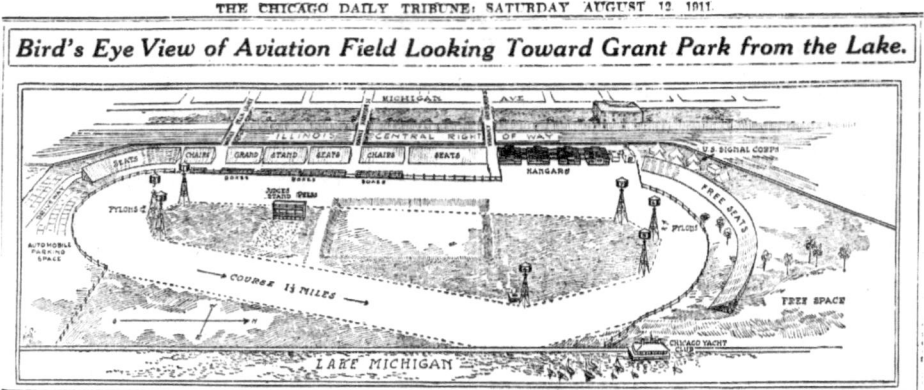

Sketch depiction of the course layout (*Chicago Tribune*, August 12, 1911).

4. "The Windy City"

The morning of August 12 started with rain, something that was not in the weather forecast, but Lake Michigan had other plans. A lake as massive as it offered its own unique weather that could not be predicted, and that morning it was not. When colder air travels over the warmer water of the lake, it produces a lake effect, thus contributing to Chicago being the Windy City. It was overcast, drizzly, and breezy all along the lakefront, delaying the opening of the meet until three thirty in the afternoon. Luckily, the cloud cover receded, and sunlight broke through, bathing the city in warmth. Aviators arrived early that morning and lingered in the hangars waiting out the weather. The massive crowd cheered as pilots pulled their airplanes out of the hangars. Michigan Boulevard was choked with traffic as people just parked their cars to watch, and the entire park area filled with spectators. Hometown favorite Jimmy Ward was the first airborne, and half a dozen or more aircraft quickly followed. He dazzled the crowd with a series of maneuvers. All eyes were heaven bound, and gasps of amazement filled the air as airplane after airplane took to the sky. The crowd was entertained on this day as records and airplanes started falling from the start.[8]

Within the first hour, there were multiple accidents. The first occurred when Arthur B. Stone was circling the north end of the track, which was later called "death turn" by the press. Just the previous year in Los Angeles, a similar turn that proved deadly was named "dead man's turn." Stone was skimming along in front of the stands at about seventy-five feet when a gust of wind off the lake hit his airplane and

A postcard picture of an unknown aviator practicing the week before the meet began (author's collection).

turned him upside down and into the ground. The crowd was horrified for several minutes until Stone slowly rose from the wreckage and gave a thumbs up. A picture of Stone's upside-down aircraft was published in the paper the next day. The second happened just minutes later on the ground, when a biplane being driven by French aviator Rene Simmon

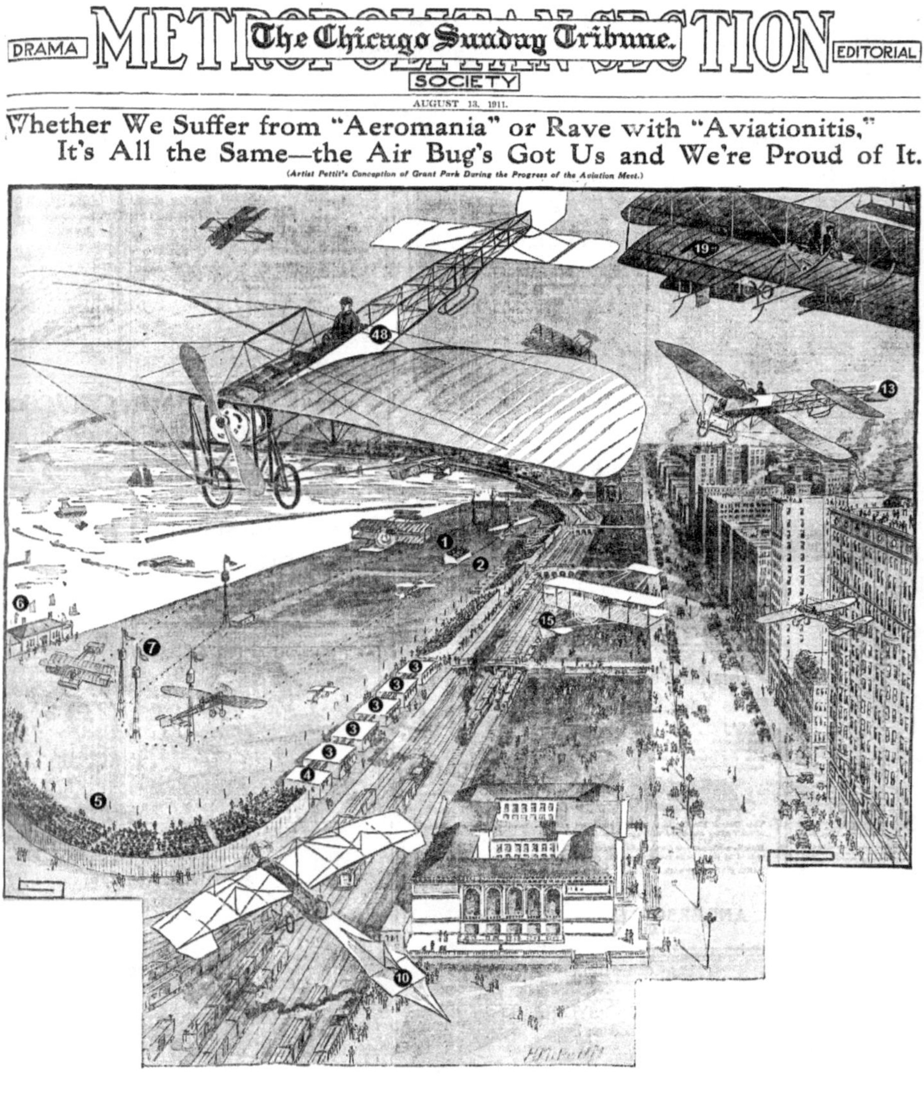
DRAMA METROPOLITAN SECTION EDITORIAL
The Chicago Sunday Tribune.
SOCIETY
AUGUST 13, 1911.

Whether We Suffer from "Aeromania" or Rave with "Aviationitis," It's All the Same—the Air Bug's Got Us and We're Proud of It.

(Artist Pettit's Conception of Grant Park During the Progress of the Aviation Meet.)

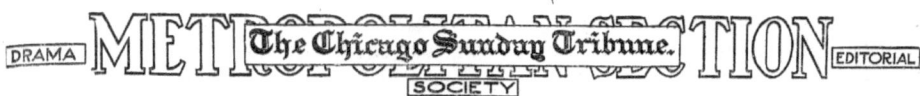

Artist depiction of Grant Park during the race (*Chicago Tribune*, August 13, 1911).

struck the wing of Wright flier Frank Coffyn, who was about to take off, destroying part of it. Coffyn tried to avoid Simmon, but the wet ground didn't allow him to stop in time. Then, moments later, just as the crowd looked back up into the sky at the airplanes, they witnessed James V. Martin in his Grahame-White biplane hit an air pocket, lose control, and plummet into a fence at the south end of the field. He was uninjured, but his plane was destroyed, ruining his chance to compete for the endurance prize. The final crash of the day happened when St. Croix Johnstone rumbled down the muddy runway attempting to lift off. But the mud caked so badly on his wheels that he couldn't clear a lamppost. His left wing struck the post, clipping it off but also spinning him around before crashing down on his right wing, skidding to a stop some hundred feet away; the pilot fortunately was just bruised and cut.[9]

Mesmerized by the airplanes, one boy, Zito Partitillo, forgot to go home after watching the meet's first day and instead stayed at the park with a mate. They snuck around trying to get a look at the biplanes and monoplanes. His mother, filled with worry, called the police and reported him missing. There was a search party, and an all-points bulletin was put out looking for the young man. Luckily, he returned the next afternoon unscathed, with his mother telling the newspaper he was grounded from the air meet for the rest of the week.[10]

After an uneventful Sunday, the next day, August 14, resulted in several dramatic incidents that also miraculously resulted in no deaths. "The half million people who made the lakefront a human sardine box" enjoyed the excitement of close races and harrowing crashes. To start things off, two planes went down into Lake Michigan before lunch was served. Both pilots were safely rescued; one was found floating on debris, smoking a cigarette. They were both rescued by hydroaeroplanes from land—a first in aviation history. Then later, a biplane flown by J.A.D. McCurdy struck a telegraph wire and exploded; miraculously, the pilot jumped to safety. A short time later, a fourth airplane clipped its wings and smashed into the ground. And the fifth and final crash of the day saw a pilot lose all power and glide to the ground before coming to a stop after a minor accident.[11]

The fourth day turned out to be the deadliest. William C. Badger, a young pilot from Pittsburgh, died after crashing into a ditch and being crushed by his plane's engine. Badger was entertaining the crowd at the north end of the track with exciting yet dangerous maneuvers when he dipped down from three hundred feet to "buzz" the crowd, descending rapidly. He leveled off and cranked up on the elevator, but the plane couldn't handle the angular acceleration (g-force), and on the rapid ascent, the support beam for the wings collapsed, causing him to

A *Chicago Tribune* photograph of McCurdy's burnt-out plane (August 14, 1911).

nosedive into the ground from fifty feet. Luckily, no spectators were hit. Badger was briefly conscious but died while en route to the hospital in an ambulance. One of the more popular pilots at the meet was another hometown favorite, St. Croix Johnstone. He was dazzling the crowd with stunts over Lake Michigan at 3,500 feet when his engine exploded or malfunctioned. He lost control and plummeted into the lake, his airplane dragging him underwater. The stunned crowd stood in horrified silence for twenty minutes until another race was restarted early to distract them. Hugh Robinson was flying a Curtiss Hydroaeroplane when he witnessed the fall and immediately put down on the water at the spot of Johnstone's crash. He frantically looked for the pilot, but by then the airplane was gone, with only some floating debris left behind. Boats arrived later, and eventually the airplane and pilot surfaced. Johnstone's death was especially tragic, because he had openly stated that this was his last meet; he was done with the sport, citing how dangerous it was.[12]

There were other crashes and accidents during the day, including one that involved Lincoln Beachy, one of the world's most well-known pilots. During a speed race, as the airplanes whizzed around the mile-long track, Beachy clipped the wing of a competitor and was penalized for the foul. Luckily, neither pilot lost control nor crashed. Beachy managed to finish and win the speed event for the day. Later

4. "The Windy City" 43

ST. CROIX JOHNSTONE, of Chicago, American. Holder of American duration record, 4 hours, 1 minute, 54 seconds. Moisant-Gnome monoplane.

A postcard of St. Croix Johnstone during the Chicago 1911 meet (author's collection).

in the day, J.C. Mars escaped serious injury when he also crashed at the north end for reasons never identified. However, the incident was severe enough that it ended his meet due to the damage that the plane sustained.[13]

After Johnstone's death, there were calls to cancel the meet. Some felt it wasn't safe, and the location itself was criticized, because it was not suitable for simple takeoffs and landings. The calls for stopping the event challenged the notion that these pilots were advancing science. Editorials appeared in both the *Chicago Examiner* and *New York Times* in favor of and opposed to the meet continuing. Aviation was still in its infancy; it was only eight years prior that the first manned flight had taken place. More advancement was needed before allowing such reckless attempts at flying and encouraging it with meets and large purses. Nonetheless, the crowd came every day en masse. They wanted action, and that's what they got.[14]

Not only were pilots falling, but records fell as well. The first occurred on day one, when the endurance mark with a passenger was established, and then days later it was bested by G.W. Beatty. When his plane came to a stop after breaking the record, Beatty was carried on the shoulders of the crowd to a table in front of the judges, where he bowed and waved to the adoring crowd. On August 19, records for speed, duration, climbing, and weight were all broken. In all, ten American records and three world records were established.[15]

For the wives and families of aviators, the constant news of crash after crash and of pilots perishing took its emotional toll. After the deaths of Johnstone and Badger, the wife of Eugene Ely suffered from an anxiety attack bad enough to require medical attention. Her aviator husband stayed by her side and did not fly for the rest of the day. When their loved ones were airborne, nothing around them mattered. They stood stoically watching as they soared across Lake Michigan, not relaxing until they swept down upon the park and safely landed. Then came the rush to greet them, thankful the day was over.[16]

Even Thomas Edison was asked during the Chicago Aviation Meet about flying safety and the strides made in aeronautics. He felt the aviation meets were mere "sport" and unsafe. He didn't call it a profession, as some aviators insisted it was. The science of airplanes and their pilots was still wanting. That the men and women who flew put their lives on the line for the pleasure of a vulgar crowd was a reasonable conclusion. Edison suggested the further development of parachutes to be installed in the machines for safety, which was something that would over time be adopted almost exactly as Edison described. Perished aviator Johnstone's father was an educated man, a doctor, and was interviewed about his son's death. The heartbroken father was blunt. "It is perfectly obvious that this frail machine will break with the terrible strain put upon it." He urged that safety devices be perfected and installed on airplanes to protect pilots, and until this was done, he called for a "stop to all public flying."[17]

Calbraith Perry Rodgers was one of the least experienced aviators at the meet. So little was known about Rodgers that his name rarely made it into press releases and coverage reports leading up to the meet. But by the meet's end, he was one of its all-stars and perhaps the most talked-about pilot. He finished third in prize money, taking home $12,285 and winning the overall title for endurance, staying in the air for an astonishing total of twenty-seven hours, almost a full three hours more than the second-place finisher. The endurance and altitude prizes were the most coveted and garnered the most press.[18]

Cal kicked off the meet, leading the endurance category after the first day's flying. Pilots could go up and down as much as they could stand it. The weather was unseasonably cool, not reaching the seventies until toward the end of the week. At altitude, it was freezing cold. In a back-and-forth battle with G.W. Beatty, Cal stayed in the air for an incredible eight hours and thirty minutes on the last day of the meet to easily win. Cal had established himself as the strongest pilot, able to endure the elements of prolonged flight.[19]

4. "The Windy City"

After Tuesday, as Cal had established himself as the leading contender for endurance, his wife, Mabel, was asked by a reporter if she worried about Rodgers when he flew. That day, the deaths of Johnstone and Badger had cast a gloom over the meet. She told the reporter that "Cal's lack of nerves helps me keep calm." Cal showed little emotion about anything, and his calm and steady demeanor allowed him to focus and endure when others simply could not.[20]

It was that laser focus that made it almost impossible for any other aviator to best him in the endurance challenge; however, on Thursday, someone tried. George W. Beatty, a Wright team flier, got up early, took off before Cal, and beat him for the day in endurance; still, Rodgers was leading overall. At the end of the meet, Rodgers bested the competition, but the press criticized his lack of daring. "Rodgers in his old Wright 'wagon,'" made no "death dips or sensational spirals," nor did he cause the crowd to "gasp by sensational dips." He simply ground out, like a machine, the endurance mark, winning $10,000 for the record alone.[21]

Harry N. Atwood flew into Chicago on the first day of the meet, landing at Grant Park to a raucous and jubilant crowd. He received what could only be described as a hero's welcome. When he landed, a throng of spectators rushed to his airplane, lifted Atwood from it, and carried him to the stands. Cal had to have watched with amazement at the crowd's reaction and Atwood's being treated to a hero's welcome. Atwood was on his way from St. Louis to New York, a distance of 1265 miles—a mark that would crush the long-distance aviation record. His journey sparked conversations about doing a transcontinental flight—or *coast-to-coast*. His stopover in Chicago was much anticipated and no doubt helped Cal decide that he wanted to attempt a long-distance flight. Atwood would make the trip to New York in twenty-six hours and thirty-one minutes over the course of twenty flights. His arrival in Chicago was the first leg of his tour, covering 286 miles that day.[22]

Cal left the track ruminating on the possibility of accomplishing the first ever coast-to-coast journey. "It was Cal's success" during the Chicago meet, noted Mabel years later, "that convinced him of his ability" to take on any aviation challenge. What he knew for sure was that he had to try something epic, something worthy of a Perry or a Rodgers. Having suffered through a childhood of sickness and loneliness, crushing rejection in his teens, and the constant struggle for acceptance because of his disability, doing something great would wash away all the heartache and disappointment. Yet even after the meet and his success, no one expected greatness from Cal. So that was exactly what he was going to give them.[23]

5

"[The] people below seemed to belong to the past"

> "[The] people below seemed to belong to the past, to a period when man walked miserably or rolled uncomfortably in primitive autos over the rough surface."
> —William Randolph Hearst,
> after flying for the first time.

When completed, the Woolworth Building soared sixty stories into the Manhattan skyline. In the fall of 1911, as construction started, New Yorkers marveled at the engineering feat being accomplished before their eyes. It represented progress on a colossal scale. It would be the tallest skyscraper in the world until 1930. When construction was in full swing, a story and a half per week was raised into the horizon. The behemoth was an amazing achievement, a testament to the advancement of the Industrial Revolution of the late nineteenth and early twentieth centuries. By the end of the year, an entire nation would marvel at the feat that one Calbraith Perry Rodgers had accomplished on his transcontinental journey—one just as monumental and important.

In 1911, America was steamrolling into the modern era thanks to the Gilded Age—from harnessing electricity to mass producing Ford's Model T cars to the advent of skyscrapers, and soon after, the airplane. Between 1880 and 1910, New York's population tripled, and its economy boomed along with it. As late as 1880, there was still no sewer system, no electricity, and, of course, the radio, automobile, and airplane were nonexistent. Cast iron pipes and running water were just starting to be installed. All this changed in just thirty years—a revolution in the way people lived—a transformative change in a relatively short period. Refrigeration and air conditioning alone changed the quality of life. Mass production and mass consumerism made more products available from coast to coast. The retail business exploded by 1900, with

5. "[The] people below seemed to belong to the past"   47

options and products unimaginable a decade before. The *Sears Roebuck and Company* catalog was fulfilling one hundred thousand orders a day, from anvils and ironing boards to furnaces. Hospitals and schools proliferated, providing better health care and education, and medical advancements and new medical procedures dramatically improved life expectancy.[1]

American industrial output was the largest in the world. Andrew Carnegie had perfected the Bessemer process, and American steel production surpassed even that of Great Britain. In 1911, the United States Patent Office issued its one millionth patent as America's economy diversified and exploded with innovation. American industry in the 1910s was the most transformative on the planet because of industrial tycoons and visionaries. People were leaving their rural farming communities and moving to the cities where they could find these new industrial jobs. Still, by 1912, only 16 percent of houses in major cities had electricity. And though the 1920s was the truly transformative decade for America in the first half of the twentieth century, the transformation's origins were in the 1910s.[2]

William Randolph Hearst was born into money. He was not an especially beloved man, and if you are aware of Orson Welles's cinematic loose portrayal of him in his 1941 masterpiece *Citizen Kane*, you know at the very least a caricature of him. In the movie, the famous motif *Rosebud* was supposedly based on either Hearst's love of flowers or his pet name for the genitalia of his Hollywood mistress, Marion Davies. Regardless of how he came into his money or how much he was liked or disliked, he was a by-product of the Gilded Age. Hearst was the son of a wealthy aristocrat and attended Harvard but was expelled for apparently hosting one too many "beer house" parties. During his lifetime, millionaires were captains of industry or robber barons, depending on how you viewed them. His father, George Hearst, and he joined their ranks, though most assuredly they thought of themselves as captains of their respective industries.[3]

New York was the city of millionaires; nowhere else in the world claimed as many as the future city that never sleeps. Industrialists, philanthropists, inheritors, and everyone in between tried to stake their claim to success in the big apple. There were some four thousand millionaires in the United States by the late 1800s, and half of them lived in New York. The modern industrialized world was created not only by mass production but also by mass consumerism and mass media. Hearst, along with Joseph Pulitzer, dominated the newspaper industry. With the Spanish-American War and yellow journalism, the power and prestige of the media—of newspapers—brought with them conglomerate newspaper producers such as Hearst. Controlling the largest newspapers made him not only wealthy but influential and powerful. Pulitzer and Hearst developed the concept of sensationalism in journalism, allowing them to yield such influence that they could help start a war and convince Americans it was in their best interest.[4]

Hearst owned the *Los Angeles Examiner* and, in January 1910, sponsored the first international air meet at Dominguez Field outside Los Angeles. Hundreds of thousands attended over the ten days the meet was held. Hearst himself flew for the first time with renowned French aviator M. Louis Paulhan. "The sensations of flying are hard to describe," Hearst said afterward. "I felt that great sense of exhilaration which all aviators describe." He continued to describe the experience in true Hearst fashion: "The little people below seemed to belong to the past, to a period when man walked miserably or rolled uncomfortably in primitive autos over the rough surface. I felt it was a shame anybody should have to walk when he can fly." Flight had captured the great newspaperman's imagination and inspired him.[5]

So moved by his experience, Hearst put up a $50,000 prize for the first aviator to make a transcontinental coast-to-coast flight in thirty days or fewer. When Hearst made his challenge, he wasn't playing to the showmanship of sport, of the air meets, or to garner publicity; he was challenging the art and science of aviation. He had fallen in love with flight and wanted to see it become an American scientific and cultural pastime. Only under pressure can something change, evolve, and be perfected. He knew this all too well and wanted to see aviation succeed. For someone to successfully fly across the country, it would indeed be worthy of great press coverage but would also stimulate the masses and inspire others to want to fly—that is how innovation occurs.

Hearst's announcement of the richest prize ever offered in America came just after Harry Atwood completed what was then the longest North American journey: 1,965 miles flying from St. Louis to New York. He accomplished it in eleven days, making the prospect of a continental trip in thirty days seem very doable. The prize offer would stand until October 10, 1911. Anyone who wanted to challenge for it, had to start by that date. By the second week of September 1910, aviators started putting their hats in the ring, stating their intention to challenge for the enormous prize. Hearst's offer started a wave of large cash prizes in Europe for cross-country jaunts as well. Prizes were offered for the first to fly across the English Channel and the winner of races from Berlin to Paris, all paying upward of $50,000 and $75,000.[6]

There were a few important rules for the transcontinental flight: Once started, you had thirty days to complete the journey. The entire

5. "[The] people below seemed to belong to the past"   49

distance had to be covered by air. You were only allowed one airplane, but you could rebuild it as much as needed, and as all those who attempted the challenge quickly learned, rebuilding would be much needed. The winning aviator had to start in either Boston, New York, San Francisco, or Los Angeles and pass through Chicago. Pilots could land and take off as often as they wished. Other than that, the first to accomplish the thirty-day feat won the $50,000 prize.[7]

Jonathan Ogden Armour, too, was a product of the post–Civil War Industrial Revolution that gave birth to the Gilded Age. His father, Philip Danforth Armour, was described as the "greatest swine-slayer of the nineteenth century." After the Civil War, Armour made money speculating in pork and later became extremely wealthy when he converted a Milwaukee, Wisconsin, grain house into a meat packing factory that helped him create an empire. Eventually, he moved the company to Chicago, where Jonathan was born in 1863. Philip died in 1901, and Jonathan took over as president of Armour and Company, and by most accounts, he excelled. He was not just a privileged son inheriting a fortune; he expanded the business. He was also not just a product of privilege; he was intelligent and authored two books on business. Armour was shrewd—some would say ruthless—but he also had an eye for development and marketing. So, it made sense that when he was in his private box watching the Chicago International Aviation Meet, he would have noticed someone like Cal Rodgers. And it would have been during evening dinner parties or mingling with the aviators on the field when Armour met Cal Rodgers.[8]

After Cal crushed the endurance competition, Armour sought an audience with Rodgers to discuss Hearst's coast-to-coast challenge. Armour wasn't interested in the money to be won, of course, but in the publicity it would mean if his company backed the right aviator. He was launching a new beverage, the Vin Fiz grape soda, and it must have occurred to him (or one of his associates) as he watched the biplanes fly around that their wings could easily be turned into flying billboards. Armour knew a winner when he saw one; airplanes were no fad, and the massive turnout at the air meets in Los Angeles and Chicago was just the beginning.[9]

The day after the meet ended, a group of fliers held a charity event for perished aviator Johnstone's widow. Appropriately, there were gale-force winds that limited participation, but some aviators, including Cal, took to the sky and did what they could. Most, however, did not take part and began the process of shipping their aircraft home. They managed to raise $8,000 for her, an incredible sum considering the conditions. The next day, Cal was going to fly his airplane out of Grant Park to an airfield in Cicero, Illinois. He was in his machine with the engine running when a group of police officers waved him down and told him he could not take off. Flying out of the park had been banned due to the weather. He was dumbfounded, telling one newspaper that "suddenly, an aeroplane is dangerous."[10]

The next day, he transported his airplane to Cicero, where he gave flights to prominent society members for a fee. Numerous women from the various prominent social circles as well as sports figures and politicians flew with Cal, enjoying their first flying experience. Mabel didn't object to Rodgers's newfound popularity from his success at the air meet, but she did feel compelled to point out to him that she had yet to fly. "Do you realize I've never been up in an aeroplane?" she informed him. Cal wasted no time and took her up into the air. A photographer apparently captured the event. "You're my best publicity agent," he told her.[11]

The participants in the Hearst transcontinental challenge saw it as being worthy of the science of aviation. Atwood expressed his concern that meets like those in Chicago and Los Angeles "invite too many spectacular attempts with fatal results." There was frustration with the exploits of the flying meets and how they allowed almost anyone with an aviator license to fly, whether they were ready or not. "It is more credit to civilization that a man can fly across the continent than he can turn a flip-flop in the air."[12]

The two giants of the American aviation scene, Glenn Curtiss and the Wright brothers, outwardly applauded Hearst's prize offer. "It will be tremendously stimulating to aviators," said Curtiss. He declared that the prize would help to further the science of aviation but also, as Hearst intended, it would set forth another example of American progress: "This contest puts America in the very forefront ... for the development of aviation." The Wrights were more reserved but still praised the challenge. Wilbur stated it was an attainable task but questioned if airplanes were capable of the challenge, noting that "[airplanes] can fly from 50 to 500 miles in one day," but the problem was that there would be plenty of intervals when they would not be able to fly and would need upkeep. Certainly, an engine would not hold up and would require constant rebuilding and replacement. But, for the most part, in the press at least, they applauded the timeframe and that fliers could routinely repair their planes and maintain safety. That was important. Still, the person who completes the journey "will be exceptional, physically and intellectually," said Wilbur.[13]

As Armour Company representatives were meeting with Cal and his manager to hash out the details to sponsor Rodgers's trip, Harry N.

5. "[The] people below seemed to belong to the past"   51

Atwood announced that he was chasing after the Hearst prize, and the media went wild. He was destined to win the prize, they said. Atwood had traveled 1,965 miles from St. Louis to New York, shattering all previous records for cross-country and distance flight. Many considered him to be one of the greatest aviators in the world. He was also handsome, charismatic, and articulate, and the press adored him. Though Cal was described as handsome with a slow-drawing smile that was appealing, his awkward vernacular and shyness did not help endear him to the media, at least not at first. It would take, over time, his undeterred confidence and forcefulness of character.

The *Chicago Examiner* ran a front-page story on September 3, announcing that the rush was on for the "great transcontinental dash." Robert G. Fowler was already on his way to San Francisco to start his attempt. Harry Atwood, though in New York, intended to move his plane via train to San Francisco as well to begin his quest. Three new entrants into the great transcontinental dash were Chicago's very own Jimmy Ward, Phillip O. Parmelee, and Cal Rodgers. Ward intended to start from Boston and head for San Francisco, while Parmelee was aiming to take off from Los Angeles. Rodgers was going to start his race for the Hearst prize from New York. There was a mad rush to get started because the winning aviator had to start before October 10 and had to declare they were entering in writing fourteen days before starting. The clock was ticking.[14]

The Wright Company was working feverishly on building specialized biplanes for Fowler, Atwood, Ward, and Parmelee. They would be smaller and lighter than the popular Model B. Ward had been flying a Curtiss airplane but defected, filed a lawsuit against the company, and joined the ranks of the Wright fliers. Word came that Rodgers, too, wanted to get a modified Wright plane, but the company was focused on Fowler and Atwood. The Wrights wanted their planes to be perfect because they felt Fowler and Atwood had the best chance at success. They were the favorites to make the journey; after all, they were proven commodities. When Rodgers approached the Wright brothers, they were not overtly enthused and even tried to dissuade Cal from attempting the feat. Eventually, Cal won them over (most likely once they learned that Armour was sponsoring Rodgers), and they offered to get him a modified biplane just like the others.[15]

In early September, the Hearst challenge and the aviators taking part were making the rounds of newspaper headlines in most major cities. Tucked into a side column, just below a diagram of Fowler's proposed path and stopping points across America, was another headline, "Frisbie Killed as Jeers Force him to Fly." Aviator J.J. Frisbie competed in the Chicago meet, where he won one of the more outrageous events, the "bomb throwing" contest—anything to excite the crowd. He flew a biplane that he had designed and built himself. He was in Norton, Kansas, performing at the county fairgrounds for several days to make some money. On his second day, while performing, he came down unexpectedly in a hard landing that shook him up but didn't cause any harm. The next day, his machine was not acting right, and he announced that he would not fly. This threw the crowd into a frenzy of boos and name calling; they shouted "faker" over and over. Frisbie tried to explain that his machine was not running properly, but the crowd only grew more raucous. They broke him; even with his wife, son, and daughter in attendance, he told the crowd he didn't want them to leave thinking that "he was not willing to do his best." He climbed aboard, started his airplane, and took off. Frisbie got airborne, elevated to approximately one hundred feet, and when he tried to bank, something went wrong. His plane tipped so much that he lost control, plunging down, clipping a barn, and crashing into the ground—the biplane partially collapsing on top of him. His wife watched in horror and was rendered "prostrate" with shock, according to a newspaper reporter in attendance. His crew rushed to the crash and found him pinned under the engine, barely alive. Physicians on the scene could not revive him, and he died not long after.[16]

Frisbie wasn't a coward or afraid; he had spent years flying balloons and jumping from them in test parachutes. But he was a proud man, one of conviction, and one who did not want anyone to leave thinking that aviation—that aviators—were not giving their best. In the days after the tragic crash, the actions of the audience were rightfully and severely criticized:

> Frisbie was undoubtedly sacrificed to the whim of a Kansas mob, which, notwithstanding particular demonstration of the fact that a flight would be dangerous, howled for a flight and taunted poor Frisbie until he flew and was killed.[17]

The nature of Frisbie's death rocked many in the aviation community and could not have gone unnoticed by Rodgers and the others as they prepared for their daring, yet extremely dangerous, transcontinental race. It was a fraternity, a brotherhood; those who dared to fly and advance the science of aviation knew full well the ever-rising, somber death toll, especially in 1911. Early September was notably deadly, as in Europe, four aviators perished, one horribly while still in flight when a leaking gas tank exploded. There were three additional crashes reported in the United States on September 1, 1911, alone. Death was everywhere; they were well aware of it and lived among it as aviators.[18]

All the coast-to-coast fliers were going to use special trains to carry the necessary spare parts along with mechanics, other crew, press, and family. They would use the system of railroads weaving throughout the county as their iron compass, following the tracks to lead them whenever possible to their destination. Aviation was so new that there were no maps or airports available for pilots. If they had any hope of sustaining a transcontinental journey financially, they would need financial backing to afford such a caravan. Fowler was being backed by millionaire C. Fred Grundy, whom Fowler first had to teach to fly before receiving his backing. Gundy also served as Fowler's manager. Fowler announced that he was taking the northern route, which would take him from California over to Laramie, Wyoming, and on to Chicago—an extremely daring and challenging route, but also a potentially much quicker one. Weighing risk versus reward was a constant struggle for aviators. Everyone else thought the southern (and longer) route, thus avoiding the Rocky Mountains, was the most practical. Fowler believed he could make the coast-to-coast trip in twenty days of actual flying if the weather and his machine held up.[19]

Jimmy Ward looked like a teenager. The Chicago native, however, was anything but a boy when flying. He was a skilled and technically sound aviator. "I know Jimmy will win," his wife said, "because he told me so." Ward was also a darling of the press, he exuded charisma and confidence. "When I start," he boldly stated, "every other contestant will know that I am in the race." Ward planned to start in Boston, head straight to Chicago, and then south. The east-to-west route wasn't the most popular, but for Ward, getting to his hometown quickly was his goal. He envisioned landing in Grant Park to a raucous crowd—an emotional moment that would carry him westward and to victory. Ward spoke about "pleasing the crowd" and looked forward to bringing the Hearst prize "back to Chicago."[20]

Phillip Parmelee predicted he would need twenty-six days of flying, with the caveat that both the weather and his airplane cooperated. "I have chosen the logical route," Parmelee announced. "I will not encounter any rain until I reach Kanas." It was probably the most practical route, starting in the arid and warmer west and going east, as, indeed, one could expect a lot less rain and less bad weather the first third of the journey. Starting in New York meant that weather would probably play more of a factor right away. "Those who travel from east to west," he said, "have little or no chance of completing their flight." The wind, he said, would constantly be against them. He planned to follow the Southern Pacific Railway from Los Angeles down into El Paso, Texas. The Wrights were closely monitoring and advising Parmelee, one of their best team fliers and one who absolutely had the toughness and skill to win the prize. They even made sure that his special train had all the needed parts on hand for quick and easy repairs. The Wrights gave all their fliers special attention, save Cal Rodgers, at least for the moment.[21]

But this thorough examination of their biplane and the costs that would be incurred to send an aviator across the continent gave the Wrights cause for concern. "Our expenses for preparing for such a race will be fully $25,000," they said, making the $50,000 prize seem less appealing than they initially thought. "And it will probably take [the parts of] two or more machines to finish." They concluded that most aviators would never have the financial means to finish the challenge. Even if they were right, Hearst wasn't concerned about every aviator being able to take on the challenge. He wanted companies like the Wrights' to support the challenge and take on the task of serious assessment of their aircraft to make them more efficient, more durable, and much safer. And this, Hearst successfully accomplished, whether anyone actually finished the challenge, let alone won it. The Wrights modified their biplanes for longer journeys but in the end felt their machines would simply "rattle themselves apart" when trying to go thousands of miles.[22]

Rodgers was going to start in the east and head west into the rain and wind. The reason for starting in the east probably had more to do with the Armour Company than sound aviation judgment. Parmalee was right; starting in the east was almost setting oneself up for failure; the wind alone was a major issue. J. Ogden Armour was making the transcontinental journey a national advertising campaign, and he had no idea how far Cal would make it. Therefore, he wanted Rodgers to start in the more densely populated east, guaranteeing the most press and eyes on Cal's biplane. His plan, however, was to head straight for Chicago and then swing way south. "I want to cut off as much distance as I can," Rodgers said, "but think I will save time by taking no chances with the Rocky Mountains."[23]

Cal was not thrilled that he had to go through Chicago, and besides Ward, no aviator really was. It added hundreds of miles to the journey and meant staying north longer than desired. "I would be glad to pay $10,000 to eliminate that stop, as it is to my mind the only serious obstacle to my winning the prize," Rodgers complained.[24]

Pilots wanted to stay south as long as possible in the relatively better and certainly warmer weather. He was going to take every precaution he could. "There will be very little left to luck," Rodgers naively stated. But there was going to be a lot of luck involved, a frighteningly large amount of luck, and on more than one occasion, as he would see.[25]

5. "[The] people below seemed to belong to the past"

Newspapers and Aero Clubs nationwide promoted the challenge of a transcontinental flight. The aviation editor of the *New York American* lauded the Hearst's challenge as having helped to stimulate interest in aviation and promote safety. Aviators had to plan safe and clean flights without stunts in order to successfully traverse the nation. The science of aviation was being advanced more than ever. Just a few months before the Chicago meet, Hearst received the highest honor from the Aeronautical Society of America "for his services in the interests of science" by offering his transcontinental prize. Hearst envisioned a day when aviation would reach the masses and when people would "sail in serenity and safety, in comfort and contentment through this new illimitable empire of air."[26]

6

"It was the only one of its kind the Wrights ever built"

"It was the only one of its kind the Wrights ever built."
—Charlie Taylor on the *Vin Fiz* biplane.

While waiting to start his journey, Cal stayed in the Chicago area performing mini-air shows at Lima Driver Park and giving rides to paying customers to raise money. One afternoon in late August, Rodgers unintentionally broke an aviation record. The wife of Ben Roller, a famous wrestler and professional football player, showed up and asked for an airplane ride. Roller had earlier that year defeated Charles "Kid" Cutler to win the American Heavyweight Championship. "I wanted to see how it felt up in the clouds," she told Rodgers. To have a famous athlete's wife as a customer must have been a little intimidating. Still, he agreed and took her up. Once in the sky, he ascended to a few hundred feet, leveled off, and circled the field. At a nice, safe altitude, he checked to make sure she was okay. She smiled and pointed up, so up he went. He leveled off at five hundred feet, and again, she pointed up. He asked if she was sure, and she was. So, he elevated to a thousand feet, leveled off, and she pointed up again. And then again and again, until Cal had reached 2,700 feet. It was the highest altitude for a female passenger ever recorded; Cal had set an American record. She only stopped pointing up because it was terribly cold at that altitude, and she finally pointed down.[1]

"I had not planned to go for the altitude with a woman passenger," Rodgers said later, "but Mrs. Roller kept insisting." Mrs. Roller was so excited that she reportedly headed for the nearest telephone afterward and called her famous wrestler husband, asking that he himself purchase an airplane. It is unknown if he ever did.

Rodgers's mother, Maria Sweitzer, was visiting from New York and

6. "It was the only one of its kind the Wrights ever built"   57

went up into the sky with her son. She had never been in an airplane, and after some coaxing, Cal got her to agree to go up. Though he didn't dare take her above a few hundred feet, the experience won her over. It was a revelation, as it usually was for first-time fliers. "I am a convert now myself," Maria admitted. "If I were young I'd buy myself an aeroplane and sail through the air." She didn't expect to enjoy it and assumed the fear would simply be too much. The only reason they didn't stay up long was the cold. "I would have wanted to stay up longer," she said.[2]

Cal also took "the Kid" Wiggin up and let him fly the biplane, something the Wrights would not do. It was Wiggin's second flying experience with Rodgers. Though Wiggin was only a teenager, he was becoming not just Rodgers's helper and go getter but a trusted companion that he would rely on during his upcoming journey. It was also during his Lima exploits that Frank Shaffer approached Cal and offered his assistance with aircraft maintenance. Shaffer was the mechanic for a carnival that was also set up in the park. Thousands of people watched Cal fly and enjoyed the rides at the carnival. At first Rodgers was standoffish, but not long into their discussion, he could tell that Shaffer wasn't some flunky engine tinkerer. He had expert knowledge of engines and generators and was excited about the Wright biplane and its mechanical intricacies. After days of assisting Cal and Wiggin with the biplane, Rodgers hired Shaffer to be his mechanic, along with the Kid, of course.[3]

On September 3, Rodgers agreed to take his airplane two hundred miles up to Appleton, Wisconsin, and perform in an air show organized by his future manager Fred F. Wettengel. Cal was paid $2,000 and performed numerous stunts in what was Wisconsin's first air show. Thousands of people attended, and Rodgers gave rides to those willing to pay twenty-five dollars. He also took up the first woman in Wisconsin history when businessman George Whiting paid for himself and his wife, Elizabeth Graves Whiting, to go up for a ride. After a successful weekend, Rodgers returned to Chicago and began preparations for entering the Hearst transcontinental race.[4]

The Wrights were more than happy to sell Rodgers their most advanced biplane. They weren't going to fund his journey, however, but he didn't need them. He just needed a biplane that was a little lighter, more maneuverable, and capable of going a little farther each day. Thanks to Cal's specifications, the aircraft they came up with was a specially designed Wright EX biplane with a wingspan of thirty-two feet and, according to one record, weighing about 903 pounds. It had a longer wingspan, a larger gas tank, and as rigid a construction as possible. Rodgers, his naval aviator cousin John, and Wiggin aided in the design modifications, along with Charles Taylor, the Wrights' brilliant mechanic. The framework was constructed of spruce with reinforced wire and covered with cotton duck fabric sealed with linseed oil. It was a nimble and quick machine with a capacity for longer flights. "It was the only one of its kind the Wrights ever built," said Taylor, "and was smaller and faster than the Model B."[5]

The aircraft's air-cooled, thirty-five-horsepower motor wasn't designed for the workload Cal was going to ask of it, which is why they carried an entire car full of spare parts in the *Special*, a special train that followed Rodgers. By comparison, the most powerful engine at the time was a European seven-cylinder, fifty-horsepower Gnome. As noted, the Wright brothers thought Cal's (and the others) attempt at history a bit crazy, because no aircraft was designed for a four-thousand-mile trip. "The damn thing will rattle itself to pieces," they mused. "It won't stand the trip." Rodgers inquired about their mechanic Taylor, who had helped build the *Kitty Hawk* engine. The Wrights told Rodgers, "You sure as the world" will need him. Taylor was uncommitted at first and simply wanted to help modify the biplane and get it ready.[6]

"Charlie, she's a beauty," said Rodgers once the EX was completed. Taylor agreed; the EX was yet another step in the advancement of aviation. "How about coming along with me to keep her working right?" Taylor had been won over by Rodgers, and he believed in him enough to take a leave of absence from Dayton and join Cal on his journey. Taylor would be well compensated at twenty-five dollars a week (twice as

Cal Rodgers standing in front of the *Vin Fiz* during his coast-to-coast journey (Library of Congress).

much as he was making working for the Wrights), and once in California, he would reunite with his wife on vacation. Having Taylor was a minor coup for Rodgers, because Taylor was a brilliant mechanic, and if anyone could keep a motor running, it was him. Cal was unwavering in his confidence that he could make the journey, and that confidence attracted someone like Taylor, who had also come to believe in Cal's ability.[7]

Years later, Taylor described the decision to help Rodgers:

> There weren't so many mechanics around at the time who understood the Wright motor and plane thoroughly, and since I had built the first engine and helped with the airships, Rodgers wanted me to act as chief mechanic.... Orv and Will consented to give me a leave of absence.[8]

The engine churned two massive eight-foot propellers, pushing the aircraft forward (instead of pulling it) through the air at fifty-five to sixty miles per hour, depending on conditions. The propellers were a Wright-patented development made of spruce, intricately glued together and laminated, and driven by a sprocket-driven bicycle chain from the engine. Cal would routinely push the engine's limits, making stretches at sixty miles per hour or more. The Hearst prize stipulation that only one aircraft could be used meant that constant rebuilding would be required. However, rebuilding an engine had its limits.[9]

On September 10, Chicago newspapers officially announced that "Armour will finance [Cal Rodgers's] air flight." That Armour didn't back the hometown kid, Ward, is telling; it speaks to his belief in Cal. Rodgers now had a major sponsor, a wealthy and powerful financial backer with deep pockets, which would prove vital. The architects of the sponsorship were E.B. Merritt, an advertising executive for the Armour Company, and Charles H. Dickenson, head of the soft drink division. How involved Mr. Armour was in the final negotiations is unknown, though he was quoted as saying the details were left up to Merritt and Dickenson. Later in the week, Stewart I. DeKrafft, Armour publicity manager, stated that Mr. Armour became "deeply interested in aviation at the Chicago Meet" and was impressed by Rodgers's success. Merritt and Dickenson negotiated the details along with Andre Roosevelt, an Armour executive who would go along on the transcontinental journey, riding in the train to oversee everything. Fred Wettengel, Rodgers's acting manager, assisted Cal in the negotiations. There are no records of the meeting, but it reportedly only took twenty-five minutes before a deal was brokered. Wettengel was to travel with Rodgers and act as his manager as well as his publicity frontman along with DeKrafft.[10]

Cal Rodgers (*left*) and Charles H. Dickenson, September 1911 (Library of Congress).

Dickenson spearheaded the campaign, seeing it as a great opportunity to roll out their new soft drink beverage in a big way. "It is an advertising proposition. The machine in which Rodgers is to fly will be named after our new drink we are making," he said. "And the name will be printed on the biplane where it can be seen by everyone witnessing the flight across the continent." Rodgers had the first advertising sponsorship of its kind, like today's NASCAR drivers who carry their sponsor's name on their cars. The product was the Vin Fiz grape-flavored soda drink. The company was hopeful it could compete with Coca-Cola. Backing a highly publicized publicity stunt was just the way to announce the soda, Dickenson believed. And not just the biplane, but the Palmer-Singer touring automobile Cal would be chauffeured in, and the *Special* train that would follow Cal's journey all carried a sponsorship slogan and logo. It was going to be a massive advertising campaign, the largest ever of its kind.[11]

As of September 10, Rodgers was still in Dayton, working alongside Wright mechanic Charles Taylor to make final adjustments to the EX. Excitement grew in Chicago and elsewhere as word of Cal's entrance into the race spread. DeKrafft informed the press that Rodgers was making final preparations but would soon head to New York to start

6. "It was the only one of its kind the Wrights ever built" 61

his journey. Rodgers was hands-on with the design specifications of the Wright EX biplane. Taylor was impressed with Cal's growth as a pilot and his knowledge of the machine. Still, there were plenty of doubters about Rodgers and his quest.

"Not everyone at the time shared Cal's certainty," Mabel revealed years later. "The airplane was still in its infancy, and the Wright brothers were unconvinced that it was capable of making a 4,000-mile flight."[12]

DeKrafft was going to help handle publicity but also act throughout Cal's journey as a co-manager and liaison of sorts, negotiating landing and takeoff locations with city officials, which would also be a key component of the *Vin Fiz* team. Lawrence Peters acted as co-manager, often going out ahead of the *Vin Fiz* and negotiating gas and oil suppliers for each stop and whatever else was needed. Fred Howard was assigned by the Armour Company to manage the train, and by all accounts, he ran a tight ship and kept everything running as orderly as possible. It was no small task to negotiate their travels along the massive railroad system that crisscrossed the country. There was also a small contingent from the *Vin Fiz* production branch that came along for the ride. Finally, there was Frank Shaffer, chief mechanic, and Charles "the Kid" Wiggin. Shaffer, Taylor, and Wiggin would be Cal's inner circle, advising him on the conditions for flight and the condition of the machine. The *Special* train sleeping car was fully loaded but had more than enough room to keep everyone comfortable.[13]

DeKrafft was the nephew of Rear Admiral J.C.P. DeKrafft, who for several years commanded the Flagship of North Pacific Station, which was most likely a source of comradery for him and Cal, and they bonded

Calbraith Perry Rodgers, circa 1911 (Library of Congress).

immediately. DeKrafft was a talker and a drinker (which Cal didn't care for but accepted), and on more than one occasion, he allowed both to get the best of him. After the team decided on a route, Peters or Roosevelt and sometimes DeKrafft set off ahead of the train in the Palmer-Singer automobile to arrange where and when Rodgers would land. As Rodgers progressed, these locations became attractions, and cities paid for the privilege of having Rodgers and the *Vin Fiz* land, sometimes even paying him to perform flying maneuvers for the crowds.[14]

When the Wright EX biplane, or, as it would be known during the journey, the *Vin Fiz*, was completed, it was painted. On the bottom wing, its stabilizer and rudders carried the advertising slogan, "Vin Fiz, The Ideal Grape Drink." It was indeed a flying billboard. People from below looking up would see the logo and slogan, and when it landed, the slogan was on the top of the wing as well. Vin Fiz soda company reps handed out samples and materials about the soda at every opportunity.

The race for the Hearst prize kicked off in earnest on September 11, when the dashing Robert Fowler, flying a Wright biplane with his own motor, took off from San Francisco. He was going to make Los Angeles his starting point, because the city had offered him $10,000 to do so. In need of money, Fowler initially accepted, although he preferred to depart from San Francisco because it was his hometown, but money

Cal Rodgers (*center*)and unknown children (*left*), circa September/October 1911, location unknown (Library of Congress).

6. "It was the only one of its kind the Wrights ever built"   63

talks. "However, the $10,000 which has been offered in Los Angeles is an inducement that cannot be overlooked," he told the press, hoping to get a response from his hometown. It worked. Just days before he was scheduled to start, San Francisco matched the offer, and the hometown kid agreed. This didn't go over well with Los Angeles or the *Los Angeles Examiner*.[15]

The six-foot aviator was, in his own right, a physically strong pilot capable of enduring the grueling journey. Early on, Fowler was the darling of the press, and many were optimistic that if anyone could succeed, he could. He was the national news story in aviation early on. The day of his sendoff in San Francisco, as Fowler made his way through the crowd at Golden Gate Park, women threw themselves at him; one grabbed hold of him, kissed him, and placed a "Women's Suffrage" badge on his jacket; he kept declaring his support for their cause. Reaching his Wright biplane, Fowler inspected the machine, then addressed the media. "I have every hope that I will reach New York and do so before anyone." With that, he kissed his mother, pulled himself up into the machine, waved to the surging crowd that the police held back, and took off down the runway. Fowler that day made 129 miles, reaching Auburn, California, at the base of the Sierra Nevada. It was a fantastic start to his historic attempt.[16]

The *Vin Fiz Special* train mechanics' car, where all the spare parts were kept (San Diego Air & Space Museum).

"I have planned for 20 flying days," he said after landing in Auburn. "My average is set at 175 miles, but I hope to have a couple of days of 500 miles or better."[17]

At about the same time, in Chicago, Illinois, Fred Howard nervously boarded the *Vin Fiz Special* train heading to Dayton. He was solely in charge of logistics for Rodgers's *Vin Fiz* coast-to-coast expedition. Howard noted in his diary his excitement at being assigned the *Vin Fiz* coast-to-coast journey: "I was to be in charge of the train and its movements, issue proper transportation to the various conductors and make myself generally useful." It arrived in Dayton the next day, carrying the Palmer-Singer automobile in the hangar car. The train also pulled a mechanical car of spare parts, basically a complete additional spare biplane, and tools. There were also two cabin cars and a dining car for all the Armour representatives, press members, crew, and Cal, Mabel, and his mother.[18]

Rodgers was getting antsy; there were departure delays that kept the *Special* from leaving Chicago before the twelfth. The only thing for him to do was dismantle the *Vin Fiz* and prepare it for loading into the hangar car of the train. Taylor, Wiggin, and Rodgers carefully removed the wings, skid, and tires and arranged the machine for safe packing. The *Special* arrived the next day, and on September 14, they headed out to New York. The hangar car containing the *Vin Fiz* was not attached but instead was hauled by itself a day later, due to yet another delay in needed parts.

After reaching Auburn, the next day Fowler headed up the mountain range toward Donner Pass, using the Southern Pacific Railroad tracks as his guide. Standing like sentries, the rugged, towering mountain range loomed before him. The wind shot from the peaks, making his ascension a slow and tedious climb. Somewhere near Colfax, his vertical rudder-control wire shredded. "All I could do was go around in a circle," Fowler said later.[19]

Using only the wing-warping lever, he managed to avoid losing complete control and volplane, or circle, down. However, there was not a suitable landing spot in the rugged mountains. With no other options, he wound up hitting treetops and crashing outside the village of Aha, California. Though he avoided serious injury by jumping from the biplane as it careened into the ground, he did hurt his back, as he later admitted. His biplane was almost completely destroyed and required a major overhaul, including the engine. "It will take three or four days to rebuild the machine," he said after the accident. He was confident and determined and didn't want to admit that his biplane was a total wreck. He would be grounded for twelve days, all but ending his chances.[20]

6. "It was the only one of its kind the Wrights ever built"   65

On September 13, Jimmy Ward put on his leather football helmet and climbed into his Curtiss biplane, waved confidently to the crowd, and took off from Governors Island in New York Harbor. The wind can be tricky in the Northeast, and just after takeoff, Ward had issues. "It [the wind] kept me so busy with my machine," said Ward, "that I could only look down once in a while." As a result, he got lost. Once over New Jersey and its maze of railroad tracks, he was to find his special train car (much like Cal's) and follow it. By the time he found it, he was hours delayed and ended up landing in Paterson, New Jersey, just twelve miles from Governors Island. The next day, Jimmy made it into Middleton and was greeted by a large and enthusiastic crowd, so excited that upon landing, they surged, and he nearly ran over some of them. Crowd control was a constant issue for early aviators, because spectators simply ignored safety precautions and barricades. The wonder kid was already a day late, so the crowd was antsy that morning when he was delayed due to engine trouble, something that would plague his entire journey.[21]

Ward was described as the "boyish aviator," and he did look like he should be a passenger, not the pilot. But he had the respect of his fellow aviators and the press. On September 15, he was ready to continue his journey, but a thick fog hugged the earth like a "white shroud," making takeoff impossible. Ward was itching to get back into the air; he wanted to get to Buffalo and take advantage of Fowler's misfortune. On the sixteenth, he got off early and made fifty-six miles to Susquehanna, New York. The next day, he made Owego—101 miles—stopped for a short break and took off again. But after about a hundred yards in the air, his engine failed, and he smashed into the ground, hitting with enough force to restart his engine, which then dragged the shaken pilot and his plane through a wire fence before crashing to a stop. The aircraft was severely damaged, and Ward was lucky to be alive.[22]

Meanwhile, Fowler was stuck in Colfax, California, waiting on a new tail section when a fire broke out in the hotel in which he was staying—a deadly one. It was a bad omen. One person died, another clung to life in the hospital, and a third suffered two broken legs, having jumped to safety. Fowler himself barely made it out before his floor was consumed. There were no fire sprinkler systems required in hotels then. Earlier that year, on March 25, the infamous Triangle Shirtwaist Factory fire occurred in New York City. There was no fire sprinkler system, and the fire engines that showed up weren't equipped with ladders tall enough to rescue the female workers on the upper floors; one hundred and forty-six women perished, some jumping to their deaths.[23]

By the time Cal was starting his race, Ward was waiting for repairs on his wings and skids.[24]

Upon hearing about Ward's trouble, Cal sent a playful telegram:

TOO BAD OLD MAN. SORRY TO HEAR YOU ARE DOWN AGAIN. GRIT LIKE YOURS IS BOUND TO KILL THE JINX AND WIN. A GRAY KITTEN CAME INTO MY CAR THIS MORNING AND CHASED THE HOODOO. HOPE TO TAKE THE AIR THIS AFTERNOON. VERY BEST WISHES.C.P. RODGERS

Though competitors at heart, there was still sportsmanship and comradery among these aviators. They all faced death, bad luck, or, as they often said, the "hoodoo." Ward was making progress as Fowler floundered and Rodgers got underway. Ward was forced to stop at Addison, New York, due to more engine trouble. The next morning, five minutes after takeoff, his engine again quit, and he plummeted fifty feet, his biplane completely wrecked, and miraculously, the boyish aviator just bruised and sore. But that was enough; as Ward pulled himself from the wreckage, he had an epiphany. The next day, his manager announced that Ward had withdrawn from the race. It seemed an impossible task—going up day after day, trying to fly in the same machine. He was done.[25]

A frustrated Fowler had to wait until September 23 to resume his journey. Having spent ten days stranded, any hope of making the race in thirty days was over. Still, he was determined to continue. He took off and attempted to ascend the Sierra Mountains again, but his engine wasn't up to the task and failed. With the wind currents howling off the mountain and the thin air, his motor was simply outmatched. On the twenty-fifth of September, he tried again, only to fail once more to conquer the mountain range. Three times, Fowler hurled himself in strident determination to conquer the Sierra Mountains. It was a bold try that established him in one reporter's view as the greatest living aviator. But it was over. Fowler was soon on his way back to Los Angeles, failing to conquer the mountains and the wind.[26]

Though he did not know it, as Rodgers started his journey, he was the only aviator who was truly in the race. All the others had failed either to start or to make it very far before giving up. Failure was not an option for him. He was fearless, determined, and would not be denied.

7

"Carried by Rodgers aeroplane, Vin Fiz"

The United States government saw potential in airplanes for military use. It was no coincidence there was a bomb throwing competition at the Chicago meet; the United States military was very interested in the practicality of air machines carrying and dropping bombs. Hearst criticized the government's interest in developing airplanes to carry weapons when instead they could "equally well carry a case of American-made merchandize"—a person truly skilled at business always sees the value of something. He thought that the focus on war machines should also include the refinement of American commerce and trade, and that the future of airplanes was in commerce, not war. He would be both correct and incorrect.[1]

The United States Postal Service had already started to test the possibility of using airplanes for mail transport. In New York, the postmaster general gave the go ahead for airplanes to carry mail in a limited capacity to gauge the viability of air carriers. "Cal also had the idea for a long time of carrying mail in the air with him," Mabel wrote years later in an article describing their travels. Rodgers even approached the United States Postal Service in Washington, DC, about air delivery during his journey. Though they were interested, they couldn't do anything at the time, as they were still struggling with getting the "regular mail out via the railroads."[2]

Still, Rodgers was determined to carry mail throughout his transcontinental flying. "Get yourself a mail bag," he told Mabel. She was tasked, in her words, to be the first "airmail postmistress." She would collect mail from those interested in Cal carrying it, and she even made special stamps and envelopes. "We decided to have a rubber stamp made, 'Carried by Rodgers aeroplane, *Vin Fiz.*'" So, throughout Cal's journey, he always had a bag of mail aboard the *Vin Fiz*. "I'll deliver mail by air all across America," said Cal. And he did.[3]

Rodgers standing in full flight gear with "Betsy" (*Vin Fiz*) (Library of Congress).

"Enthusiasm ran high," said Mabel about carrying mail. Everyone wanted to own a piece of mail that had flown on the *Vin Fiz*. By the time they were flying, "I had not only my bag full of airmail," she said, "but a box full too." When Cal started his journey, they had 263 pieces of mail that he carried. Not all the "130 pounds" of mail fit on the plane, so he had to rotate which letters were with him. And, of course, some were delivered to their recipients along the way. The amount of mail varied due to crashes as well, where mail was sometimes a victim of collateral damage. The mail bag was tied to the gasoline tank, and on one occasion, the mail that was onboard was lost when it "came loose" and letters sprinkled down all over parts of Indiana. What a sight it must have been for those below as mail fluttered down seemingly from the heavens. Some of the fallen mail actually found its way to its intended recipient thanks to good Samaritans on the ground.[4]

The enthusiasm for Rodgers's airmail was real. Hollywood actors and prominent businesspeople paid to have letters flown. It became so popular that Mabel hired "two mailmen, to sell photographic cards," which they charged twenty-five cents for. After Cal unintentionally delivered mail across Indiana, there were only seventy pieces left that stayed with him the rest of the way and became known as "all the way" airmail delivered from New York to California.[5]

7. "Carried by Rodgers aeroplane, Vin Fiz"

The *Special* train that followed Rodgers comprised three cars, usually pulled by a Baldwin 4-4-0 engine. The Baldwin pulled a Pullman passenger car with two estate rooms, one of which was reserved for Cal and Mabel. There were a dozen or so cabins that held up to four people. The Pullman was luxurious, with hand-carved wood molding finishes and high-end furniture in every room. The parlor contained a private culinary section manned by two stewards, both named George. At the end of the car was a viewing platform with a small spiral stairwell to go up for a panoramic view of the countryside. In all, somewhere between forty and fifty passengers were always on the train. Behind it was a day-coach car for eating, drinking, and lounging. The final car was the massive hangar car that carried all the spare biplane parts and the Palmer-Singer auto.[6]

There was a group of about twelve "hustlers," as one newspaper described them, who were part of the Vin Fiz Company advertising team that scattered ahead of the *Vin Fiz* biplane, handing out advertising materials at most landing and takeoff points. They swarmed over every venue and town promoting the soft drink and offering samples. They handed out leaflets, flyers, and coupons.[7]

8

"I Endure.... I Conquer"

"I Endure.... I Conquer"
—Cal Rodgers's Tombstone Epitaph

At three o'clock in the afternoon on September 17, 1911, a large gathering assembled at the Sheepshead Bay Racetrack, just east of Brooklyn near Brighton Beach. It was easy to identify Cal Rodgers as his six-four frame towered above the crowd. He was led to his biplane by his cousin, naval Lieutenant John Rodgers, along with a contingent that included his wife, Mabel, his ace mechanics Charles Taylor and Frank Shaffer, Charles "the Kid" Wiggin, Amour Company representatives, including several members of the publicity department, and twenty-five or so members of the press corps. Maria Sweitzer, Cal's mother, was also present but would return home to Long Island after his departure. After Lieutenant Rodgers politely asked observers to step away from the airplane, a ceremony began.[1]

Though history would know the aircraft as the *Vin Fiz*, Cal affectionately called her "Betsy." He was known to pat Betsy's wings as if they were the head of a child and speak to her in a reassuring manner. Cal started the journey in his typical flight attire: business suit, leather jacket, long leather leggings, a cloth cap, and goggles. He carried with him a few letters and a brooch from his wife that he was to present to Carrie Jacobs Bond, a famous composer who lived in California. Unknown to him, there was also a bottle of Vin Fiz soda crammed down beside his seat, put there by one of the publicity managers. It would be his trusty companion on his entire trip.[2]

There was no safety harness in these early planes. Fliers believed it was best to be thrown clear, because the engine was either directly behind or beside the pilot and often broke free on impact, crushing the pilot to death. The pilot's seat was a shallow, twelve-inch-square wicker platform with a straight back and was usually directly in front of or

8. "I Endure.... I Conquer"   71

beside the engine. The pilot's feet rested on an outrigger extending in front. For comfort, Cal Rodgers often just let his long legs dangle.[3]

As mentioned, the *Vin Fiz* was a flimsy aircraft that is archaic by today's standards. When actress Amelia Smith went to christen the aircraft with a bottle of champagne, Cal gently grabbed her arm, telling her, "You want to break that bottle sweetheart, break it on a rock." And so she did. Laughter and roars filled the air, but few really understood just how serious Cal was. After the ceremony, Cal lit an El Ropo cigar (his cigar of choice), acknowledged the crowd, and climbed aboard his aircraft. As he did, the crowd swarmed too close again, but they jumped back when the plane roared to life.[4]

Cal wasn't just chasing Hearst's $50,000 prize—he was chasing destiny. In a way, he was in a race against himself. He desperately wanted to do something big, something important, and live up to the family name. The money, though it was substantial and would be welcome, wasn't the main motivation. The Armour Company was going to pay him five dollars for each mile he flew east of the Mississippi River and four dollars per mile west of it. The *Vin Fiz* was a flying billboard, and Cal went out of his way to land in towns and cities to promote the soda. He quickly learned he could profit from these pit stops, because some places offered handsome sums for him to drop in for an appearance or to perform mini airshows. And sometimes he literally did *drop in*.[5]

Cal Rodgers and the *Vin Fiz* taking off at Sheepshead Bay Racetrack, New York (Library of Congress).

Rodgers checked the runway one last time, turned to his mechanics, and yelled, "Let 'er go!" He waved to the crowd and thundered down the makeshift runway lined with spectators. The Kid probably ran behind Cal for a few moments before he stopped and watched. He looked at the crowd and smiled at their faces of joy and excitement. Cal banked west over the East River toward Manhattan, where the streets were filled with onlookers who waved hats and umbrellas. After several laps around the Manhattan skyline, aided by the swirling and gusting air currents, he veered west again, crossing over the Hudson River and Jersey Shore heading for Middletown. He quickly found the Erie Terminal and followed the tracks, eventually crossing the Ramapo Mountains and the two-thousand-foot summit.[6]

Traveling just a little under a mile a minute, he arrived in Middletown at six o'clock after an hour and thirty-two-minute flight covering 104 miles. When he neared the landing site, he could see the sprawl of over ten thousand people gazing up at him. As he landed, the crowd again swarmed the aircraft, lights flashed as photographs were taken, and reporters pushed and fought their way to Cal. Police Chief John McCoach had a contingent of men with him to help quell the crowd as people sought to touch Cal and his flying machine.[7]

Cal rarely said much. He often couldn't. When there were crowds, he could not make out what people were saying to him. So, he politely waved and smiled, and then one of his managers quickly escorted him away. Some in the press would find him aloof and distant, but as he continued on, facing adversity, he would win over even the staunchest critic.

It was a tremendous start, prompting questions about how fast he could make his coast-to-coast trip. After such a start, there were some on the *Special* that felt Rodgers's winning the prize was a foregone conclusion. In Chicago, he had already proven himself the toughest aviator in America. His wonderful first day simply reaffirmed what they believed. "We were all very jubilant that night," Taylor remembered years later. The success of the day's flight "made us think Rodgers would average at least 200 miles per day," making the journey easily within the thirty days required.[8]

When asked what he felt his daily average could be in such ideal circumstances, Rodgers declared, "I can make 200 miles a day." The feeling in the air was electric and full of excitement. Hopes soared that Cal could pull off the impossible and make the ocean-to-ocean jaunt in thirty days or less. "Well, it's a start anyway," added Cal. "I'll get away early tomorrow at sun-up." Cal loved the ocean; his family were sea captains and sailors. Before starting his journey, he took Betsy to the waters

8. "I Endure.... I Conquer"   73

there in New Jersey and rolled her along the shore. He was determined to land on the sand and beach somewhere in California, come hell or highwater. For Cal, it was truly a coast-to-coast trip.[9]

Cal was always optimistic, and this kind of start only fueled his intense desire to make history. "No man ever had a truer machine and a more perfect engine than I did today," he said. "There was not a miss of the cylinders and not a swerve of the machine." As a matter of fact, "it's Chicago in four days."[10]

Mabel was excited and confident as well. She didn't fret over the dangerous nature of the journey Cal had started. "To start, the prize has been Calbraith's sole ambition since he learned to fly," she told Thomas Hanly of the *New York American*. "He has a perfect machine and perfect control. The weather is perfect too. A few days of this and he'll make the records fly."[11]

A reporter questioned why Cal talked so little, insisting that he had a speech impediment. His sister defended her brother, saying, "Because Cal talks so little," people have spread rumors that he has difficulty talking, which was untrue. "You should hear his words fly when he is

Cal Rodgers (*center*) smoking one of his trademark cigars standing with members of the *Vin Fiz* team (*left*) (San Diego Air & Space Museum).

speaking of aviation," she quipped as she walked away. The exchange must have angered her, because she was never quoted again, or no one ever dared say something around her.[12]

Cal's mother, Maria, was asked how she felt about his odds of winning the Hearst prize. "I am certain Calbraith will win," she said. "Of course, I am opposed to my boy flying [for the prize]," because it was dangerous and risky. She constantly fretted and worried but never unnerved Cal, who was almost always stoic. She continued, "The Wrights have told me Calbraith is very careful." She always called Rodgers *Calbraith*. The newspapers flipped between *Cal* and *Calbraith*. She just wanted Calbraith to reach California in one piece, then she'd relax, she said.[13]

That night, Cal and Mabel, along with a small contingent from the Armour Company, including its president, Davison, attended the Drum and Bugle Corps dance at Linden Hall in downtown Middletown. As they entered, Cal immediately became the center attraction. The dancers asked for a photograph, and he spent much of the evening being introduced to local community members. Most did not know that Cal struggled to make out names or sometimes even understand what was being said. He was never comfortable in such situations due to his hearing impairment and was awkward in his answering of questions—the few he could make out. He probably just smiled and shook hands, praying for it all to end. Thankfully, the band began to play, rescuing him from the spotlight. Mabel walked over, took Cal by the arm, and escorted him back to her table.[14]

Cal was up early the next day, before sunrise, and woke his crew. "Up and at 'em, fellas," he called out in the Pullman car, "let's get flying." The crew dressed and readied themselves. Cal kissed Mabel goodbye and was driven to the field by chauffeur Jimmy Dunn in the Palmer-Singer automobile. By six in the morning, a large group of spectators was already at the Orange County Fairgrounds as Cal prepared himself for flight. The biplane was pushed to the south end of the field to take off into a northern wind per Charles Taylor's instructions. After a while, the crowd grew so large that it encroached on the runway, giving Rodgers only the minimum length required. The moistness of the ground would also hinder his takeoff. Additionally, willow trees at the far end swayed back and forth in the breeze, which almost seemed to be driving down instead of north. Cal hesitated for some time as he studied the wind and the movement of those damn willows. There was an additional delay because he and his crew had to constantly plead with the spectators to stay off the runway. After discussing the situation with Taylor and Shaffer, Cal climbed aboard the biplane, the spectators were

8. "I Endure.... I Conquer"

herded back, and he barreled down the field toward the trees. Taylor, as usual, reminded Cal to "take off into the wind." He needed its lift, and Cal did not always remember to do so.[15]

What no one could have foreseen were the sudden downdrafts that were occurring, so when Cal's plane started to ascend, the wind was not providing enough lift but was instead pushing the machine down. As Cal approached the willows, he had to get to forty feet quickly, but his aircraft was floundering on takeoff. The crowd gasped as Cal barely cleared the trees, narrowly making it through by cutting over and between a set of smaller ones—a truly incredible maneuver in itself as he disappeared over the tree line. There, he immediately had another obstacle: telegraph wires. He swooped downward, trying to get under them, and then back up and over a tree in someone's yard.[16]

Henry VanCuren lived at 92 Fulton Street and was in his backyard with his wife, gardening, when the roar of an engine thundered from the sky. They looked up, dumbfounded, as the *Vin Fiz* headed right for them. They scattered out of the way as it came barreling down into their backyard. Cal was able to dip under the telegraph wires but could not fully crest the top of the hickory tree. The *Vin Fiz*'s wheels or the rudder (reports at the time vary) smacked a large branch, tossing the airplane into the ground, folding it onto itself and into a chicken coop, pinning Cal underneath the wreckage, and killing several chickens in the process.[17]

The *Vin Fiz* being moved into takeoff position in Middletown, New York (San Diego Air & Space Museum).

As the feathers, letters, and dust settled, VanCuren's wife reportedly scolded those who would listen about why a machine fell from the sky and crashed into her chicken coop. Fred Howard had to talk Mrs. VanCuren down and offered, of course, to pay for the damages. Most of the time, a hard crash killed the pilot from being crushed by the engine, which is behind or to the side of them (on the *Vin Fiz*, it was beside Rodgers). Miraculously, Cal narrowly escaped being crushed but was cut up and bruised. As he was pulled from his plane, cigar still in mouth, Cal mourned the condition of his airplane, "my beautiful Betsy." She was decimated. The engine was detached and damaged, along with a broken chain case, a damaged rudder shaft, smashed wheels, and a cracked gasoline tank—days of work, to be sure. It would not be Chicago in four days.[18]

Back at the field, the crowd rushed in great angst to the crash site. The worst must have been feared by all. Mabel and Maria arrived a short time later to find Cal removed from the wreckage. They were relieved that he was alive, but blood from a nasty cut drew Maria's instant attention. He was bruised and battered, but relatively uninjured. As Maria fretted over Cal's condition, Dr. Henry McBriar and his son, who happened to be nearby when the accident occurred, were already on the scene. Years later, McBriar claimed that he and his son Lawrence drove Rodgers to the hospital. But there was also a Dr. M.A. Stivers who was present as well, at least according to reports, which defies logic, because that is an awful lot of doctors nearby. Regardless, we know Stivers took care of Rodgers at the hospital, discharged him, but ordered twenty-four hours of bedrest, which Cal would of course ignore. After discharge, Mabel and Maria loaded Cal into the Palmer-Singer with the help of chauffeur Jimmy Dunn and drove him back to the Commercial Hotel. Once back at the hotel, yet another doctor, T.D. Mills, followed up with Cal to make sure he had no signs of internal bleeding.[19]

Though Cal was not deterred or shaken, his mother had seen enough and urged her son to quit. Her conversion to his flying had ended. "Give it up now, Cal," she said. "You were providentially saved from death." Cal was unmoved; he wasn't overtly religious in the first place. She continued to argue that the trip was now a lost cause, but she could not deter him. At the very least, he "will be killed or seriously injured," she said in tears. "For me," she even pleaded.[20]

Cal most likely embraced her and assured her he would do no such thing as die. Rodgers already knew that everyone from the Wright brothers to his own mother thought him crazy to attempt such a dangerous thing as a transcontinental journey. It was suicidal, some said, an overreaching attempt to become famous by someone from a heroic

8. "I Endure.... I Conquer"

Jimmy Dunn behind the wheel of the Palmer-Singer (San Diego Air & Space Museum).

family bloodline who could not get into the Naval Academy because of his disability. They doubted him and his abilities as an aviator. Cal's dream of following in the family lineage probably never died; instead, it fueled his desire to excel at flying. He was hell-bent on making a name for himself, and nothing would stop him. Quitting was never an option. Mabel understood this and never wavered; she supported him to the end.[21]

Wettengel told DeKrafft that he thought the day's events meant "the end of the line." He demanded they meet with Cal and urged DeKrafft to order a second EX and have Cal go back to New York and restart. The *Vin Fiz* was in bad shape, and days of rebuilding would be a serious delay and ruin their chances of success. DeKrafft wired the Wrights and even inquired about the possibility of obtaining a second craft. But Cal would have none of it. "We're in race," he said, noting the others that were still flying (Ward hadn't quit yet, and Fowler still intended to continue). After this meeting, Rodgers went to Taylor and Shaffer and told them they "had to put Humpty Dumpty back together again." Only the radiator and gasoline tank were without damage; it would truly be a massive rebuild. But if anyone could do it, Taylor could, and Cal knew it.[22]

As he began his historic journey, Cal quickly gained a growing following wherever he landed. Just days into his attempt at history, Rodgers was already making a name for himself. In 1911, the population of the United States was 98,863,000, and only 2 percent had ever seen a flying machine. It must have been a wondrous thing to see an airplane carrying a man floating through the heavens above the small towns and hamlets he passed over. As news spread of his journey, time seemed to stop wherever he flew. Below, onlookers always stopped what they were doing mid step and gazed up as the "Birdman" drifted by.[23]

9

"Once you have left the ground to fly through the air"

> "Once you have left the ground to fly through the air, you never quite come down to earth again."
> —Cal Rodgers

At dusk, a steel gray storm rolled in over a crimson sky as Rodgers's crew started working on his severely damaged plane. The rain was pouring down and wouldn't let up all night. The wrecked airplane had been loaded onto the back of a truck and taken to the armory. There, they hung electric lighting for the crew to work under. Local townspeople helped transport the spare parts from the train to the warehouse. The mechanics team, led by Taylor, Shaffer, and "the Kid" Wiggin, worked nonstop well into the night. The mayor of Middletown offered Cal's crew whatever they needed. Even the Middletown Electric Railway put up $1,000 to help offset Cal's expenses. Everyone wanted him to get back in the air as soon as possible. There was constant commotion in the armory all night as crews took shifts working on the *Vin Fiz*.[1]

The next morning, Cal's cousin John Rodgers left for Dayton to expedite the shipping of desperately needed parts. The Wrights originally told John that it would take days to get all the new parts to them; needing them sooner rather than later, he decided to go there himself. When Cal awoke, he immediately wanted to check on the status of his plane. Jimmy Dunn chauffeured Cal to the armory in the Palmer-Singer tour car, which was hard to miss because it had *Vin Fiz Flyer* stenciled on either side of the hood along with *C.P. Rodgers* on the driver and passenger doors. Cal arrived at the armory with his customary cigar in his mouth. As he entered, he stopped and looked around in amazement; the plane was literally surrounded by mechanics and people wanting to help. "Wiggy, get her fixed up; I'll be ready," said Cal.[2]

"No layman can understand the wonderful work of mechanicians," Cal told the local newspaper later that day. "When I looked at it [it was so badly wrecked], I said goodbye to it, and my first thoughts were for a new machine." John Rodgers was thinking the same thing as he traveled to Dayton to see the Wright brothers, but per the rules of the Hearst prize, they had to use the same aircraft for the entire journey or restart with a new one back at the original departure point and reset the thirty days. They could rebuild the craft as extensively and as many times as needed. As the parts were being packaged for shipment, the crew working on Betsy fixed what could be and prepped the *Vin Fiz* for the arrival of the rest. Though she wasn't perfect, she was more than flight ready. "[Other than] a few minor defects, the machine was perfect," said Cal. "[The defects were] nothing vital, but all demanding vigilance."[3]

Though stuck in Middletown, the president of the Vin Fiz Company, Charles Davidson, had pennants and extra cases of the soda delivered so the marketing crew could span out in the area to advertise and promote. He asked Cal and Mabel to go out in the Palmer-Singer with Jimmy Dunn and promote the product as well. Maria, two inches taller than Mabel, reportedly towered over her in a very intimidating manner and informed her she would also go and sit next to Cal, no doubt to continue to try to talk some sense into him. Harry Sweitzer later observed from the incident that Maria could "have given Stonewall Jackson a few pointers in tactics."[4]

Middletown Police Chief Higham took DeKrafft and Rodgers to scout a possible field for his departure. They could not use the same field; it was clearly not suitable, which Cal had found out the hard way. Higham escorted them to the Orange County Fairgrounds. Having sufficient runway length as his main concern, Cal got out and looked down the vast field next to the fairgrounds; it was perfect. The proposed runway offered plenty of room, and Cal agreed it would be the spot, later confirming that there "was a good long stretch of ground for the take-off."[5]

Not even a week into Rodgers's journey, things became perplexed by a situation that arose between DeKrafft and Wettengel, Rodgers's personal manager. Disputes over locations for *Vin Fiz* departure and landing locations were common, and the two had already had disagreements. But what apparently set them off was Wettengel's continued insistence that Cal give up the race and restart. It became heated to the point of DeKrafft's punching Wettengel. The altercation was severe; Wettengel was knocked down and ended up pressing charges. DeKrafft was fined but paid up, calling it "cheap." Whatever was said, Wettengel was apparently in the wrong, because the Armour Company paid

9. "Once you have left the ground to fly through the air"

DeKrafft's fine, asked Wettengel to step down as Rodgers's manager, and sent him home, apparently without any objection from Cal.[6]

A series of telegraphs confirmed a new engine had been shipped from Dayton along with all the needed spare parts. Two days later, the parts arrived. Lieutenant Rodgers returned just before Cal's scheduled departure from Middletown on Wednesday, September 21. That evening, another storm swept over Middletown, causing Cal to worry, "The fates are against us. It is raining ... and I do not want to make a big jump tomorrow." With such weather, the ground would surely be wet, and his wheels would slip, making takeoff tricky.[7]

"Hope you have the best of luck," Jimmy Ward telegraphed Rodgers. He wished Cal happy flying and hoped that the luck "changes for both of us." Ward would encounter more bad luck and, not long after, be out of the race to the coast. At this moment though, Ward was a threat, and Cal was eager to get back in the air.[8]

Reporters asked if his mishap and subsequent delay ruined his chances of winning the Hearst prize. Cal scoffed, "Oh ... I'll make up for this. The machine should be fixed soon; wait until then and I'll do some tall flying." The machine had been badly damaged; the engine had buried itself in the earth. The only thing not seriously smashed was the steering apparatus. He reassured the reporters that the new parts were in place and that the *Vin Fiz* had been rebuilt even better. "We have the best mechanician in the world—Charlie Taylor. We will be ready for the start tomorrow."[9]

Taylor was indeed one of the best. He came from humble beginnings; he was born on a small family farm in Illinois to an uneducated mother and father on May 24, 1868. He was a talented and instinctive mechanic who had built the Wrights' first airplane engine for the Kitty Hawk. He even helped build the first military plane years later. Taylor was the first airplane mechanic inducted into the US Air Force Aviation Museum Hall of Fame. The Federal Aviation Administration honored him by creating the "Charles Taylor Master Mechanic Award" recognizing senior aviation mechanics and their achievements. "Almost every evening after a hop we had to completely overhaul the [*Vin Fiz*] engine," Taylor said years later. Rodgers was lucky; he had one of the best airplane mechanics on the planet helping.[10]

As the *Vin Fiz* was being finished and prepped for the continuation of the race, rumors circulated that the reasons for Rodgers's recent troubles were because of "the influence of liquor." The *Middletown Daily News Press* quickly squashed this as a "vicious falsehood," because they knew Cal to be a man who "takes the best care of himself." Usually, newspapers had no trouble spreading rumors, but they had gotten to know Cal so well that they felt compelled to publish a rebuttal against such lies. His only habit was well documented: he loved to drink milk—lots of it—daily, and his only known vice was the constant cigar he smoked or rolled in his fingers as he smiled and conversed.[11]

The next morning, the weather conditions were better; the ashen sky was replaced with shades of blue and enormous, expanding clouds that indicated a calm morning breeze. The field was wet, but not enough to halt Cal's departure, because the runway was longer than needed. He planned to leave in the afternoon, and by then, the grass would be almost dry. Nearly the entire town of Middletown came out to the fairgrounds to see Cal off. The *Vin Fiz* team published an editorial thank you to the town for their hospitality. Rodgers would be a favorite of the community, and the Middletown newspapers dutifully tracked his progress throughout his entire journey. The engine was checked again, a loose fuel line tightened, and Cal gave the signal to "Let 'er go." Cal's mechanics, led by Taylor, had gotten the spare engine off the train just the day before and repaired everything vital that evening. They tested it repeatedly, making sure the magneto and fuel lines were perfect. The Wright biplane ascended gracefully with little trouble. "From the moment I left the ground I was climbing, and I never stopped until I was about 1,800 feet," Cal

Charles Taylor, circa 1904 (Caltech Archives and Special Collections).

said later. "The model EX climbs like a cat, and in one swing I was high enough."[12]

"This afternoon," wrote the *New York Times*, "one of the most successful [flights] ever made by an aviator" took place in front of "thousands" of spectators. Cal reportedly told his crew that he didn't care if they had to wait a week to get the *Vin Fiz* right; he didn't want them to rush the repairs or the installation of the new engine. It was a telling remark, because it indicated that maybe he wasn't as concerned with winning the prize as some. He was keenly becoming aware that attrition would be key to making it across the country. Trying to make it in thirty days was the problem; hurrying repairs and taking chances in weather were true obstacles for all those trying to win the Hearst prize. Cal would most certainly have liked to win the prize, but what he wanted more than anything was to make history and create a legacy for himself. In his mind, being the first to make a transcontinental journey would be the stuff of legend.[13]

"The wind was a little choppy at the first, but I was soon above that and off for Port Jervis," said Rodgers. "Twenty-two miles away I could see the white smoke of the whistles as I crossed over the main part of Middletown."[14]

The next stop was Hancock, New York, ninety-five miles from Middletown. "I was above the air currents going faster than the wind, and the engine went on singing a sweet song. I lit a fresh cigar and let 'er go," said Cal. When the weather was right, Cal could feel the hum of the engine and, of course, slightly hear its roar. Betsy was running in top form, and his optimism for making up time soared. Not only did she soar high, but Cal's confidence did as well. If he could make up some time, he could reach Chicago in a few days and swing south for warmer air, a less cluttered landscape, and easier landings and takeoffs.[15]

Cal had little trouble finding the Erie Railroad tracks, and with the breeze at his back, he started to make up time. "I was hitting up fifty miles before I left Middletown ... as a nest of houses slid under me." Soon he ran into an obstacle: the Port Jervis hills. Though only 400 feet, it was a range with a steep slope that caught Cal by surprise. "I saw them almost before I caught the glint of the Delaware [River]," Cal later said. "I turned a little to the north west ... [and] caught the air currents from the hills right there and shot up over them." And he was on his way, making excellent time.[16]

The sun glancing off the railroad line cut a ribbon of silver through a countryside steeped in woods, small towns, and hamlets. Rodgers often commented on the feel of flight, stating, "Once you have left the ground to fly through the air, you never quite come down to earth again." The feeling must have been like a natural high—an adrenaline rush for these early pilots—why else did they do it? For Cal, the reasons were more complicated, but certainly the allure of flying and looking down on everything with the wind at his back must have touched him deep in his soul. "I was shooting into the sun," Cal was quoted as saying about his flight that day. He was up in the sky with the rays of the sun and only the wings of birds as companions, where so few people dared to venture in 1911.[17]

10

"I hope I never have any more trouble in the air than I had today"

> "I hope I never have any more trouble in the air than I had today. It was the real thing in the danger line."
> —Cal Rodgers

Rodgers was about ninety miles from Middletown, skirting the Pennsylvania state border and making excellent time, when he saw the town of Hancock on the horizon. "Town followed town," Rodgers said later. In this part of the country, towns and hamlets dotted the landscape. He was lulled into a funk, drifting with the wind, sailing above nothing but woods and hamlets, when a spark plug went out, the engine sputtered, and the plane gyrated. He didn't have long to avoid burning out his engine and had to put down quickly in a wet potato field where a farmer and two field hands were harvesting the potatoes. They stopped and watched as the flying machine plowed into the ground, skidding across the earth before coming to a harmless stop just feet from their rows of potatoes. With a shrug, they went back to work pulling potatoes, seemingly unimpressed with Rodgers or his plane. "I went over to them and asked where I was," Cal later said, amused. "One of them told me between grabs." Though the farmers weren't impressed, the sight of a biplane going down alerted everyone in the area. "Of course the crowd came seemingly out of the mountains," he said later.[1]

Rodgers had to wait for the *Special* train to catch up to him. As he did, locals kept coming to see what the fuss was all about. Soon trucks and cars choked a nearby dirt road as people trudged over the field to get to Cal and his biplane, trampling some crops in the process. Rodgers apologized to the farmer and offered to pay for the ruined crops. About an hour later, Shaffer, Taylor, Wiggin, and a team from the train arrived to shoo away the crowd and retrieve the *Vin Fiz*. It's not hard to imagine the ordeal of having to fight their way through the crowd, which often deteriorated into disputes and disagreements with the onlookers.[2]

The next morning, the weather was gloomy and gusty. It was eleven in the morning before Cal got off and started to ascend to two thousand feet. "Because of the wind against me," Rodgers reported later, "that meant all kinds of [air] pockets." It was a bumpy ride navigating the wind and the sudden pockets of dead air. Cal had to get up to 2,500 feet before he found a calm stream to fly in, but up there, "it wasn't the warmest," and he had to constantly swing his feet back and forth to keep them warm.[3]

In his efforts to find some calm air, Rodgers lost his way and ended up heading south into Pennsylvania. "Pretty soon I came to a good sized town," Cal said. If he had stayed on course, it would have been Binghamton, but as he dropped to get a better look, he saw something that troubled him: coal mines. "This gave me a shock. I had studied the route enough to know coal mines didn't belong in Binghamton." Cal had gone forty-five miles off course and was approaching the town of Scranton, Pennsylvania. Realizing he had to find out where he was, he put down in a field outside of town.[4]

Once again, it didn't take long for a large crowd to arrive from all over. Wherever Rodgers went, people showed up, even when it wasn't a planned stop—hundreds and sometimes thousands, depending on how long he was stuck. The massive congregation was unruly. "This crowd went crazy," Rodgers told his managers later. The crowd wanted to touch the machine, even sometimes take a piece—as absurd as that sounds—and almost to a person write their name on the cloth wings. "In ten minutes there wasn't an inch free of pen marks," Cal complained later. He nearly lost his temper as he fought off the mob. "They didn't mind climbing on it to get a good spot." Rodgers even had to physically restrain one gentleman who carried with him what he described as a "chisel" and was intent on getting a piece of the history-making *Vin Fiz*. He had no regard for safety or for what might happen once Rodgers was back in the air. If something was ripped or broken, the result would have been catastrophic. Eventually, he recruited the help of a few good men to steady the plane, and he took off, heading back where he came from, most certainly relieved he was getting out of Pennsylvania; he had seen enough.[5]

Not long after being airborne, Cal again struggled with air pockets and gusting wind, having to get all the way to three thousand feet before he found some peace. Again, the air was freezing cold, and it was all he could do to stay warm. He managed to go about forty miles before he was forced to put down at Great Bend in order to find some fuel and

10. "I hope I never have any more trouble in the air" 87

eat his meager sandwich for lunch. Rodgers got some fuel, ate, and again dealt with a crowd before getting back in the air. He reacquired the railroad and headed out toward Elmira, his destination for the day. "I made out the town," he said later, "and then started looking for the fair grounds." But it was dusk, and the sun hung low on the horizon. The fairground was the prearranged landing location, but it was getting too dark to find it. "There wasn't a big field in sight, and I sailed away up over the town, looking around, and then swung around to look for the special." He was running out of time.[6]

As he floundered, looking for the fairgrounds, he could not find a suitable landing spot. But then he got lucky and spotted a short train with a white stripe on top; he had found the *Vin Fiz Special*. Not only that, as he crested a hill, he spotted a field next to a large pond. He put down gently and waited for his crew. It did not take long for them to get there, and as usual, they had a litany of questions about where in the hell he had been. Cal's hop to Elmira was 173 miles, and a hundred of them were out of the way—not a great day.[7]

That night, word came that Jimmy Ward had once again suffered engine trouble that caused him to crash land. With another spent engine and serious damage to his biplane, Ward was forced to pull out of the Hearst prize race. Cal did not celebrate Ward's demise; "it was the hoodoo ... it's been pursuing him ever since he started," he humbly noted. He knew how much Ward wanted to at least make it to Chicago, and he never got close. For the most part, there was a camaraderie among these early fliers. They felt kindred, a brotherhood, so few risked their lives as they did. Cal's mother used the occasion to celebrate one less competitor but also to point out to Rodgers that he needed to consider doing the same, for his luck was not faring much better. According to some witnesses, her reaction caused a stir among the *Vin Fiz* team and even Cal himself. Mabel, meanwhile, remained steadfast in her support for her husband and might have even had words with Cal's mother about her constant negativity.[8]

That evening, Tayler, Shaffer, and the Kid removed the new engine and replaced it with the rebuilt one in order to work on the spark plug issue. It is unclear if this was under the direction of Rodgers or if they ran into trouble that night while prepping the *Vin Fiz* for the next day's flight.

On the morning of September 23, as Cal awoke, he was notified that there was a heavy fog. It was so misty, the earth seemed to be swallowed up by it. He didn't even leave the train; instead, he lay back down and slept another hour. At nine, he rose, had coffee, and headed down to the field. Once at the field, Cal was concerned, because not even the sun's rays could penetrate the gloomy mist. "I want to get away as soon as possible," said Cal. "Time is precious." No doubt, time was on his mind. "If weather conditions help me, I am confident I can beat yesterday's trip." Cal told reporters that his goal for the day was four hundred miles—an incredible goal, but one he surely thought he could accomplish.[9]

After an hour or so, the mist evaporated and the sun broke through, unfurling a luminous day of golden light. Cal conferred with Shaffer and Taylor, and they agreed it was their best chance to get airborne. But they had to first get the crowd to move and open up a suitable strip of runway for him—into the wind, as Taylor made sure. The field was a flood plain "edged by a bluff," and because the crowd would not fully remove themselves, Rodgers headed toward the wrong slope. He needed to get over some trees, avoid the pond, get in the air, and then head toward the Erie Railroad. However, when he "topped the bluff," he was immediately confronted yet again by telegraph wires. "My old friends," Cal later remarked. He drove the *Vin Fiz* down hard, barely avoiding the obstacle and almost repeating the crash from days before. Still, he landed with such force that the wings reverberated, snapping several support wires. Though the *Vin Fiz* was not seriously damaged because he had avoided a nosedive, the repairs would still cause yet another delay.[10]

"I got over this [bluff], dipped in a puffy wind and then rose to find my old friends, the telegraph wires, in front of me," Rodgers reported later to the newspapers. "I dodged them by aligning just nine inches from a tree directly in front of me and three feet from a ledge. The only thing I suffered were a few brace wires that pulled out."[11]

Shaffer inspected the damage and then headed back to the *Special* to find wires and grab tools. The Kid and Taylor began removing the snapped wires and inspecting the rest of the aircraft. A short time later, Shaffer returned, and they went about replacing the wires, this time double enforcing them. Cal stood off to the side with Mabel, checking the time, and watching the repairs. At one point, he joined in and helped with the wires. After two hours, Taylor declared the *Vin Fiz* ready to go. They wheeled the aircraft to a knoll in a clearing.[12]

That afternoon at 2:13, when Rodgers finally took off, as usual, a large crowd was in attendance. For a while, the journey was smooth and uneventful, when after about forty-five minutes, he noticed the engine wasn't running properly because the aircraft kept losing power and dipping. He could not always hear the difference—he could only feel it. When he looked at the engine, he noticed a spark plug was fouling and working itself loose from the magneto. He cursed his luck; the magneto was going to be the end of him, he must have thought. In order to

10. "I hope I never have any more trouble in the air" 89

keep the plug from falling out, Cal had to keep one hand on the plug and operate the biplane with the other—not an easy task. Unwilling to land and fix the engine, Rodgers held on for an hour with his arms spread eagle until he simply could not take the strain any longer. Still, Cal was roaring along at sixty miles an hour, making good time; he was desperate to keep going.[13]

As Rodgers drifted over one hamlet after another, everyone stopped and looked up at the sky. Fire bells, whistles, and horns alerted all that the great Birdman was approaching. First, it was Addison at 2:57 p.m., then, five minutes later, he soared over Rathbone, where horns and whistles reverberated, and all motion in town ceased as everyone gazed skyward. Then, it was Cameron Hills, its hillsides dotted with people in their automobiles and on their horses waving and cheering as he passed. By 3:22 p.m., he had reached Adrian, and just five minutes later, he could see the outskirts of Canisteo. By this time, there was a large caravan of people in cars and buggies and on horseback trying to keep up. People followed the *Vin Fiz* to Canisteo, where they could tell Rodgers was clearly looking for a place to land as he circled around.[14]

Cal released his hand from the plug and descended quickly before it dislodged. "I picked out a field above Canisteo and sailed down," Rodgers later wrote. "The plugs stayed in until I was about to hit the ground, when they jumped out again. That stopped my engine before I was ready."[15]

"I hope I never have any more trouble in the air than I had today. It was the real thing in the danger line," Rodgers wrote in his press release. "At least it seemed so to me, and that I came out of it with nothing worse than a smashed left under

Rodgers looking over the support wires of the *Vin Fiz* (San Diego Air & Space Museum).

plane was lucky." It was a miserable hour as he held in the plugs and worked his aircraft with just one hand. It is unclear if he was able to light a cigar this time as he flew. "Finally, I was obliged to keep my right hand back all the time, while I tried to work the two levels with my left hand." As the engine died on his approach, the biplane slammed into the ground.[16]

The caravan of automobiles, buggies, and horses saw him dive northwest of Canisteo and all rushed to the scene of the accident. Cal had been thrown from the plane when it came to a stop but was fortunately uninjured. The first to arrive was Theodore Cobb, a local businessman, who was driving the fastest car. Reportedly, he found Cal standing by the *Vin Fiz*, but he was in some distress because he didn't want his mother and wife to be worried. It was a stupid, minor accident. Cal asked Cobb to speed off for the *Special* train and tell them "where I am and tell my mother and wife that I am not hurt." As Cobb left, the rest of the caravan emerged up the road. Cal had to once again stop them from taking parts of the plane as souvenirs. John Rodgers was one of the first to reach Cal from the train in the Palmer-Singer with Jimmy Dunn. He was relieved to find his cousin safe and sound. Not long after, the rest arrived via the *Special*, along with Mabel, who carried with her a quart of milk. Cal kissed her and finished the milk in one long drink. Cal's mother embraced him, fretted about his cuts and bleeding, and insisted he seek medical care. He, of course, refused, lit another cigar instead, and joined Taylor, Wiggin, and the rest of his crew to assess the damage to the aircraft. The skids were splintered, the lower left wing was broken along with its supporting wires, and the fabric was ripped. His day was well short of his four-hundred-mile goal.[17]

The *Special* followed along, usually well behind the *Vin Fiz*, as Rodgers stuck to his iron compass as much as possible. They had organized in advance a system of notifications. "We kept track of his progress from bulletin boards in railroad stations," said Mabel, "which we read as the train slowed down as we passed through towns." The boards were updated by station agents who saw Rodgers pass by. Jimmy Dunn was usually the one to read the message and relay it to the others. A typical message read: "Plane with Mr. Rodgers arrived at 4:23 pm, it was going west.... God bless him (signed) the Station Agent."[18]

The headline next to Rodgers the next day in the *Chicago Examiner* mentioned the death of a twenty-three-year-old aviator named Frank Miller, who had crashed outside of Troy, Ohio, in bad weather after the crowd had spurred him on. According to newspapers, he wasn't going to fly, but the crowd verbally assaulted him, calling him names. So

10. "I hope I never have any more trouble in the air" 91

Miller went up, and not long into the flight, his engine stopped, and he dropped, plunging straight into the ground, the plane exploding on impact. Miller was trapped underneath the engine and burned to death, if the impact hadn't already killed him. Cal's mother noted his death to him and Mabel, pleading with them both for him to stop and give it up. Was he doing all this just for fame or the love of the morbid masses? Every other day, it was something—a crash, a mid-air crisis— that was nerve racking for her. No, it was suicide, surely. She reminded them of the Wright brothers and their insistence that it was foolhardy. The biplane was literally shaking itself to pieces, as they had predicted. Miller was the fifty-sixth aviator to perish in 1911 alone. Rodgers had already crashed several times and was sure to crash again and again. But Cal was unshakable, and Mabel was always by his side. Still, the feeling of despair had to haunt her with every takeoff and landing. She was incredibly strong.[19]

Alfred Slawson owned a nearby blacksmith and carriage shop in Canisteo and offered it to Taylor and his crew to conduct needed repairs. They hitched the aircraft to a set of horses and towed it into town. Taylor, Wiggin, and their team immediately began working on the *Vin Fiz*. The magneto issue had to be dealt with before it got Rodgers killed. As his mechanics worked on the aircraft, Rodgers was approached by locals, who declared that his plane could "fly to the moon." Cal smiled for a moment before his mother appeared with a local doctor, whom she insisted examine him. He obliged but was not too happy about it. Cal stayed at the shop for a time, overseeing the repairs, not leaving until they agreed that it would be ready by the morning. With that, Jimmy Dunn and the Pullman-Singer automobile whisked Rodgers to the Sherwood Hotel where he reunited with Mabel. Later that night, Taylor, Wiggin, and the rest of the crew joined Cal, Mabel, and his mother for dinner; it was Cal's treat for all their hard work.[20]

Rodgers wrote of the day's events before bed:

> Something went wrong with me all day.... It opened with a fog that wouldn't rise until after 9:30 o'clock. I would have been off by 6 if they hadn't told me then that there was a thick mist over the valley. I rolled over then and woke up at 8. I got down to my machine soon after 9 o'clock, and by that time they had changed motors for me. I wish I had kept the new motor now, but the mechanician wanted to give it an overhauling.[21]

Because of the magneto issues on the new engine the day before, the mechanics, led by Taylor, decided to swap it out with the one they had rebuilt. Rodgers seems to lay blame for the engine trouble perhaps on Taylor and his insistence on removing the newer motor. Clearly, frustration was building for Cal as the days came and went. He should already be in Chicago; now it was still days away.

As Rodgers's popularity rose at each stop, the Armour Company managers demanded he do more promotions and press events—that he take advantage of every opportunity to give the *Vin Fiz* exposure. By the end of September, he was the only aviator in the running for the Hearst prize, and, day by day, he was gaining more and more publicity. There were also demands from Taylor and the *Vin Fiz* crew, not to mention his wife and mother. Still, Cal was in his element.

11

"There were five thousand pairs of eyes"

> "There were five thousand pairs of eyes scanning the
> eastern horizon for the first glimpse of the birdman."
> —*Wellsville Daily Reporter*

The next day, the goal was to reach Jamestown, New York, 116 miles away. Cal took off from a field outside of Canisteo on Mr. Flint's farm, where two thousand spectators showed up. Apparently, Mr. Flint didn't know what he had bargained for when he agreed to allow Rodgers to take off from his farm, because his crops were trampled. Upset, he threatened legal action. Cal got in the air without incident and headed west.

The *Wellsville Daily Reporter* gave a detailed description of the anticipation and revelation of seeing Rodgers and his biplane as he passed over Wellsville not long after leaving Canisteo:

> By a prearranged plan a fire alarm was sounded at the time [of Rodgers's passing] ... within a few minutes after the alarm had been given many roofs of buildings, telephone poles, bridges and nearby hills were dotted with human beings anxiously watching for the approach of the first aeroplane to ever fly over Wellsville. There were five thousand pairs of eyes scanning the eastern horizon for the first glimpse of the birdman.[1]

The allure and attraction that followed Rodgers wherever he went during his transcontinental journey cannot be overstated. When the *Vin Fiz* was finally spotted at 11:07 a.m. floating above the hills to the east of Wellsville, the newspaper reporter noted that "it appeared like a large bird over the horizon." The article continued, "It made a turn cutting across and over the hills east of the village," before heading west. The newspaper noted that Cal could be seen for about twenty minutes before disappearing over the horizon.[2]

Rodgers had been airborne for two hours and thirteen minutes but had only traveled sixty-five miles due to a strong headwind. After hours of "bucking the bronco wind," as Cal described it, he was exhausted and hungry, but more importantly, he knew that he needed gas. As he approached the city of Olean, he saw a good spot to land at the fairgrounds, so he eased the airplane down and landed. It took but minutes for a crowd to gather around Cal, who was looking over Betsy while eating his lunch. He discovered that he was indeed low on fuel. About this time, the town mayor arrived, along with the Chamber of Commerce president. Cal endured handshakes and photographs and then asked if anyone had some petrol. The *Special* was not close, and he did not want to wait for it to get fuel. The owner of Olean's bicycle factory and garage, Frank Close, spoke up and volunteered to get some fuel. Cal was obliged, and as he waited for Close to return, he noticed a loose wheel on his airplane but was able to fix it. Close returned with a large ten-gallon milk canister full of gas. Soon the *Vin Fiz* was fueled up and ready to go. Cal bid everyone farewell and took off. In all, he had only been delayed by about thirty minutes.[3]

But not ten minutes after his takeoff, the *Vin Fiz* started to waver as the motor began to miss and sputter, and more importantly, Betsy lurched and dipped, causing Cal to look at the engine. "I hadn't gone more than eight or nine miles when the magneto began to show signs of trouble," Cal said later that day. He had no desire to repeat yesterday's theatrics and quickly looked for a place to land. He found a field that was suitable and put the airplane down. Rodgers landed in yet another farmer's field near a barn. As he climbed out of his biplane, he noticed someone. An American Indian with a native headdress approached and pointed at the *Vin Fiz* and then to the sky and said in broken English, "Big bird ... biggest I ever saw." Cal had landed on a farm in the Allegany Seneca Indian Reservation at a place called Red House. Soon, Seneca Indians were emerging from all over to look at the *Vin Fiz* and its big Birdman.[4]

Red House was just outside of Salamanca, New York, where traveling evangelist Billy Sunday was giving a rousing fire and brimstone sermon to a packed house in a makeshift tent off Main Street. Sunday was a popular religious figure in the early twentieth century and traveled all over the country giving rousing sermons. He was once a professional baseball player for the Chicago White Sox but gave up a lucrative career and became a preacher. Being a former baseball player helped him generate interest in his religious revivals. But on this day, not even that would be enough. The congregation first heard the whistles of the *Special* as it approached in the distance, then a few moments later the

11. "There were five thousand pairs of eyes" 95

humming motor of the *Vin Fiz* could be heard. As the crowd started to shift in their seats, a murmur arose as Sunday continued his service. The town knew from newspapers that Rodgers would pass over at some point that day, and the excitement of seeing the great Birdman and his big bird was simply too much. Within moments, the congregation began to dissipate; apparently, not even the appeals of Sunday to stay did any good, because soon he was virtually alone. "This world is going to hell so fast it is breaking the speed limit," the enigmatic pugilist was quoted as saying.[5]

Back at Red House, Cal had an audience of natives from the Seneca tribe as he worked on the engine; his six-four frame towered over them, prompting one to say, "Big man," and all agreed, which probably made sense—a big man in a big bird. After about thirty minutes, he was able to get the plugs secured and ready to take off. Yet again, he was having issues with his magneto, which was unsettling, causing him to push the limits of his machine by just flying. He inspected the field and noticed it was soft ground, almost mushy, due to long flattened and matted grass—which would surely hinder his takeoff speed. At the far end of the field was a tall, double-layered fence—an ominous obstacle. He asked for two men to hold his machine as he started the engine, then hopped in and barreled down the field. But not long into his attempt, he switched off the engine because he was unsure about his speed and the fence line. At this point, the Seneca chief offered to remove the fence, but Rodgers demurred. "No," replied Rodgers, "I can get over it." Cal tried a second time but again shut off his engine and turned back. Frustrated, he looked at the time. He had not traveled far and needed to keep moving. His third attempt was his last of the day; he kept the engine on and pulled as hard as he could on the elevator lever, the fence line rushing at him. But he wasn't using the wind, and the field conditions made it impossible. He careened into the first fence and then became ensnared and thrown into the ground by the second line. The *Vin Fiz* was in shambles again. As Cal staggered out of the wreckage, the Seneca Indians came running over to check on him. The chief looked at the wrecked big bird and then at Rodgers. "I said we'd take the fence down, big bull head."[6]

The *Special* pulled into the Salamanca Railroad Yard, where its passengers were informed of Cal's crash. The ramps to the Palmer-Singer car were lowered, and the automobile was backed out and quickly off to Red House. As usual, with Jimmy Dunn behind the wheel and Taylor, Wiggin, and Shaffer inside. Mabel and Maria were assured that Cal was unhurt, so they stayed behind and waited.[7]

The Palmer-Singer was on the scene about thirty minutes later, and they quickly began assessing the damage. While Cal waited, locals informed him that he was just outside of Salamanca. At that point, he had traveled only ninety-one miles. Both propellers were shattered, and the wings torn to "ribbons." Hopefully, the engine was not seriously damaged, but it was too early to tell. Taylor most likely stood observing the crash scene, calculating whether Cal had taken off into the wind.[8]

As Cal stood in the wreckage, he noticed the glint of light under the smashed biplane. It was the bottle of *Vin Fiz* he was carrying. He looked it over, and miraculously, it was not broken. The soda was still securely contained inside. He must have smiled at it because he kept it as a good-luck charm the rest of the way. Still, knowing that there were easily two days of work to be done and how little distance he had covered since he started, the feeling that the Hearst prize was escaping his grasp had to be settling in.

Taylor and Shaffer had the *Vin Fiz* taken into Salamanca. Once there, the biplane was moved to the Salamanca Engine Works garage, where reconstruction started in earnest. "Fix her up, boys," said Cal, "and I'll be ready." When pressed by a reporter, Cal admitted his attempt to take off in that field was foolhardy. He was pressed for time and took a chance, and now, because of the crash, he was running out of time.[9]

12

"The panorama of little villages spread out ahead"

> "The panorama of little villages spread out ahead of me looked like a set of black checkers on a monster board."
>
> —Cal Rodgers

Rodgers had dinner at the Palace Café with Stewart DeKrafft, Lawrence Peters, Fred Howard, and other senior members of the Vin Fiz and Armour Company. Mabel and Maria stayed behind at the Dudley Hotel in Salamanca and had a quiet dinner. Maria was noticeably upset the entire afternoon and again was rumored to have pleaded with Cal to give up the journey. Cal, as he would every time, appeased her with words but had no intention of stopping; besides, Mabel was a rock of support, which probably irked Maria even more.

A crowd started gathering outside the café to get a look at the first aviator to ever visit Salamanca. The meeting was most likely a somber one, because they surely discussed the situation. There was unwavering support for Rodgers, but a growing sense of frustration had to be present. Cal was seven days into his Hearst transcontinental challenge, and the prospect of success was not looking hopeful. He would have to make it all the way to Chicago by Friday at the latest, which was not even the halfway point. Making it to Chicago by Friday would mean getting to Kent, Ohio, by Thursday, and on Friday, September 29, taking a massive jump to Chicago, which was a little over 380 miles away—making the total distance 1,100 miles in twelve days. That would mean about another three thousand miles to make it to the Pacific Ocean in the remaining eighteen days—doable, but not likely, based on the first week of traveling. Cal sat mostly in silence, trying to absorb as much of the conversation as he could. Surely, his mind wandered as he thought about the importance of the upcoming week. The challenge was daunting but not insurmountable. He had already overcome so much of his adversity; he would handle this. At some point, the gathering crowd outside caught his attention.[1]

When the crowd outside the window at the Palace Café grew restless, he excused himself and went out to say a few words and shake hands. Jimmy Dunn in the Palmer-Singer soon swung up and rescued Cal to take him back to the hotel. But they didn't get far; Main Street became choked with onlookers who had heard that Rodgers was there, so the drive turned into a parade of sorts, with Rodgers shaking hands with hundreds of people as they slowly drove.

It took two days and virtually all the spare parts they had to get the *Vin Fiz* airworthy. They ordered more spare parts from Dayton that they would pick up in Marion, Ohio. Andre Roosevelt had to readjust the scheduled departure points and cast out his team to make the arrangements. On the second day, Rodgers and Mabel stayed the night in Jamestown after learning of the excitement there the day of his accident. The entire community had gathered the day before to watch Rodgers pass over, waiting for two hours for him, only to never see the *Vin Fiz*.[2]

By Wednesday, September 27, the repairs on the *Vin Fiz* were complete. The ripped canvas on the wings and the support wires were replaced, and the engine was reinstalled. The elevator plane and rudder were not attached until the biplane was taken out to the field. Then, for the final piece, the propellers were reattached, which could all be done in less than an hour. "With any kind of weather I ought to make 33 miles to Jamestown in short order tomorrow," Rodgers said. "If everything is working right I'm going to strike out towards Meadville, Pa., [another] seventy miles beyond." That evening, a raging thunderstorm swept in, putting a damper on the *Vin Fiz* crew.[3]

Cal was asked about his stay in Salamanca, and he spoke of the hospitality he had received thus far on his journey at every stop. The questions then focused on the repairs and the accident. He noted all the spare parts were used up and that they had ordered more, and as for him, well, "all except a new aviator" had been ordered. They were stuck with the one they had; "the old one had learned his lesson, he hopes." No more pressing the issue; take what was given and stay the course.[4]

The rain had stopped, but there were still the remnants of an early morning fog as Jimmy Dunn drove Cal to the field. Cal usually sat in silence. He had to have gazed out at the mist, thinking about the importance of the next forty-eight hours. He absolutely had to make Chicago by Friday, and to make that even a possibility, he had to make it to Kent today, 203 miles away. When the car turned onto the grounds, a large

12. "The panorama of little villages spread out ahead"   99

crowd was already waiting. Betsy stood at the far end of the field surrounded by Taylor, Wiggin, Shaffer, and the rest of the mechanic crew. The sun bathed her in a glorious glow of white and orange. As he stepped out of the Palmer-Singer, the wind was gusting too much to take off.[5]

An adjacent field near where Rodgers had his accident at Red House had been selected for the takeoff point. This time, the field was long, and there was no fence to deal with. At 10:30 a.m., the wind was gone, and Taylor, Shaffer, and Wiggin steadied the plane as Cal climbed aboard. He started the engine and throttled it, testing it for several minutes. Taylor and Shaffer were satisfied; Cal nodded and gave the signal. "Let 'er go!" He roared down the field lined with bystanders, including the Seneca Indians.

"With the weather as nearly perfect for the machine as it can be," said Rodgers, "I succeeded in getting past the hills, which have been my constant companion since leaving New York, and into the level country." Because of his recent inflight issues, Rodgers was training himself to always be aware of the landscape and to look for good places to make an emergency landing. He did not want to be caught with a dead aircraft and no place for a suitable landing. The journey through western New York was an arduous one, to be sure. Rolling hills and outgrowths of the Allegheny Mountains extended from Pennsylvania and occupied most of the southwest part of New York, at times as high as 2,500 feet. There were long stretches where no suitable landing spot existed, and if he had engine trouble, it would have simply been a crash landing into trees or fence-lined fields of tall crops, brush, and grass.[6]

Rodgers passed over Jamestown, Pennsylvania, at a rate Cal claimed later was "faster than a minute" a mile. The *Vin Fiz* was humming. Not content, he kept at it, reaching Corry, sixty-two miles out from Salamanca. "I made the fastest run of the day," said Rodgers. After 104 miles, he was to stop at the Meadville Country Club. They were to have lined the field with white cloth, but at three thousand feet, Rodgers had trouble finding the location. Even as he came down, he saw nothing and ended up stopping at the Meadville Racetrack. He stayed for a couple hours for rest and recuperation and was off by 1:20 p.m. toward Akron. He came into a bit of trouble west of the city because the railroad tracks he was following became jumbled up and then ran around a "mountain" that he had to follow. After another hour, he needed gas and looked for a place to land at Warren. He picked out a level field and put Betsy down but damaged a skid on some tall grass. He had to wait for the *Special* to catch up for the repair. It took only minutes for a crowd to materialize, and the onlookers were more aggressive than usual this time. "Women are the worst offenders," Cal observed, "and I can see they do it without thinking." As already noted, the most common thing was people wanting to sign the wings (and sometimes take something off the plane), sometimes even trying to climb on. "When you think of the weight of a good size person," Cal said, and the fragile nature of the wings, it could be destructive. Cal was sometimes blunt, and the spectators sometimes belligerent, not understanding the damage they could do. No matter how hard Cal tried, he could not keep people away from the *Vin Fiz*. When he landed in Mansfield a few days later, a member of the press observed, "The plane had the appearance of being covered in thousands of names." Rodgers would be stuck in Warren for another hour and not leave until after four o'clock.[7]

The view from 2,500 feet was often breathtaking, Cal told the *Chicago Examiner*. He said that he was "fond of watching the crowds" that gathered beneath him as he passed over. The mass of humanity in the "thousands congregate at every farm house and village," and they waved to Rodgers as he passed by. So strange and exhilarating was the sensation of flying—how distorted the earth looked. "The panorama of little villages spread out ahead of me looked like a set of black checkers on a monster board." In the distance was a billow of "curling smoke" from a contained fire that "shot up" into the sky and then drifted away until it disappeared. Cal was joined by a "flock of birds ... [they] started up at me at one place and then turned and flew off as hard as they could. Like

Rodgers taking off at an unknown location during his transcontinental journey (Library of Congress).

12. "The panorama of little villages spread out ahead"   101

they had thought me a new kind of hawk." It would not be the last time birds would fly alongside the *Vin Fiz*.[8]

A message was sent from the *Special* to Akron to make bonfires to light the way for Rodgers, but it never made it. Cal wanted to press on as long as possible as the sun sank in the distance and dusk set in. Not seeing any lights toward Akron, and with Kent virtually dark below him, Cal managed to see the silhouette of a meadow, and, without knowing if it had fencing, he had to set the airplane down. "I picked out a little meadow as I shot across Kent," Cal described later. "I came down mostly on faith." He had to gamble; he had again pushed the limits, staying airborne longer than he should have, but this time it paid off. Cal took chances regularly; how much his experience at Red House truly affected him is debatable. The further he went, the more chances he seemed willing to take.[9]

Rodgers had accomplished his longest hop of the journey so far: 204 miles. Chicago tomorrow was a real possibility, and that would get him back on track to still make the thirty days to win the Hearst prize. He was optimistic that he could push even harder. "It is only 382 miles from Kent to Chicago, and I would not be surprised if I pressed that distance pretty close tomorrow," Cal said. "Give me the wind and a smooth working machine, and I will try hard at any rate." He trusted himself almost with arrogance in his ability to succeed. But the media never described him as arrogant, though some thought him to be ignorant of the dangers of flight.[10]

Thursday night, a powerful storm blew into central Ohio, producing gale-force winds. The *Special* was rocked badly enough to awaken the Kid and Shaffer, who grabbed Taylor and headed out to the *Vin Fiz*. They feared the wind would damage the biplane that was sitting in the open, and for hours they held down the biplane against a fierce wind and driving rainstorm.[11]

Most of the country endured a heatwave during the summer of 1911, with temperatures in much of the Midwest in the high nineties throughout most of July. Combined with incredible humidity, the air was hot and insufferable. In New York City alone, 211 people succumbed to heatstroke, with newspaper reports of people being literally driven "insane" by the heat. People were left dying in the streets, while one man jumped off the pier in an apparent suicide attempt. By October, the unusual weather pattern continued when a massive northern cold front from Canada rocked the Midwest, particularly Indiana. Winds were reported to reach over fifty miles per hour in places. Tempest storms caused rivers and streams to overflow, bridges were swept away, and tornadoes were reported. Perhaps an El Niño effect was still in play toward the end of September.[12]

Full of confidence, Rodgers woke at four, and immediately his heart must have sunk. He could feel the howling wind scraping the outside of the *Special*. He opened the curtain and saw rain pelting the window. "You can't fly against a gale of wind in any kind of flying machine yet invented," said Rodgers. "The Machine is in perfect condition, but only because the men who were watching it last night won a four-hour fight against the wind." The wind never let up, and another day was lost.[13]

Rodgers finished his telegraph with optimism, as usual. "I want to get away tomorrow morning, but cannot unless the wind dies down. I have received a very flattering offer to make a detour to Canton, where there is a meet tomorrow morning. It will all depend on the wind in the morning."[14]

Rodgers was to perform briefly at an air show in Canton, Ohio, for a fee. But because of the delay and the continued weather issues, Rodgers did not take the detour to Canton and did not leave Kent until almost nine the next morning. Still facing a fierce wind, he made slow progress, taking twenty-four minutes to reach Akron, just ten miles away. There was no way he would get to Chicago today. Still, wherever he went, he was drawing larger and larger crowds.[15]

At first, he was just a speck floating on the horizon. Soon the "whizzing of propellers" and the *Special*'s whistles could be heard. The entire town of Mansfield shut down as everyone gathered near the landing spot. Thousands of people topped roofs, filled fields, and lined the streets in every direction. So many automobiles choked into a street that led to the fairgrounds that there was a traffic jam "more than a mile long." Never had the town seen such a massive turnout. Cal, as he usually did, circled the town, sometimes waving and performing a stunt or two. Cal circled again and began his descent. He landed at the fairground on the north side of town, next to William Isley's farm. The crowds gasped as he appeared to narrowly miss some telephone wires, but he was well above them. He swooped down and made a soft, near-perfect landing. Rodgers, by all accounts, gave a "fine show" with stunts and maneuvers above the city.[16]

Rodgers came to a stop and immediately got off the plane, where he was soon met with a police contingent to help keep the large crowd from tampering with the biplane. From this point on, whenever possible, the *Vin Fiz* team alerted the local authorities to get help with crowd control, because it was becoming unmanageable.

Cal was shivering with cold and moved about rubbing his shoulders and arms. The crowd gawked at Rodgers; some commented on how tall he was. They always envisioned fliers as smaller, much like a jockey. Mr. Isley invited Rodgers over to his home to warm up. Cal thanked him and

12. "The panorama of little villages spread out ahead" 103

took him up on the offer once the police were adequately protecting his plane. He didn't stay too long, noted a newspaper reporter, before going back outside to the *Vin Fiz* and inspecting it. They had gasoline waiting for him. His stay in Mansfield was a little over an hour before he was back in the air heading for Huntington.[17]

Not long after leaving Mansfield, the air currents shifted and pushed Rodgers west so much that he made his best time thus far, covering forty-one miles in twenty-four minutes—an incredible time. As Rodgers approached Decatur, Indiana, his engine began acting up, causing the aircraft to sputter and dip. He was at about 1500 feet, and "my motor commenced working badly," Cal told a reporter later that night. "I decided I better make a landing. I could see hundreds of people on the streets of the little village." He ended up landing in Red Hilpert's field outside of Bobo, also known as Rivare, about three miles east of Decatur. The carburetor was shot and needed rebuilding, and Cal was stuck until the *Special* could catch up.[18]

It was after four in the afternoon, and Rodgers was twelve miles ahead of the train. Still cold from the freezing flight, he briskly walked in "violent exercise" to warm himself. The *Special* was notified of Rodgers's location once it reached Bobo, where Taylor, Shaffer, and the Kid drove to the airplane with their tools and began working on the engine. Quickly, they discovered that it needed more work than could be completed right away, and Rodgers departed via the train for Huntington, where he would spend the night—yet another setback. Rodgers, Maria, and his mother, along with the *Vin Fiz* and Armour representatives, were invited to the Huntington Chamber of Commerce banquet at Sheller's Café that night. As they were entertained, two crew members stood guard over the biplane because sightseers were everywhere.[19]

When Cal was interviewed before attending the banquet, the questions, of course, focused on whether he could still make it within the thirty days. Time was like sand through the hourglass, and it would not stop until it was out. "I expect to make the Sierras within twelve days," he said. He wasn't focused on Chicago anymore; that was a foregone conclusion. He had to look forward to where he could make up time. He would make it to Chicago tomorrow, he stated, and land in Grant Park in front of tens of thousands. Once in the Sierras, he would have his "greatest obstacle," as Cal opined, "the great mountain chain." Rodgers's thoughts had already turned to the Southwest and the daunting task of the mountains and long stretches of desert he would have to navigate. If he could get through Texas and into the mountain range in twelve days, he could then leap over to California and make the coast.[20]

13

"I breathed when I sailed over the edge of the cloud"

> "I breathed when I sailed over the edge of the cloud and saw the misty land beneath me."
> —Cal Rodgers

As usual, Calbraith Perry Rodgers was up early. When he opened the window drapes, a monochrome sky and a rainstorm greeted him. As he dressed and had his morning coffee, Cal was determined to attempt to cover as much ground as possible. He had to; time was running out. As long as the wind stayed temperate, he would give it a shot. Rain was a nuisance, but unless a massive downpour was occurring, he could still take off. At the moment, taking off wasn't possible, but if the rain subsided, he could.

However, the thought had to be setting in that Chicago was most likely unattainable in such conditions. A hundred and seventy-eight miles to Grant Park was obviously doable if the weather would cooperate. His mother, as she usually did, probably implored him not to fly. Rodgers always did his best to comfort her when she fussed, but she was a constant worrier by most accounts throughout his journey. The *Special* took Rodgers back to Rivare, where the *Vin Fiz* was being guarded by two crew members. Despite the weather, a sizable crowd had gathered near the field to watch Rodgers take off.[1]

The *Chicago Examiner* had several reporters following Rodgers, who described him as an excellent pilot who performed "with ease" the skill of flying. On days like today, he would need to be excellent. Rodgers was known for fearlessly releasing his hands from the control levers, digging into his pockets for a cigar, and lighting it while in flight—a skill (or hazardous risk, depending on how you saw it) that astonished and dismayed people. "Oh, there is no danger," Rodgers laughed when questioned. "I watch her [Betsy] pretty close."[2]

13. "I breathed when I sailed over the edge of the cloud"   105

Unfortunately, though the rain had stopped, the wind had picked up by the time Rodgers arrived at Rivare. Cal's crew questioned whether he should even attempt to fly this morning. His mother was most likely beside herself when he told them he would be flying. As they readied the plane, at about 8:45 a.m., the rain broke and the wind subsided. Rodgers shoved newspapers inside his leather jacket for extra padding because the cold the day before had been almost unbearable. He put on his leather gloves and hat and climbed aboard the plane.[3]

He barreled down the field and swooped up into the ashen sky, heading southwest toward Decatur. "I was up in the air by 8:55 in the morning as I wanted to make good and get into Chicago at some time this afternoon," said Rodgers later. But it wasn't meant to be. He leveled off at one thousand feet, and not long after, he came face to face with the head of a monster—a fast-moving storm.[4]

Then a tempest of wind rocked the *Vin Fiz* as he slammed into the front. "The weather had been playing a joke on me," Rodgers said later. Once he got airborne, it was even worse. Cal had to hold on tight to the levers and ride the shaking airplane. The blast of wind nearly tossed him out of his seat. "I had to buck corkscrew currents, which whirled me around like a top." He lost control and swirled around the current until he escaped the wind's grasp.[5]

Then there was a calm before a violent, thunderous rain scudded across a pallid sky. "I noticed a full-grown storm coming right at me," he said. It was a large storm with "boundaries [that] were all plainly marked, so the only thing left was to try and run around it." The rain "cut and stung" him, making it miserable to just hold on and fly. Cal noted later that he had to "drive over billows higher than any I have ever met on the sea."[6]

Rodgers rounded to the outer edge of the storm cloud and made it into a sliver of clear space and what he had hoped was a way around the storm. He found himself wedged in between two storm fronts that were about to collide. There was nothing he could do to avoid being caught up in them. The airplane was being tossed around. Cal noticed a "rift" in the approaching front to his right that carried east, so he swung the *Vin Fiz* that way in an effort to "skirt the storms."[7]

The swirling winds continued to shake and rattle the *Vin Fiz* terribly, and the rain still stung and was impenetrable as he lost sight of the ground. He was flying blind. When caught in such a storm, pilots had only the string tied to a wing support beam to tell them if they were still ascending or descending. Rodgers was now in danger of being driven down into the ground gradually by the thrusting wind. The storm had trapped him; it was so bad that "for a time I couldn't go up and dared not take a chance on coming down, [it] kept me pretty busy."[8]

As the storms consumed Rodgers, the *Special* lost sight of the *Vin Fiz*, surely causing Cal's mother to fret over the safety of her son. And this time, rightfully so. Cal should not have attempted flight on this morning; he was playing with fire, or in this instance, lighting.

Rain seemed to be shooting from all directions; the heavens and the sky began to turn dark. Rodgers somehow got Betsy up to a relatively calm space. "I used the warping wire for all it was worth, [and] I used my elevating level and managed to gain some altitude." That gained him another one thousand feet, he surmised, putting him at an altitude of around 2,500 feet. He was above the high winds and stinging rain. He turned northwest, following the Erie tracks. He felt as if he were through the worst of it, but soon the atmosphere started to blacken.

The hair on the back of his neck started to bristle as electricity filled the atmosphere. He was entering what he described later as an "electrical gridiron." Lightning began to rumble and explode all around him. He had to land. He looked below and could see lightning flashing. According to one reporter, "it was now that Rodgers did his best flying." The press on the train had regained sight of Rodgers and watched as he perilously tried to escape the storms.[9]

His goggles were steaming up so much he had to remove them "for fear I might become blinded by moisture," which was unpleasant as rain turned to hail and started to cut up his face. He also had to remove his leather gloves and cover up the magneto to protect it because the moisture could cause the engine to turn off. "It was a cold and painful situation," Rodgers described later.[10]

The wires and metal on his aircraft certainly would attract electricity, and to be hit by a lightning strike would be catastrophic. He also feared that his engine would shut off at "any minute." He tried to see what was below him, but the massive storm had covered the earth. "It was lonesome," Cal said. For a time, he just flew, unsure of exactly where he was or how high he was. Then the storm parted, and the earth appeared. "I breathed when I sailed over the edge of the cloud and saw the misty land beneath me." The hoodoo was working in his favor yet again.[11]

The fear of lightning striking "burned into his brain" and caused him to react immediately. Rodgers took hold of the elevator and began a rapid descent. As he dove the *Vin Fiz* sharply, he had to again contend with high winds and a hard rain. The airplane was tossed about as lightning flashed all around him. As he raced to the earth, there was just one problem, and a major one: visibility was again almost nil. He could see the landscape but could not tell exactly what he was flying over: woods, houses, hills, et cetera. Luckily, he dropped out of the milky clouds,

13. "I breathed when I sailed over the edge of the cloud" 107

the earth rushing up toward him, and then he was "swinging sharply" to avoid hitting the ground, said an eyewitness. He had been heading south instead of west, and he was way off course. He spotted a field bordered by trees and put down. The wind was pushing and shoving his tiny biplane, but he managed to get it down safely in a "blinding rain." He was outside of Geneva, Indiana, and had to wait out the storm.[12]

For the first time, he landed without a crowd forming. There was no one around, and no one was approaching. He saw a farmhouse and headed for it. The family offered him shelter and a meal as he warmed up and dried off. The weather cleared around 2:30 p.m., and with the help of the farmer, he turned the *Vin Fiz* around in the field to take off. It's unknown if the farmer or his family had ever seen an airplane or what their reaction was. Cal assuredly thanked them for their hospitality and took off. Cal had no idea where the *Special* was and figured he should head northwest toward Huntington. He found the trolley line to Bluffton, which took him right into Uniondale and the Erie Railroad, which he followed up to Huntington, where he landed at 4:36 p.m.[13]

14

"Ambition coupled with energy is the driving force of mankind"

> "Ambition coupled with energy is the driving force of mankind."
> —Philip Danforth Armour

Just outside of Huntington, Indiana, Rodgers found a large field that belonged to farmer Patrick Gorman and put the *Vin Fiz* down. He was soaking wet and shaking from the cold. Gorman offered Cal shelter and warmth in his little farmhouse as they waited for his *Vin Fiz* team. By 6 p.m., he was taken to the *Special*, and he was not seen again that night. Rodgers had a quiet dinner and went to bed early, no doubt exhausted from the hard flying. The next morning, he slept in until almost ten, had a "hasty" breakfast, and was whisked away by Jimmy Dunn in the Palmer-Singer back to the takeoff point. Though he'd never show it, the journey must have taken a physical toll on Rodgers. Consecutive days of fighting hard winds, storm fronts, and freezing, driving rain would exhaust even the strongest flier.[1]

The storms raged across the Midwest. In Austin, Pennsylvania, the storms were so bad that a mill dam broke, wiping out an entire town, with initial reports of "hundreds dead." Of the three thousand residents, seventy-eight perished, and an entire community ceased to exist in a matter of minutes. The weather across the area where Cal was flying was going to be treacherous for the next few days, according to all weather reports.[2]

As Cal reached the field, there were over three thousand people on hand to watch, despite the foulness of the day. Rodgers inspected Betsy and conferred with his mechanic team. At some point, both Mabel and his mother approached him and suggested that he not take off with the wind so strong. Desperate to make up time and get to Chicago, Rodgers

14. "Ambition coupled with energy is the driving force"   109

insisted on trying. A reporter for the *Chicago Examiner*, Count de Beaufort, was in attendance and wrote of Rodgers:

> Hairbreadth escapes appear to have absolutely no effect upon the tall, taciturn aviator, who, having started out to fly across the continent, is sticking to it in spite of repeated setbacks.[3]

And this was before he witnessed the following breathtaking scene. Cal, as he always did, put on his hat, goggles, and gloves and patted Betsy reassuringly on the wing before kissing Mabel and his mother. He climbed aboard and lit a cigar. The wind was howling as the engine was fired up. After a moment, Cal calmly called out for Wiggin to "let 'er go," and away he went, barreling down the field lined with spectators, rows deep. As the biplane took flight, it was immediately caught in a gale, and, as if it were an automobile on ice, it slid across the skyline wildly. The crowd gasped as the plane struggled to get even fifty feet off the ground. When the *Vin Fiz* seemed to reach some altitude, like a hand from the heavens, a gust of wind tossed the plane straight down "perpendicular to the earth, while the tail was straight up in the air." The *Vin Fiz* slammed into the ground, driven down by the force of the wind. Beaufort, a *Chicago Examiner* newspaperman, recalled the events later that day:[4]

> I was a little distance away when the accident happened, but near enough to notice the terrible incline, and I am sure I was not the only one on the field, crowded with about 3,000 spectators, who feared that this time Rodgers had paid the price.[5]

Indeed, it was a price that so many early aviators paid; upward of 70 percent perished while heroically advancing the science of aviation. The accident looked bad enough that surely Rodgers was at the very least injured. Just the day before, in Spokane, Washington, yet another aviator had met his death. Cromwell Dixon crashed while performing at the Spokane Interstate Fair. Gale-force winds cutting across the field from the Pacific Ocean tossed his plane into the ground. Dixon was only nineteen years old.[6]

It is easy to imagine the distress of Mabel and Cal's mother as they made their way, fighting through the throngs of people as the crowd rushed to the *Vin Fiz*. As Shaffer, Taylor, and Wiggin arrived, Cal was holding the bottle of *Vin Fiz* soda, still, like the aviator, unbroken. Though both were shaken up, they were both still intact. "When we came up to him, there he was standing calmly, looking at the debris of his machine smoking a cigar." Cal stood virtually unscathed, with a few scratches and bumps, his cigar in mouth, and as they approached, he was heard to say, "Guess I'll have to wait a bit, after all."[7]

"Rodgers is one of the coolest and calmest propositions I have ever seen," continued Beaufort. Cal had ice in his veins, and at this point in his journey, he might have even believed in his own immortality because, time and again, he avoided the hoodoo. So many aviators had perished and continued to die, even as Cal was making his historic journey. Yet there he was, crashing and avoiding death and significant injury time and again.[8]

They put the wrecked biplane on the back of a flatbed truck and hauled it to Fraizer's Garage in downtown Huntington. "Except for the engine, the craft looked almost a complete wreck," wrote a local newspaper reporter. Cal and his crew had to virtually rebuild the entire biplane again—several days of work. One propeller was completely shattered, and one side had completely torn off the frame. The entire main framework had collapsed upon itself; it was a miracle Rodgers wasn't killed. They began repairing and rebuilding the *Vin Fiz* that afternoon.[9]

As each crash and close call came and went, Cal began to think less and less of them; it wasn't indifference but confidence. The thought of crashing never left his mind or diminished the chambers of his fear; he simply never showed fear and ultimately became comfortable with it. Aviators had to live with the fear; they compartmentalized it, and when something bad happened to a fellow pilot, it was the hoodoo or simply

The wrecked *Vin Fiz* after the terrifying crash at Huntington, Indiana. A befuddled Charles Taylor with his hands pressed to his sides looks on (author's collection).

14. "Ambition coupled with energy is the driving force" 111

bad luck. A simplistic assessment of a dangerous profession, to be sure, but an understandable reaction to the reality of the situation.

Cal's head mechanic, Frank Shaffer, recalled one flight he took with the Birdman. When they were at about five thousand feet, Cal let go of the warping lever, lit a cigar, and put his feet up. Shaffer suggested Cal be careful; the wind was still strong, to which Cal responded, "Oh, we're alright. She's ridden the wind before, and she'll do it again." Cal simply believed in his destiny; he had an unshakable belief and confidence. "The air is nothing to me now.... I've never been afraid when I'm up there." Indeed, fear had no place in the mind of an aviator if he wanted to keep his nerve while airborne.[10]

That night, Rodgers and Mabel attended a potluck banquet in Cal's honor. The next morning, Beaufort of the *Chicago Examiner* got the chance to interview Rodgers. He apparently talked him into the interview with a box of Cuban cigars. Cal didn't like to do interviews; his main communications were telegraphs, press releases, and very short interviews. It was Beaufort's first interview with an aviator, and he was excited to talk to the most popular one alive. It turned out to be a pithy and difficult discussion that left him wanting more. Rodgers's answers consisted mostly of "bully" and "maybe," the pundit complained later.[11]

By now, Taylor and Shaffer, along with the Kid, had noticed one major problem with the engines. Years later, Wiggin described the issue:

> There was no oil cup, and after 25 miles the graphite lubrication would wear off the roller bearings in the chains. When that happened, they would get hot, shake like hell and eventually break.[12]

This accounted for the Wrights' concern that the biplane would "vibrate" itself to pieces. Their engine was not built for long-distance flying, which forced Taylor and Shaffer to constantly rebuild the machine.

Rodgers did elaborate on his crash, stating that the wind threw him off balance but that the reason for his sharp nosedive was that the presence of so many people in the adjacent field forced him to put straight down quickly in what was left of the clearing. "If it had not been for them [the people], I could have glided to earth," but instead he had to "drop and take a chance of landing safely or steer right into the crowd," which would have been deadly because of the massive nine-foot propellers, let alone any kind of impact from the machine.[13]

The next day, Rodgers and Mabel visited nearby Fort Wayne, Indiana, to attend a small gala in his honor at the Anthony Hotel. They had dinner and stayed the night. The next morning, they toured the town and met briefly with reporters. When asked if he was still in the race for the Hearst prize, he said bluntly, "I am going to push on westward as soon as repairs are completed." Although making it in the allotted thirty days was another question, he wasn't about to give up the historic journey.[14]

In his regular press telegram, Rodgers wrote that night:

> With good weather tomorrow morning I will make another attempt to fly into Chicago. The Model EX has been rebuilt entirely except for the engine.... If I can get any kind of wind back of me, I will cover the 142 miles in short order.[15]

The plan was to take the Erie Railroad tracks north toward Hammond, Indiana, at the southern tip of Lake Michigan for a brief stop, then fly up over the southwest corner of the lake and continue into Chicago on a short hop to Grant Park, where Cal planned to put down around three in the afternoon, followed by a short ceremony. Early the next morning, he planned to head toward Kansas City, following the Rock Island Railroad. Rodgers needed it to play out just like that in order to still have any shot at the Hearst prize. Then he had to make up massive amounts of time heading southwest, hopefully into better weather and better flying.

The next day, Thursday, October 5, the *Vin Fiz* was ready. Again, Taylor and Shaffer put the engine through its paces. They now had two motors including the one in the *Vin Fiz*, but there would be no more engines coming, and they would have to do their best to keep them running. The hangar car was again short on parts, particularly motor parts. They had rebuilt both engines again, along with the entire frame of the plane. That morning, the cold front did not produce high winds, just frigid temperatures. Rodgers put on the heaviest jacket he had, stuffed it with newspapers, and waited until just after eleven in the morning to take off due to heavy rain. After taking off, Rodgers did several large circles over the grounds, testing out the *Vin Fiz* because she had been almost entirely rebuilt again. Satisfied with the plane, he headed out, following the railroad tracks northwest. Right away, Cal knew it was going to be a long flight. The cold penetrated his gloves and jacket, and it did not take long for his hands to numb. Soon he realized that the cold wasn't just numbing his hands; it was also clogging the fuel line from the reserve tank.[16]

He sputtered his way to his fuel stop outside of Aldin, where local farmers had mowed the field of thick tickle grass the day before so he could land. Once down, Rodgers grabbed a scythe, not only to help expand the runway for takeoff but also to help get his blood circulating and to warm his partially frozen body. When the runway was of suitable length and the airplane refueled, Cal attempted to take off

14. "Ambition coupled with energy is the driving force"   113

but hit something and broke a skid that required repair. That caused yet another delay, but soon he was able to fix the skid and get airborne, heading for Hammond. But he was hours delayed overall for the day; it would not be Chicago by early afternoon.[17]

At this point, Cal was laser focused. The *Vin Fiz* was running as well as it had the entire trip. He got up to 1,500 feet and took off toward Hammond. The *Special* was reportedly making a mile a minute, leaving Rodgers behind all day. Flying with a wind current, Cal roared off, eventually overtaking the train and getting "three to five miles" ahead of it, according to one newspaper. He reached North Judson, where "10,000 had assembled" to watch him fly over. Cal was to land at Crown Point in Hammond, where it was reported a "monster crowd" awaited. Upon arriving and circling the field, Cal found that it was so packed with people that he felt he couldn't land on the runway. He turned south and found a suitable field to put down without trouble around five thirty in the evening as dusk was settling in. The masses did not stay put, and a parade of automobiles and spectators flooded town heading for the *Vin Fiz*.[18]

Rodgers was nineteen days into his attempt to win the Hearst $50,000 prize. Of those days, he had flown nine, covering about 1,400 miles, with seven days lost to repairs and three to weather. When asked if Rodgers could still make it, Armour press chief and manager, DeKrafft, replied that they expected Rodgers to complete the journey. The plan, he said, was "night flying," which was possible in the Southwest, and they could make up significant time. The weather was better, and during dusk, the sun's glow on the western horizon hung a little longer, providing just enough illumination. They were going to push Cal to the limit; they believed in him. After all, they had selected Rodgers for this massive advertising campaign across the country because "he is the best of all American aviators." DeKrafft continued, "we [still] feel Rodgers will win the William Randolph Hearst prize for crossing the continent in thirty days." The race was still on.[19]

15

"For all of his back of steel determination"

> "For all of his back of steel determination, Calbraith's heart was tender."
> —Mabel Rodgers

According to DeKrafft, it was the most expensive and largest advertising campaign in history. "Before we reach the coast this flight will have cost us $150,000," he said. "It is the most gigantic advertising scheme ever undertaken." It was the first of its kind and by far the most complicated and extravagant advertising campaign ever attempted: a flying billboard, a billboard on a moving train, and another on an automobile. Everything was painted and detailed. A dozen salespeople splayed out at the beginning of each leg of the journey to hand out advertising materials and samples wherever the *Vin Fiz* happened to land. Cal carried with him a bottle of Vin Fiz soda as a good-luck charm, though initially as a requirement. As he approached Chicago, the soda company was in full force in the streets, advertising their product and giving away samples.[1]

Rodgers was skimming over Hammond, following the Erie tracks, when he noticed four men lounging on a handcar on the tracks looking up at him. This event wasn't unusual; as a matter of fact, nearly the entire city was looking up at him. However, what these men didn't know was that just a mile or so away, the *Special* was on the same track bearing down on them. "I shouted at them, but they either did not hear or comprehend," Cal said later. So he spiraled down and yelled out again, pointing at the approaching train. The men barely got out of the way in time and surely would have been killed had the *Special* rammed into them.[2]

That night, Rodgers, Mabel, and his mother joined a small party

15. "For all of his back of steel determination" 115

and had dinner at the Majestic Hotel, where they were staying. The dinner parties were usually kept small whenever possible, which was the way Cal liked it. His exact state of mind is unknown, though several newspapers noted his growing frustration. The discussion must have involved the reality of not winning the prize but still completing the historic journey.[3]

The next morning, Rodgers and his crew were met again with extremely high winds. Taylor and Shaffer arrived at Heckman Field (where the *Vin Fiz* had landed) and quickly deemed it not suitable for takeoff. So they broke down the plane and wheeled it four miles to Douglas Park. As they reassembled the *Vin Fiz* and prepared for flight, the Police Commissioner informed them that due to the high winds, they could not use any property within city limits; it was unsafe. By the time they found another field outside the city, it would be too late in the day to take off, and again, Rodgers lost another day.[4]

As he experienced more crashes and accidents, there were reports that some towns started to dictate whether Rodgers could take off by calling in their police chief to ground him. Cities controlled the use of their property, so if the weather conditions were bad, they could deny use of their land and facilities. No one wanted to be the town where Cal Rodgers, the transcontinental aviator, died. "Since leaving New York," Rodgers complained, "I have been treated so inconsiderately" by some cities—an exaggeration to be sure. But his frustration that city officials were dictating his departures was understandable. "Chicagoans are true sportsmen, and I know they will be at least courteous," he said, expressing his growing frustration.[5]

"As soon as I land in Grant Park," Rodgers continued, "I will prepare to start for Springfield, and with an even break with luck I'll be there by tomorrow night." The Chicago Aero Club had planned a big to-do with Rodgers's arrival that now had to be modified due to his need to get back in the air immediately.[6]

Later that evening, Rodgers expressed his frustration concerning the weather, telling a *New York Times* reporter that the winds were indeed "too dangerous ... [and] weather permitting I will make my start early tomorrow and be in Chicago before noon." Cal, upon reflection, clearly agreed that the weather was too dangerous to have flown in. He would lose two full days of flying stuck in Hammond because of gale-force winds.[7]

The morning of the eighth, the weather was calm and the sky clear. The *Vin Fiz* crew found a suitable field but could not obtain permission from its owner, William Norman, to use it. The farmer at first agreed, but seeing the massive crowd gathering, he was worried his cow pasture

Cal (seated) with Frank Shaffer (standing in front), preparing for flight (San Diego Air & Space Museum).

would be ruined, so he asked them to leave. Yet another delay. The large crowd followed the crew as they wheeled the plane to a new field down a dirt road. This one belonged to Daniel O'Conner, who was apparently very willing to allow Rodgers to depart from his land.[8]

The crowd cheered and waved "an enthusiastic goodbye" as Rodgers got up in the air about eleven o'clock. He had to circle back and find the Erie Railroad, and after a couple laps, he found it and headed over Hammond and toward Lake Michigan. Rodgers was over the city and could see people in the streets, on rooftops, and in cars waving and cheering.[9]

The excitement as he ascended into the air and saw Lake Michigan and the "smoke and houses of South Chicago" had to put a grin on his cigar-chomping mouth. Navigation was easy at this point as he headed right for the lake, swooping out over it, and then followed the shore, heading up into the city.[10]

At Grant Park, two days of anticipation left the large crowd anxious as they waited for the Birdman to appear on the horizon. At first, there was just a black speck at two thousand feet; countless times, birds in the distance had been misidentified as the flier, but soon, one speck hung level and then started to get bigger and bigger. Then came the hum of the engine; they knew it was the *Vin Fiz*. Cal was scheduled to land at noon and did not disappoint when he touched down at precisely 11:57 a.m.[11]

Tens of thousands lined streets and rooftops and waved as Rodgers

15. "For all of his back of steel determination"   117

passed over. Even churches ended service early as thousands poured out into the streets in their Sunday best. Rodgers landed in the park near the spot where his old hangar had stood during the aviation meet in August. Police again had to hold back the crowd that tried to swarm Rodgers and the *Vin Fiz*, wanting to touch the aviator. He warmly greeted the crowd, waved, and smiled. After a short ceremony, he was whisked away to the La Salle Hotel for lunch with city officials, Mr. J. Ogden Armour, and members of the Aero Club. As he was driven around the city with his wife and mother, "large crowds followed." Rodgers was described as a "popular hero" whom people looked up to and admired for his bravery and determination.[12]

Rodgers delivered letters he was carrying to E.B. Merritt, Mr. Armour, and others. "Rodgers is demonstrating the possibility of carrying mail by aeroplane," declared the *New York Times*. During his journey, Cal was doing much more than that. He represented determination, heart, and the spirit of the underdog. It wasn't just the allure of seeing an airplane that drew people; it was the chance to be in the presence of the Iron Aviator, the great Birdman.[13]

Cal was scheduled to take off around two in the afternoon, and by the time he arrived around three thirty, an "immense crowd" estimated at eighty thousand had assembled to watch. The police again had to clear people away to allow his car to get him to the *Vin Fiz*. While Rodgers and his crew started the plane and prepared it for takeoff, the police had to clear the runway of an overeager crowd that was swarming. It took thirty minutes to clear a strip and allow Rodgers enough room to depart. He took off at 4:01 p.m. as the "crowd cheered itself wild." He circled the park twice and then steered out toward Peoria to the southwest. Not long after turning southwest, he was blown off course by a gust of wind and then became engulfed in smoke from a forest fire and got disoriented. It took him some time in the maze of tracks to find the Chicago and Alton Railroad and orient himself. Around 5:20 p.m., he landed at Dellwood Park on the outskirts of Peoria.[14]

That evening, Rodgers met with his team and Armour Company reps and determined that the Hearst prize was now out of reach and really had been for days. But from the beginning, the money had never been what motivated Cal. He wanted to make history, and that was still attainable. Both Atwood and Ward had pulled out of the race; he was the last birdman flying. Atwood still held the distance record at 1,265 miles, which Rodgers would exceed if he made it to Missouri as planned. The Armour Company had created a "gigantic" advertising campaign that was simply too big to fail at this point. Besides, Rodgers and the *Vin Fiz* were steadily capturing the entire country's attention and imagination.

If Rodgers could make it to the coast, he would make history, and the *Vin Fiz* would be right there with him. Everyone agreed that there was no stopping; they would press on no matter how long it took.

Of course, the morning after Rodgers's announcement, he was greeted by clear blue skies and a calm breeze. It was Monday, October 9, and Rodgers was hoping to break Atwood's record by making Springfield, Illinois, and then Marshall, Missouri, the following day. He headed out that morning around seven, and, as usual, a large crowd saw him off. Once in flight, he circled back and found a peculiar sight. Warden Murphy of the Peoria State Prison had allowed the inmates into the yard that morning to watch Rodgers pass over. They waved and cheered as the Birdman flew by, some no doubt wanting to hitch a ride out of there.[15]

"For all of his back of steel determination," recalled Mabel years later, "Calbraith's heart was tender." He had known the prison was there. The week before, while going over his itinerary and keeping landmarks in mind in case his iron compass failed him, he saw that he would be near the facility. "He told me to call the warden," Mabel said, "and ask to have the inmates out in the yard." She called, and Warden Murphy agreed. "I'll circle over the pen," Cal said, "and give them a glimpse of their first airplane." He didn't just circle; he put on a show. "He gave them a magnificent demonstration of acrobatic flying." He did rolls and dives, much to the delight of all below. Later, he told Mabel that he "uttered a prayer for the imprisoned men" as he left them that day. Rodgers himself had felt imprisoned in a world without sound as a boy after his illness, so his sensibility toward the inmates is not surprising.[16]

The clear skies and no wind allowed Cal to make extremely good time, at some points possibly as fast as seventy miles per hour. He reached Springfield at 5:20 p.m., landing at the State Fair Grounds. He was escorted into the city by another biplane flown by Clifford Turpin, a Wright flier whom Rodgers knew. Rodgers discovered a slow leak in his radiator, but it didn't slow him down. That night, Taylor, Shaffer, and the Kid easily patched up the leak and had the *Vin Fiz* ready for flight the next morning.[17]

By flying the 230 miles from Springfield to Marshall Rodgers the next day, he would be the first aviator to cross three major rivers in one day: the Illinois, Mississippi, and Missouri. The weather was good, with a little wind, when he took off at 8:35 a.m. Unfortunately, at altitude, a headwind slowed his progress for much of the morning. It took him two hours to get to Nebo, a distance of seventy miles, where he stopped to refuel and quickly eat. The *Special* reached Nebo ahead of Rodgers, and Taylor and crew were waiting with gasoline and oil. He was reportedly only there for fifteen minutes. The *Vin Fiz* soared back into the

15. "For all of his back of steel determination"

sky, and Rodgers climbed to a reported altitude of seven thousand feet. Below him, the massive Mississippi River cut across the Midwest. He traversed the mile-wide behemoth and out over the "tablelands of Missouri." Below him was the seventh state he had crossed since his journey began.[18]

The headwind continued as he reached Louisiana, Missouri, and passed over Mexico, Missouri. A half hour later, swinging toward Marshall, he was finally going with the wind and started to pick up his pace. Below, the entire community of Mexico was out "in force" to witness the Birdman as he flew over; the crowd waved and cheered. Rodgers was scheduled to land and fly low over the city, but he failed to do so. In town was a *Vin Fiz* representative, C.M. Clay, who telephoned the *Vin Fiz* manager at Thompson, where the *Special* was following Rodgers on the C & A Railroad. They alerted Cal, and he graciously gave up precious time (he wanted to try for Kansas City), turned around, and headed back to the tiny hamlet where a "large crowd" from all around had amassed. As he approached, he swooped down and buzzed the field, where the "roar of his engine" electrified the crowd. For ten minutes, he performed a series of maneuvers that thrilled and awed the crowd. It was an "exhibition of aviation," wrote a newspaper reporter in attendance, "from which they will date time in the future." Rodgers had again "delighted" the crowd, and it was reported that some there were unconvinced that machines could fly until they saw Rodgers that day.[19]

After his exhibition, Rodgers circled around, waved goodbye, and straightened out for Marshall. He roared across Missouri, making seventy-five miles per hour with the wind at his back—one of his best stints in his coast-to-coast journey. However, as he approached Marshall, the magneto control broke, and again, he was having spark plug issues. He dropped to 1,200 feet, reaching back and trying to fix the control and plug. Before he could fix it, a cylinder popped off. Cal was helpless as, moments later, a second one stopped as well. He dropped to three hundred feet, skillfully gliding the biplane down, circling until he made a "beautiful landing."[20]

Rodgers landed at Marshall Fair Grounds, where a crowd of eight thousand had amassed to witness history. As he lowered himself out of the *Vin Fiz*, a "human avalanche" fell upon the aviator. Rodgers became lost in the mass of humanity as the town police chief tried to stem the crowd. Quickly, Rodgers's crew, led by Taylor and Shaffer, jumped in and protected the *Vin Fiz* from treasure hunters wanting a piece of history.[21]

Cal had broken the distance record and was no doubt ecstatic. "I am happy to know that I have flown all told 1,642 miles since I left New York ... which breaks all records for cross-country [and distance] flight."

Though only credited with 1,391 miles, he still broke Atwood's record. Though it was again a hard day of fighting the wind, it was still better than battling a cold front and its storms. "It was a bully day for a flight," Rodgers told reporters. "If I had started out earlier this morning, I would have tried to reach Kansas City tonight." But as it went so many times, things didn't align for him to make that jump. It would have to be tomorrow.[22]

16

"All the population that could get out of doors gazed"

> "All the population that could get out of doors gazed steadfastly towards the heavens for a glimpse of the flying machine."
> —*Chicago Examiner*

Back in New York, Thomas Edison was giving a demonstration that would help transform America and the world. The Electrical Exposition of 1911 opened on October 11 at the new Grand Central Palace. Hundreds were in attendance for a luncheon, and afterward, they convened on the first floor for a short ceremony. Edison gave a speech and then flicked the switch, turning on five thousand light bulbs and illuminating the magnificent building. For two days, people toured the building and its six rooms of household items powered by electricity, from dishwashers to curling irons and everything in between. The modern era was in full swing. Daily life and how people lived were transforming before their very eyes.[1]

Fourteen hundred miles away, Calbraith Perry Rodgers was also making history and doing his part to revolutionize civilization. After landing in Marshall, again electrifying another massive crowd, The mayor and a caravan of automobiles took Rodgers into town to the Elks Club. All along the way, people lined the streets to get a look at the great Birdman. He was the guest of honor for a dinner and a ceremony. Although he was always awkward and felt out of place, Rodgers did his best to endure the proceedings.[2]

That night, Taylor and Shaffer fixed the magneto, but both agreed the entire engine needed overhauling, which would have to wait until Kansas City, where they could most likely get any additional spare parts they needed. That night, Rodgers went to bed early and rested after what was another grueling day of flying. By now, the physical toll that he was enduring was evident. He had lost weight, his face was drawn, and his smile was more subdued. But again, his size and strength aided him and maybe even saved his life during a few of the crashes.[3]

Cal wanted to take as direct a route as possible now that he was in the heart of America. But the Armour Company wanted him to adjust to get as many eyes on the *Vin Fiz* and the marketing campaign as possible. The "Armour Company, for publicity reasons, wanted Cal to depart from his intended, more direct route," Mabel revealed years later. They wanted him to go to Kansas City, though it was essentially out of the way. Most likely, DeKrafft was instructed to tell Rodgers to make for the city.[4]

Kansas City was eighty-four miles from Marshall, and Rodgers wasn't scheduled to land there the next day or even to fly over the metropolis. Not everyone wanted Cal to make for Kansas City. Taylor asked him not to; he told Rodgers no one had yet flown over the city for fear of divergent air pockets because of the Missouri River's extreme bluffs that lay to the north of the city. The bluffs redirected the wind into the city's tall buildings. The swirling airstream had thus far scared off all other aviators and caused Cal's team to worry. If he attempted to fly over the city, he would encounter dangerous air pockets that could be deadly. Not only did the wind concern them, but the terrain was equally bad because there were few suitable fields close enough for Rodgers if he lost power, which was something that had happened on two occasions already. Numerous newspapers, as well, described what they felt were "treacherous" air pockets above Kansas City.[5]

The *Vin Fiz* soared into the sky at precisely 8:24 a.m. As Rodgers left Marshall, it was the usual sight for him: wide-eyed faces pressed up against the sky watching with amazement. The world was being transformed before their eyes. The automobile had started the process of shrinking time and space, and within only decades, the airplane would revolutionize travel. Most onlookers wherever Cal passed over had never seen a flying machine. Some simply didn't believe they existed. When the *Vin Fiz* flew, it was a revelation to all—a radical readjustment to what was possible and what the possibilities of the future held.[6]

The wind was favorable, and Cal was making good time as he reached Higginsville. He circled the town twice, giving all spectators a chance to gaze up into the sky. Later, about an hour into his flight again, the magneto acted up. A spark plug blew out. The plane lurched and dropped as it sputtered across the sky. Rodgers was forced to put down in a field at Blue Springs, Missouri, around 9:50 a.m., luckily without

16. "All the population that could get out of doors gazed" 123

incident. Eventually, nearly the entire community amassed in the field outside of Blue Springs as Rodgers ate a quick lunch and fixed the spark plug. After an hour, he was ready to take off. Locals volunteered to hold Betsy's wings as he fired her up. The crowd eagerly watched as Cal called out for them to "let 'er go," and he raced down the field and into the clear cobalt sky.[7]

It was a good day. The weather was ideal for flight, and the allure of being the first to fly over Kansas City was no doubt tempting to Rodgers, but the spark plug issues should have been enough to deter him from even considering it. He crossed over the countryside at a high rate of speed, the *Vin Fiz* seemingly running perfectly now. Cars below couldn't come close to keeping up as he crossed the Big Blue River before reaching Independence, Missouri. At this point, he was skirting along the Missouri River when he could see the landscape rising up to the bluffs lining the northern side of the river. Directly ahead was Kansas City. Cal wasn't reckless, as some accused him of being; he was adventurous and confident in his skills, and he was a skilled flier. By now, 1,400 plus miles and weeks of flying had sharpened his skills and his senses. Rodgers's growing prowess as a flier was noted time and again in newspapers. His confidence, combined with his skill, allowed him to attempt things others would not. The fact that his employer wanted him to go and the allure of being the first to fly over Kansas City were too much, so he went for it.[8]

The excitement in Kansas City at the possibility of seeing the transcontinental flier that day was palpable. A ten-year-old boy named Walt Disney (yes, that one) lived in Kansas City and heard

Rodgers and the *Vin Fiz* flying into Kansas City (San Diego Air & Space Museum).

about the incoming historic flight. Having "been intrigued by aviation," he couldn't resist. So, he and his older brother ran two miles to see Rodgers and *Vin Fiz* land. As lookouts from Independence began reporting Rodgers's flight path, which appeared to be heading directly to the city, the excitement grew. He wasn't scheduled to fly over, yet here he came. The entire city shut down, "all business activities ended," and once again, streets filled, rooftops were populated, and the countryside amassed. All eyes gazed skyward to the east in anticipation.[9]

At first, there was just a speck on the horizon as onlookers cheered and pointed. Not long after, the wings became recognizable, and the hum of the engine audible. A newspaper correspondent described the scene:

> All the population that could get out of doors gazed steadfastly towards the heavens for a glimpse of the flying machine. Belle whistles and automobile sirens made a terrific noise. The aviator came towards the city by way of the Missouri River. When he reached the Kaw River he darted towards the stock yards, where he arrested a live stock show.[10]

After disrupting the stock show, much to the amazement of the cowboys, he circled over Union Station and the courthouse, and headed out over the business district at the center of the city. He followed Grand Avenue to Swope Park and the residential district. Amassed at Swope Park was a massive crowd of ten thousand. They gasped and cheered as the *Vin Fiz* came swooping down from the sky and landed on the canvas-strewn runway that the Aero Club had quickly laid out for him.[11]

Rodgers and the *Vin Fiz* were swarmed as the local police did their best to quell the onslaught of the mob, a futile effort. After the spectators had been calmed and a contingent from the *Special* had arrived to watch over the biplane, Rodgers was taken away to do a quick interview. He was asked about his unplanned stop in Kansas City. "I did not intend to go over, but when I saw the city ... I just couldn't resist," he said, "so I just jumped over the bluff and took a circle or two." Cal was also a showman and loved to entertain. He could not resist giving Kansas City a show, and he certainly wanted to be the first to fly there.[12]

Once again, Cal was doing what some thought was impossible. He took chances, but they proved time and again to be calculated and well executed. After lunch at the Evanston Golf Course, Rodgers took off, heading for Overland Park, not far from Kansas City, where he was scheduled to conclude the day's journey. He took off and headed south but was immediately blinded by the low sun, something that he was unaccustomed to. Rodgers flew in the wrong direction for a time, saying later, "I was really lost." He regained his bearings and headed for the park in short order.[13]

16. "All the population that could get out of doors gazed"   125

At Overland Park, Rodgers was feeling good about his machine and had a little fun. Mabel apparently wasn't impressed. "Calbraith put on a hazardous exhibition display," she recalled later. He wanted to "show off," according to her, and he did. He thrilled the crowd with dips and turns and soared over the area for a time. But it put unneeded wear on the machine and took a toll on the engine.[14]

That evening, Taylor, Shaffer, and their mechanical team tore apart the engine for a complete overhaul, one that would hopefully fix the magneto issues for good. Taylor was growing frustrated with Cal's antics, for sure, but he was also impressed by the aviator's strength and determination. "We were constantly repairing about the ship," he noted years later. "Oil lines broke, cracked cylinders and crystalized intake valves," to name a few. It was getting to be dicey work.[15]

By now, Rodgers was making front-page headlines from San Francisco to Boston. The entire country was becoming enraptured by the "daredevil," the "Birdman," the "Ironman." He was now halfway to the Pacific Ocean.

Cal publicly acknowledged numerous times that he no longer had any chance to win the Hearst prize. "Of course, I am sorry I will not be able to win the rich stake," he told a local reporter, "but that fact is not going to deter me from being the first aviator to cross the American continent." Making history and doing something never done before were always his goals; the prize would have been a nice bonus.[16]

Center middle left, **Charles Wiggin and** *center middle right,* **chauffeur Jimmy Dunn, others unknown (San Diego Air & Space Museum).**

17

"[Cal] is going to master the air and fly to the Pacific coast"

> "[Cal] is going to master the air and fly to the Pacific coast, because he has the courage and confidence to do so."
>
> —Mabel Rodgers

The plan was to continue working south from Kansas City, through Kansas, and then down into Oklahoma. The reason was simple: to avoid Colorado and the Rocky Mountains' massive range of fourteen thousand-foot summits that were impossible for the *Vin Fiz* to cross over. Rodgers would continue to follow the tracks of the Missouri, Kansas, and Texas railroads (the Katy) and head down into San Antonio and then the Southern Pacific Railroad into California and the coast.[1]

Rodgers's wife, Mabel, was rarely heard from but occasionally expressed her confidence in Cal, especially after the success at Kansas City, where she thought him a bit reckless. "Mr. Rodgers is going to master the air and fly to the Pacific coast, because he has the courage and confidence to do so," she said. She was always a supporter of Cal, perhaps even loyal to a fault, but now she was a true believer in his incredible will and determination. His apparent invincibility was becoming something openly spoken of among his crew. "He has already had several severe accidents, but he has never given up. I think it is second nature to him," she said of Rodgers's spirit. To never give up was ingrained in his Rodgers and Perry DNA.[2]

Rodgers's love for speed didn't just end when he landed his biplane; it was not unusual for him to take the touring car for a fast spin around the countryside. In the evenings and some afternoons, when time afforded it, he would take the car and find a lonely dirt road to drive fast.

17. "[Cal] is going to master the air"   127

But nothing beat the speed and thrill of the biplane; it was always calling him back.³

A heavy fog delayed Cal's departure from Overland Park, Kansas, until almost noon. Rodgers headed east back to Swope Park, not far away, where a thousand or more were waiting. He wowed the crowd with two figure eights and then swung back around and headed west toward Overland Park. He passed Lenexa at 12:20 p.m., and though fighting a headwind of eighteen miles per hour, he soon passed over the *Special*. He put the *Vin Fiz* down in a field at Moran, Kansas, for fuel and oil—a fairly isolated place. Still, a decent crowd had materialized but was "manageable" and well-behaved, according to Rodgers. The field bordered the railroad, and a short time later, the train arrived. Taylor, Shaffer, and Wiggin got to work quickly. Not long after, Cal was back in the air, heading toward Parson, Kansas.⁴

People had started arriving at the fairgrounds at Parson three days before Rodgers was scheduled to arrive. By the time the big day came, there was a camp of ten thousand anxiously waiting for the aviator. As Cal approached Parson, he noticed a massive storm with distinct edges pushing fast from the south. At that point, he had a decision to make. Rodgers could tell that if he tried to land, he'd be engulfed in the storm, and getting out of there would have been impossible, so he swung wide of Parson and the storm. It was moving so fast, he still "struck its edge," and the wind rattled and shook the *Vin Fiz*. Cal managed to stay the course and get free of the weather. As he did, the sun cut through the clouds and illuminated the countryside. He wrote about it later:

> The sunset was beautiful, and the storm clouds banked up on the horizon in a most peculiar manner. There was lightning playing all around me, and I was mightily glad I had not landed.⁵

Rodgers kept his line for Oklahoma. Around five thirty in the afternoon he had to make a pit stop for more gasoline. He found a "broad field" at Russell Creek and put the *Vin Fiz* down. On the other side of a hill were the railroad tracks, and not long after, the *Special* stopped, and his mechanics arrived to get Betsy ready for the last jaunt of the day.⁶

Not fifteen minutes later, Rodgers was soaring back into the sky, headed for Vinita, Oklahoma. In almost total darkness, he arrived at Vinita against strong winds and made what was described as a "beautiful landing" in adverse conditions. He had been flying for 271 minutes and covered 190 miles while touching down in his ninth state.⁷

The weather had been holding and the wind was tolerable, so the next morning, Rodgers wanted to try for Fort Worth, Texas, 319 miles distant. If he was successful, it would be the greatest distance yet covered in a single day. He got up early and was driven to the field by Jimmy Dunn, where the crew was already getting the *Vin Fiz* ready. But Mother Nature returned with a vengeance, with winds as strong as Rodgers had seen in over a week. This time he heeded the advice of his team—and his mother—and stayed grounded for the day. Though one must wonder, if the Hearst prize were still in play, would he have taken a chance? Previous decisions and his penchant for taking risks suggest he would have. The fact that Rodgers was not under any kind of ticking clock allowed him not to take chances that he had felt the need to before.[8]

A group of one hundred Cherokee Indians, led by Chief Buffington, traveled from their reservation in the hills to Vinita to witness the flying "big bird" machine. The Cherokee reportedly raced forty miles to make it in time before Rodgers resumed his flight. Luckily for them, the wind had shut him down for the day. People came by all morning and afternoon to get a look at the *Vin Fiz*. A cowboy showed up and offered Cal one hundred dollars if he could mount and ride his horse. Rodgers declined, telling him that flying "was buck enough to suit him." Rodgers met with Chief Buffington and showed his people the *Vin Fiz*. It was indeed a big bird, they said.[9]

On Tuesday, October 16, Cal got up early again, but this time the howl of the wind was gone. So he readied himself and headed out to the departure area. But the weather was not completely gone, "I noticed that it had turned very cold," he said later. Not only that, but by the time he arrived at the field, the wind was beginning to come back. Wanting to get as far as he could, Rodgers did not delay and took off around 7:45 a.m., before the wind kicked up too much. When he got into the air, there was a headwind, but he still pressed on making decent time. "It was amusing to see all the people running out to see me," he said. "They were on top of everything that had any elevation." Even in these remote areas, people came from afar just to get a glimpse.[10]

Though it was true, as Frederick Jackson Turner proclaimed, that the great American frontier was gone, in places like Oklahoma, there were still parts wild and untouched. "This was good flying country," Rodgers noted later. "There are some places with odd patches, which caused me to fly higher, so as to plan for landing." The vast, sprawling landscape was infinitely different from what he encountered when he left Sheepshead Bay, where the land was dotted with hamlets, towns, and rolling tree-covered hills. The Midwest, on the other hand, was filled with prairies, sunbaked fields, and livestock. Passing one field where cows stopped and gazed up at him, "[he] noticed that even they began to stare up at me. It seemed funny for it is usually hard to attract a cow's attention."[11]

17. "[Cal] is going to master the air" 129

He put down at Muskogee around 9:40 a.m. for gasoline and oil. The flying conditions were still rough because the wind was "growing very puffy" when he landed. They refueled quickly and restarted the *Vin Fiz*, but right away something was wrong because the engine sputtered and misfired. For two hours, they worked on it, even having to go back to the *Special* to get extra parts. Around 11:30 a.m., Cal was finally off again against the "puffy" air with a "strong quartering" wind of twenty-five miles per hour. The going was rough, but Rodgers continued. Cal took an elevation of three thousand feet to have a view of the landscape and a landing spot among the woods, brambles, and high hills.[12]

And it was a good thing Cal had kept his altitude high because the engine once again began to sputter. Moisture was the culprit because the engine started to spout steam. He spotted a farm in the distance and quickly began his descent. Luckily, a field was clear, and he touched down without incident about five miles outside of McAlester, Oklahoma. Rodgers was alone as he lumbered off the plane and began inspecting the engine. Oil and water were mixed in the oil pan. He had a little extra oil on board and was able to clean out most of the water. Though the engine would run, it could start misfiring at any time. Rodgers wanted to get to McAlester, "so I took a chance," he said later. Rodgers restarted the engine, and though there was still some moisture in the cylinders, it ran well enough to risk takeoff. He got up into the air and sputtered his way to McAlester.[13]

Rodgers finished the day having gone 127 miles, not even close to what he had wanted. That night, Shaffer and Taylor tore the engine apart and found that a cracked cylinder head was the culprit. They would be able to replace it and have the engine ready in the morning, they told Cal. "So I decided to stay there for the night," he told the media.[14]

One reporter described Rodgers's progress as "bird hopping" along in his transcontinental quest. And there was truth to that. Much like the United States' World War II "island hopping" strategy to Japan, Cal was hopping his way to the West Coast.[15]

Rodgers left McAlester at 7:30 a.m., heading toward Fort Worth. He banked and circled so he could pick up the Katy track heading south. He reached Denison around 9:23 a.m., but it was overrun with people with no suitable place to land. So he continued on, landing just a little southwest of Pottsboro, seven miles south of Denison, where he was to refuel seven minutes later. As Rodgers landed, he was dumbfounded. They had contracted with a garage to have gasoline waiting for him, but it was not there. Apparently, they required Cal to come and get the fuel and had refused to bring it to the field. The company was under the impression that Cal was to stop at Denison and have the fuel taken on there. This miscommunication caused a two-hour delay.[16]

Beulah Belle Bennett was eleven years old when Rodgers landed in Jim Bryant's pasture outside of Pottsboro. Her father, Frank Bennett, was the president of the Pottsboro Bank and offered to take Cal to get his fuel. She recalled Cal's landing years later: "Everyone who ran on into the field where the plane landed were given the chance to autograph one of the wings." Rodgers was grateful and took Mr. Bennett up on his offer.[17]

Rodgers and the *Vin Fiz* were often flying under contract to stop at certain towns and to sometimes perform short flying exhibitions. The costs for the coast-to-coast journey were skyrocketing. This produced trouble because the fuel stop was to be at Denison, and the company contracted to provide fuel refused to take it to Rodgers. Tension and competition between towns and communities to get Rodgers to make a stop sometimes rose to a fever pitch. Rodgers even accused some towns of purposely delaying his departure in order to spoil another town's visit.[18]

After refueling, Rodgers took off from Pottsboro and headed for Fort Worth. He needed to pick up the Santa Fe Railroad. When he reached Gainesville, two tracks intersected, and he mistook the other track for the Katy and headed instead for Wichita Falls. The hamlets he passed over waved vigorously, trying to get his attention and alert Rodgers that he was heading the wrong way. By the time Cal realized his mistake, he had to backtrack over sixty miles. At some point, a railroad telegrapher managed to get Rodgers's attention and signaled him about his mistake.[19]

Cal righted his path and shot back toward Fort Worth. Cal reported an interesting event that occurred while he was lost. He was flying at two thousand feet when he saw a bald eagle below him, keeping the same speed as he was, and that appeared to be shadowing the *Vin Fiz*. For miles, the eagle was just below him, hanging in the shadows of the biplane. He then noticed the eagle start to make a sharp ascent, heading right for the biplane. The bird got within feet, close enough for Cal to look the eagle right in the eye, and after a moment, it swooped away and out of sight behind him. Even the birds were confused by the flying machine.[20]

Fort Worth newspapers had been tracking Cal's progress for the last two weeks in anticipation of the Birdman's scheduled stop. It was none other than *Fort Worth Star-Telegram* publisher Amon Carter who sponsored Rodgers's flight into Texas, paying a handsome sum to have him land in Fort Worth. As word came that the *Vin Fiz* was approaching, the fire station rang its bell to alert the city. Schools closed, church services halted, and businesses ceased operating. People flooded into the streets and onto rooftops. Although Rodgers was about five hours late, a massive crowd of ten thousand lingered, awaiting his arrival just outside of town in Mr. Ryan Place's pasture, the scheduled landing spot. Automobiles and buggies were everywhere, with a row of cars from town waiting to get in. Police Chief J. William Renfro and his men formed a line to keep people off the makeshift runway. All eyes were toward the heavens as Cal and the *Vin Fiz* approached.[21]

The *Star-Telegram* narrated Rodgers's approach:

> "There he comes," exclaimed everybody simultaneously, and instantly the whistles of the roundhouses and yard engines screeched forth their blasts of welcome until their sounds were drowned by the cheering multitude as the winged "creature" hovered overhead and began to gently circle to earth.

The *Special* had arrived well before Rodgers, and two crew members were waving a white sheet at the end of the runway to get Rodgers's attention. It apparently worked, as he banked and swooped down to land. As he did, the crowd broke through the police barrier, forcing Cal to crank on the elevator and rise back up, nearly sweeping the field and doing only God knows what possible harm. It took several minutes before Chief Renfro and his men could restore order and clear the runway. Meanwhile, Cal circled three times until he could finally land. Cigar in mouth, he smiled, stepped off the plane, and was immediately swarmed. It was accurately reported that he was a man of few words because he simply said, "Howdy" to the crowd when they rushed toward him.[22]

At this point, the landscape of the continent was changing rapidly compared to the rolling timber-choked knolls of the east. The relatively flat fields with wide open spaces to land were now filled with cactus and chaparral, which could make landings extremely dangerous.

The next morning, a crowd of five thousand or more amassed at Ryan's pasture once again to watch Rodgers and the *Vin Fiz* take off. High winds again delayed Cal's departure. He had to wait until a little after noon for the winds to die down before he could take off. Rodgers passed over Arlington twenty minutes later, on his way to Dallas and the state fairgrounds. Once over Dallas, Rodgers dropped to just five hundred feet and circled the city. Onlookers packed the streets and filled the rooftops. At the fairgrounds, another seventy-five thousand people waited for the Iron Aviator to arrive. The *Vin Fiz* circled the grounds and then landed perfectly in front of the packed grandstands.[23]

The *Dallas Morning News* described the scene:

> Amid tumultuous applause from an eager crowd of 75,000 persons, Cal P. Rodgers, sea-to-sea aviator, glided gracefully down the infield of the State Fair racetrack at 1:50 p.m. [He hovered] over the fairgrounds for 15 minutes in the most thrilling exhibition of aerial navigation ever seen here...[24]

As Rodgers dismounted, the crowd overwhelmed the security detail and swarmed him and the *Vin Fiz*. People grabbed and tugged on Cal; everyone wanted to touch the great aviator. Eventually, the crowd was subdued, and Cal spent time shaking hands and pretending to hear what people were saying to him.[25]

The next morning, a large crowd gathered again at the fairgrounds to watch the *Vin Fiz* take off. It became so large that it could not be contained, and in haste to touch or get a "piece" of history, the wave of people damaged the left wing severely enough to cause a delay for repair. It was not until two in the afternoon that Rodgers pulled himself aboard and called for his team to "let 'er go!" He lifted into the air and circled the grounds as the crowd cheered and waved. Quickly, he got to two thousand feet and squared off for Waco.[26]

About thirty-five miles south of Dallas was the small town of Waxahachie. The mayor and city council desperately wanted the *Vin Fiz* to land, so they sent a wire asking if such a stop was possible. It was not, but Cal so appreciated the request that he agreed to adjust his flight plan, swing a little west, and pass over the hamlet. About forty minutes after departing, Rodgers approached Waxahachie. The town had painted the tops of some old train cars to help him find his way. They also cleared the depot so the *Special* could stop if needed. It did not stop but passed through about fifteen minutes ahead of the *Vin Fiz*. Cal sailed over the town at 2:45 p.m.; the local newspaper described the event:

> His machine glided along as gracefully as a bird on a wing, and all the machinery appeared to be working perfectly. The revolution of the propellers could be plainly seen.[27]

As he passed over at an altitude of three hundred feet, people could see the cigar in his mouth. The entire town "congregated in the streets" as Rodgers passed by, and he was soon off to Waco.

"Them there things" won't last, said the early skeptics of manned flight. At Waco, there were apparently a fair share of disbelievers. "Whether he or she is an enthusiast and believer or not," the local newspaper proclaimed, they are "invited to come out" to watch the first "honest-to-goodness flier" land at Gurley Park. At first, there was a tiny speck on the October skyline; soon, the propellers came into view, and the excitement in town grew.[28]

17. "[Cal] is going to master the air"

The Young Men's Business League had arranged for the *Vin Fiz* to land in Waco and for Rodgers to stay the night. They offered to pay a $250 purse to Rodgers if he circled the field and landed. A thirty-foot American flag flew from a massive pole on the skyscraper the Amicable. Its rooftop was packed with two hundred onlookers who waved, cheered, and whistled as he circled the building. "The sky scraper is a model one," Rodgers noted later, "that even New York would be proud of." The Katy that Rodgers followed as he entered the city ran straight toward the Amicable building. The view from the top was breathtaking. The local newspaper described the bedlam:

> As he came over the business portion, the aviator slowed down, and he must have heard the cheering of the crowds who flocked into the streets and thronged the roofs with upturned faces. He drifted on out over the railroad line, twice as high as the Amicable, then turned north over the residences.[29]

At that point, everyone on the Amicable lost Rodgers in the sun and quieted down. They mingled and probably started to contemplate leaving when out of the sun's rays boomed the *Vin Fiz* coming right at them, this time so low they could see Rodgers "head ... looking down over the edge of the plane." The crowd whooped and hollered as he buzzed by. After another low circle over the city, Rodgers headed for Gurley Park. There he circled the grounds, packed with people, low enough for everyone to see his face. They waved and cheered as he came around to land. As the *Vin Fiz* touched down, the people "left the grandstands and swarmed upon the field." As he came to a stop, the police force holding people back was overwhelmed as the crowd thronged around the plane even before the propellers stopped. Cal shut the engine down, was literally pulled from his pilot's chair, and was placed on the shoulders of the adoring crowd. For an hour after, Rodgers shook hands, stood for photos, and was introduced to countless people, none of whom he probably heard.[30]

The mass of humanity in the park was only getting larger as Rodgers did his best to make pleasantries and protect his plane. A "solid line of automobiles" from the city created a traffic jam as people got out of their cars and "charged upon the crowd, intent on getting close to the aviator." The scene was described as a "circus," and there in the middle of it all was Cal, standing head and shoulders above the crowd, "a veritable giant, standing six foot six." Rodgers was becoming a legend, a hero, and, apparently, even growing in height and stature during his historic journey.[31]

The *Vin Fiz* was the center of attention as well. People were amazed at how seemingly flimsy it was. They noted the cloth-covered wings and "bicycle" tires. They touched and fondled the machine as Cal calmly tried to stop them from taking parts of it. The crowd at every stop continued to write their names on the wings, unaware that even the slightest cut could, once in flight, result in catastrophic consequences. "The canvas once white," noted a reporter, "is now black from the inscription of thousands of names." Cal was described as gracious but was almost always seen as awkward and uncomfortable by those who met him. The loud and rambunctious crowd made it extremely difficult for him to ever understand what was being said to him or to even answer a question if he heard it. He had a high-pitched voice that wasn't loud enough, and as a result, he came across as obdurate.[32]

People shouted out to him and asked questions he could not have heard, such as, "I didn't know a man as big as you could fly." And there were always adoring fans. "Oh, isn't he just a handsome thing?" called out one woman. Some asked if he would fly again. "Go up again mister," pleaded one six-year-old boy. One woman touched the engine and grabbed a handful of grease, proclaiming, "I'm going to let it stay on until it wears off." Cal was becoming the modern equivalent of a rock star. He was Charles Lindbergh before there ever was one.[33]

That evening, Taylor, Shaffer, and the Kid had to have spent hours going over every inch of the *Vin Fiz*, making sure no one had damaged or taken anything. The Young Men's Business League entertained Rodgers and Mabel that night at the Huaco Club. It was a pleasant evening, with Cal again the center of attention, which was something that Mabel had to have been growing tired of. At some point, word arrived of the death of Eugene Ely, which stunned Rodgers. He sat without comment for some time and then spoke quietly: "Ah, that's what gets them all if they stay at it long enough." No one said anything as he continued, "That's why I'd like to get out of it, before it gets me"—a shocking comment coming from someone who seemed so confident and proud of his ability as a flier. The festivities could not have lasted much longer, and Cal and Mabel returned to the *Special*.[34]

18

"[The] American people were melting down old heroes"

> "[The] American people were melting down old heroes and recasting the mold in which heroes were made."
> —William Allen White

The front page of the *Waco Morning News* featured a headline about Rodgers's landing and spending the night. Right next to his story was another headline, "Famous Flier Falls to Death." Eugene Ely died while performing stunts at the State Fair in Macon, Georgia. Cal and Ely had become friends during the Chicago Air Show back in August, and he was someone Rodgers admired. Ely was reportedly high up, performing terrific dives, when, on his last attempt, he kept falling and could not recover. His plane crashed into the track, barely missing two pilots in the center of the mile-long oval. He reportedly leaped from his plane before impact, but the force of the fall killed him. The aircraft was incinerated on impact with a massive explosion that sent pieces flying everywhere. The vulgar mob in attendance rushed over to grab fragments as souvenirs, and within minutes, not much was left—they even took articles of clothing off Ely's body.[1]

As a result of the mass-media revolution taking place at the time, these early aviators were some of the first "celebrities" of the modern era. Combined with the growth of urbanization and an ever-expanding market economy, along with newfound leisure time for middle-class workers, they gave their attention to things like sports and movies. The decade, which climaxed in 1910, "was a time of tremendous change in our national life," noted journalist William Allen White. "[The] American people were melting down old heroes and recasting the mold in which heroes were made." As the twentieth century dawned, you could read about the same event in a newspaper in New York that you could in San Francisco on the same day. That was new. Newspaper subscriptions were roughly thirty-two million in 1880; however, by 1909, there were over 164 million nationwide. Newspapers dominated the transmission of information; it was all there was. The first commercial radio station did not come onto the scene until 1916 in Pittsburgh.[2]

Though the term *celebrity* had been around for some time, the modern celebrity, as we know them today in sports and entertainment, didn't really exist in 1910. Cal Rodgers and other aviators were the modern equivalent of some of the first sports and entertainment celebrities. In comparison, it wasn't until 1914 that Babe Ruth played his first professional baseball game, Charlie Chaplin acted in his first silent film, and Jack Dempsey boxed in his first professional bout—three of the largest cultural icons to ever exist. Baseball, boxing, movies, and football were extremely popular and gaining national appeal because of the mass-media revolution taking place. From 1901 to 1914, by far the most-written-about subjects were the robber barons, like Rockefeller, Carnegie, and Hearst, and other leaders in business and politics. Though these captains of industry captured much of the media's attention, slowly the feats and accomplishments of sports heroes rose above them. By the 1920s, sports and entertainment stars dominated the headlines. These early aviators in 1911 were some of the first modern mass-media darlings of sports celebrities, and as they accomplished greater and greater feats, so too did they capture the attention of the nation. In 1911, no one did so more than Calbraith Perry Rodgers.[3]

He was over halfway to California, and the end was now more attainable than ever. History was right in front of him for the taking—to put his stamp on that Perry lineage and legacy and to make a name for himself. He was not going to be denied; Cal just believed and willed it into reality.

Rodgers was gaining momentum, and his popularity was skyrocketing. More and more newspapers were picking up his story and putting it on the front page. Nevertheless, the recent news of Ely's demise and how it happened must have placed a somber mood on the next leg of his journey. Would the hoodoo—would *it* get him? It was most assuredly on the mind of Mabel and Rodgers's ever-nervous mother, Maria. The next morning, Cal was informed that the Palmer-Singer motorcar had been involved in some kind of accident. It took several hours to find alternative transportation. "I did not get away from my hotel until 11:05," Rodgers revealed later.

Taylor, Shaffer, and Wiggin spent more than the usual amount of time giving Betsy an inspection. It was a good thing; they discovered

18. "[The] American people were melting down old heroes"   137

"The Kid" Charles Wiggin helping Cal prepare for flight (San Diego Air & Space Museum).

that the elevator and rudder wires were worn to the point of a breakage inevitably happening. Fixing it would take some time, but they had no choice. Cal's goal of 188 miles to San Antonio was going to be a stretch today. By 11:20 a.m., when the *Vin Fiz* lifted from Gurley Park, the crowd was again large and rambunctious. "I circled their 22-story sky scraper again for fifteen minutes," Cal reported later, "and also around town."[4]

Rodgers followed the *Special* out of town, not taking the lead until it stopped at a water tank, and then he "shot ahead," as Cal described later. He wanted the train to get out ahead of him, so he performed several large circles around the city, but after the *Special* stopped for water, he decided to push on. The weather was beautiful; he reported, "I had a fine flying day, with a slight wind back of me, a five to eight-mile breeze." Rodgers soared on to Temple, about twenty miles southwest of Waco, and looked back to see that he had lost sight of the *Special*.

So, he "started back to see if it was moving," but after five minutes and no sign of it, he turned back around and headed for Granger, where he was scheduled to stop, refuel, and perform a short flying exhibition. Rodgers was in Granger for about forty-five minutes for fuel, then he took flight and performed a series of stunts for the crowd that had gathered. "Granger is a small but very energetic town," Cal said. The crowds were getting more energetic and were usually larger in urban areas the further he flew in his attempt at history. Though the massive crowd in Chicago would perhaps never be equaled, the frenzy was palpable everywhere he flew.[5]

Charles Tew was six years old when Cal approached Austin at about two in the afternoon. Rodgers was making good time: "sixty miles an hour," he said later. Tew and some friends were nearby and scrambled up the hill to the landing area trying to spot the *Vin Fiz*. "Every once in a while somebody would say, 'there he is,'" Tew recalled years later. "And it would end up to be a buzzard. Nobody really knew what an airplane looked like." Eventually, the *Vin Fiz* appeared, and the large crowd went wild, with "lots of screaming." After he came to a stop, Cal lumbered out of the aircraft and worked on it, almost completely ignoring the crowd. A local newspaper reporter noted, "Rodgers is almost as famed for his reticence as for his flying skill and nerve." Cal's reputation for not talking caught up with him wherever he went, with very few ever realizing why he was that way.[6]

"Rodgers warmed up" to the crowd after a time, "a little—very little," the newspaper reporter complained. Rodgers was shaking hands, and people started introducing themselves and even asking questions once they settled down and it was quieter. After taking on more gas and oil, Cal was back up in the air around 3:45 p.m., headed toward San Antonio—the goal for the day's flight. But not before giving the crowd one last thrill "by circling the capitol dome" low enough for everyone to see.[7]

But about ten miles southwest of Austin, the *Vin Fiz* engine erupted. Cal described it to the *New York Times*: "Suddenly one of my intake valves blew out, and the head dropped down and broke a hole in the piston." He then meekly described the events after, "I volplaned to a good field about eight miles from San Marcos." To the casual reader, it didn't sound like much of an event. He finished his message saying the engine was being worked on and he would be back at it in the morning.[8]

But what happened was his first real scare of the 2,300-mile journey. Rodgers was at 3,500 feet, going sixty miles an hour, when the piston exploded violently, causing the *Vin Fiz* to tumble over and into an uncontrollable dive—just like Eugene Ely had two days before. His

18. "[The] American people were melting down old heroes" 139

engine dead, Rodgers held on to the elevator and warping levers with everything he had as he tried to slow his dive. He was over a wooded area; there was no place to land that wouldn't decimate the biplane and him. Then he noticed that to the southwest was the small town of Kyle, with a few fields around it that looked good for landing. Using the levers, he fought for life and death to bank his plane and volplane around toward the town, all the while falling to the earth at an uncontrollable speed. Rodgers's massive size and strength are probably what saved him. His large hands willed the rudder and elevator to turn and level as the ground rushed up at him. He got over a residential area as he miraculously leveled off, "narrowly missing the roofs of several homes," slamming into the ground in a field that just so happened to be perfect for landing.[9]

By eyewitness accounts, as the earth rushed toward him, Rodgers got the plane leveled just in time and skimmed over the houses, slashed across a cornfield, and smashed into bushes and shrubs in the field. When Rodgers was found, he appeared to be in a daze, walking around the plane, "pale white" and slightly incoherent. The *Vin Fiz* was miraculously not severely damaged. The tires and skids would need some work, but structurally, Betsy was in good order, besides the engine. Within minutes, the entire town was in the field, offering help and looking on in amazement at the Birdman who had fallen from the sky. It was a miracle. Cal regained his composure and asked that the *Special* be alerted, and word was sent off toward the railroad station.[10]

Those on the *Special* saw Cal go down fast; he was miles ahead, but they could see the speck of an airplane in the sky flounder and plummet. As to the emotional state of all on board, we can only guess how Maria and Mabel reacted. DeKrafft had the train stopped, and John Rodgers, now back on the train after being gone for a few weeks, drove Taylor and Shaffer in the Palmer-Singer auto as fast as they could in the direction Rodgers had put down.[11]

For the first time during his coast-to-coast journey, Rodgers was shaken. Though he had been truly tested for the first time, newspapers still referred to the "nerveless, man of steel" who escaped death time and again. He retired to his estate room on the *Special* and was not heard from for the rest of the night. Maria and Mabel attended to Cal and were reportedly both taken aback by his outward appearance. They noticed how the near-death experience had shaken the Iron Aviator to the core. He had a glass of warm milk and went to sleep, refusing even his usual evening steak.[12]

Taylor and crew got to work removing the blown-out engine and replacing it with the only spare they had, one that they had already rebuilt twice. A broken piston rod is what wrecked the engine, making it completely useless. The engine was leaking so much oil now that it was coating the wings. Rodgers had been pleased with the performance of the destroyed engine. "If that isn't going some," he told a Waco reporter the next day about making more than sixty miles per hour, "I am not acquainted with speed."[13]

The next morning delivered rain and wind. Even if the weather had been good, it is doubtful the plane would have been ready anyway. The newly rebuilt engine was taken from the hangar car and put into place on the *Vin Fiz*, and the day was spent going over and over the machine—starting the motor and turning it off, testing every aspect. They no doubt inspected every inch of the biplane, making sure nothing was frayed, cracked, or broken. When Cal finally emerged from his estate room, most still noticed that the man was recovering from yesterday's hop. Reporters on the train wanted to know if Cal was going to fly today; he seemed to snap at them and pointed out the driving rain and wind. Then his mother stepped in and scolded them, saying, "It is you people who keep pushing him and pushing him." Though there was certainly some truth to her statement, Rodgers did most of the pushing, but on this day, he seemed more relieved than disappointed at the weather. "I don't know which is wearing out faster," he said, "me or the machine." He dismissed himself and went to the hangar car to check on Taylor and crew and their progress.[14]

As he often did, DeKrafft stepped in and continued to answer questions. Frustration was mounting for reporters as well; one asked if Rodgers was losing his nerve from the fall that nearly resulted in a tragic accident. "Rodgers did not fall," DeKrafft asserted, "but volplaned to earth." There was a major difference between the two, he said; with the one, you end up dead. He ended the press conference by stating, "The transcontinental journey will resume as soon as weather conditions permit."[15]

It is not known exactly what was said when Rodgers entered the Pullman hangar car, but Taylor and Wiggin both noticed that the man was still emotionally recovering from the fall. And it was a fall that Rodgers somehow pulled out of and was indeed able to volplane to a miraculous landing. They updated him on the progress and expressed their confidence that Betsy would be ready in the morning even if they had to work all night. Cal most likely thanked them before retiring again to his estate car for the rest of the evening.[16]

The next day, it was sunny and clear. Cal, Taylor, and Shaffer inspected the field for takeoff. The storm the day before had drenched the black loam soil, which was still thick and wet. Loam is a silt and sand

18. "[The] American people were melting down old heroes" 141

mixture that becomes heavy and cakes onto anything that it comes into contact with. It caked onto their boots as they walked the field, pushing the plane. "The black loam clung to my wheels," Rodgers said. They decided to remove the wheels and just use the skids. They also turned the *Vin Fiz* so it would have a longer stretch of runway to allow Cal time to get his speed up. This took a little extra time, delaying his departure.[17]

Rodgers left Kyle at ten in the morning, and with a crowd of locals standing by, he flew around the area several times, much to their delight. He circled for about twenty minutes to allow the *Special* to get out ahead of him, then headed toward San Marcos, about ten miles away. "I made an altitude of 2,000 feet and found that the air, although very warm below, was almost frigid at the height." The community around San Marcos had prepared a landing strip for Rodgers, and by the time he approached, it was surrounded by a throng of five thousand spectators eagerly awaiting his arrival. The crowd was electric when the *Vin Fiz* came into sight, but as Cal approached, he was not as happy. "I found I had a bad place to land but succeeded in landing safely."[18]

As would sometimes happen, his being the first airplane ever seen in this part of Texas, when Rodgers came in to land, people sometimes ran "right underneath seemingly without a particle of fear" of the machine and its propellers. Once down, the security detail was quickly overrun as the crowd of "5,000, swarmed around the machine." It was bedlam. Rodgers was again swept up in the mass of humanity as he tried to keep them from destroying the *Vin Fiz* in their haste to touch him and the machine.[19]

Rodgers would also sometimes, well, many times, rub local reporters the wrong way with his apparent aloofness due to his deafness. He enjoyed pleasing people and being in the spotlight, but when it came to answering questions, Rodgers preferred to withdraw; at best, he appeared uncomfortable. Eventually, he got away for a short lunch before heading back out.[20]

It was Sunday, and San Marcos was southern Methodist and Presbyterian country. The people in those parts were devoutly religious, as most of the country was. In Texas, in San Marcos in particular, they took it to a whole different level, causing Cal to observe, "San Marcos is, I believe, a very religious town." It was arranged for him to be driven back to the train station, where the *Special* waited. His driver noted that Cal was the "first attraction to come to San Marcos that had ever broken up their regular church attendance." And it wasn't clear if everyone was happy about that.[21]

Cal returned from lunch and found the field still packed with bystanders. He remarked later, "I was annoyed greatly by the people persisting in standing in my way at the extreme end of the field." They eventually got the crowd to understand the danger of standing at the end directly in front of where the *Vin Fiz* would lift off. Rodgers had concerns about the conditions of the field and getting enough speed to avoid plowing into the residential area at the end of it. But he got in the air. "I was forced to fly low, and there were many trees and houses, so I was very much pleased when I got safely into the air." He made one circle and then "squared away for San Antonio."[22]

Taylor would later scold Rodgers, telling him, "How many times do I have to tell you, don't take off with the wind behind you." Cal didn't always think about it, and sometimes he just took off.[23]

Rodgers found his iron compass and followed the tracks. "I could see in the distance the Katy Special," a large train that he would overtake before dropping into San Antonio. He flew at three thousand feet with a backwind and easily made a mile per minute. The polo field at Fort Sam Houston, San Antonio, was filling up with people early that morning as anticipation for Rodgers's landing grew. There would be no disappointment today. Rodgers was making good time, and the weather was ideal.[24]

The *San Antonio Light* reported that a "huge crowd" awaited the Birdman's arrival. As the lookouts along the railroad signaled Rodgers's approach, "all eyes ever to the north" watched for the *Vin Fiz*. Bells, whistles, and horns sounded as the biplane approached. "It could be seen sailing with the ease and grace of a huge bird, excitement was rampant among the crowd." Rodgers circled the field as he usually did before landing. Learning from the fiascos at Waco and San Marcos, San Antonio brought in extra security in the form of the Texas Third Cavalry to hold the crowd back. As Cal landed at 12:40 p.m., he taxied down the runway and came to a stop. The crowd again rushed the plane but could not get past the soldiers. Rodgers dismounted and waved to the adoring crowd. The Aero Club of San Antonio was on the field to greet Rodgers, as were other local dignitaries and officers of the cavalry. After a short greeting at the Officer's Club, Cal was taken by automobile to the St. Anthony hotel for a meal and some rest before resuming his journey.[25]

Around four in the afternoon, Cal returned to the fort and lifted off thirty minutes later. He headed for Harlandale, just outside of San Antonio, where he was scheduled to perform an exhibition. First, he circled over the Alamo, then across San Antonio, heading southwest to its outskirts. He did several maneuvers for a large crowd before landing. The next day, Taylor, Shaffer, and Wiggin rewired nearly the entire plane due to the discovery of more frayed wires.[26]

18. "[The] American people were melting down old heroes"

About this time, Cal was given word that Fowler was restarting his west-to-east continental journey and was about to leave Los Angeles. Rodgers welcomed the competition, even though Fowler was far behind. "Maybe he can make a race of it, after all," mused Cal. "That would add some interest for both of us."[27]

19

"I will not stop until I have reached the Pacific"

> "I will not stop until I have reached the Pacific Ocean or am disabled by accident or killed."
> —Cal Rodgers

When he spent the day in San Antonio overhauling the support wires and not flying, rumors swirled that Rodgers had lost his nerve. The story about his treacherous mid-air engine failure had made the rounds. Others speculated that the *Vin Fiz* campaign was bankrupt and Rodgers was going to have to give up his quest to reach the West Coast. Neither, of course, was true. Rodgers and Mabel took time sightseeing and relaxing, while Taylor and his crew worked on the *Vin Fiz*. Intimacy between Cal and Mabel had been rare on his epic journey, and no doubt the time spent together and away from everything was much needed.[1]

It wasn't just about sightseeing for Rodgers; he was concerned. The country between Del Rio and El Paso was treacherous. He was starting to understand just how massive the state of Texas was. It was desert terrain with rocks, chaparral, mesquite, and cactus trees everywhere, making it a deadly landscape for any kind of emergency landing. And maybe he was feeling a bit unnerved by his near fall the other day. The *Vin Fiz* needed to run perfectly, which is why the team spent an extra day in San Antonio going over the machine. Rodgers's strategy was to get high, 3,500 feet or more on every hop, which would allow him five to seven minutes to volplane for a spot to land if he had engine trouble.[2]

A "large" crowd gathered again on the morning of Tuesday, October 24, but waited nearly three hours for Rodgers to appear because he could not find his flight gear. Rumors probably floated again that he was done—had lost his nerve. What happened to his gear is unclear; perhaps an admirer had something to do with it. The *Vin Fiz* lifted off at

19. "I will not stop until I have reached the Pacific"   145

12:35 p.m. Rodgers circled San Antonio until he got above three thousand feet, and then headed southwest out ahead of the *Special*. About twenty-five minutes into his flight, his plane encountered motor trouble. It began misfiring until it quickly shut off. Rodgers managed to get it restarted and continued for a couple miles before the engine shut off again. Having enough altitude to find a suitable spot, he volplaned down into a cotton field and landed with no trouble.[3]

Again, the magneto was the issue, and Cal had to wait for the *Special* to catch up before Taylor and Shaffer could make the necessary repairs. By this time, the farmer who owned the field appeared and, thankfully, was more curious about the Birdman than his trampled cotton. After fixing the engine, Rodgers needed to take off again, and the cotton field would be an issue. Luckily, the farmer allowed the *Vin Fiz* crew to flatten and remove enough cotton to allow the plane to get up to speed and plow through the rest. Rodgers got back up into the air at 2:25 p.m. and took his time to get up to four thousand feet because rocks and mesquite trees covered the terrain. Cal would comment later, "This is bad flying country." After gaining altitude, he pointed the *Vin Fiz* toward Del Rio.[4]

Rodgers was scheduled to stop at Sabinal, a small hamlet twenty-five miles away. Upon reaching the designated landing area, he saw that the locals had laid out white cloth in the middle of a "tiny" field for him to land in. But after flying by, he saw that it was impossible to land there. "They had not realized that I glide down but thought I could settle right on a marked spot," much like an actual bird or helicopter. At times, people truly had no concept of what an airplane was or how it maneuvered. Luckily, a suitable field was not far, and Cal put down at 3:30 p.m. as the crowd made their way over. Half an hour later, the *Special* arrived at Sabinal, and Rodgers had a quick meal in his private car while the mechanics refueled and oiled the plane. He took off around 4:30 p.m. and, twenty-five minutes later, stopped at Uvalde, another contractual obligation. This time, the field marked for landing was sufficient, and he was only on the ground for thirty minutes to meet the local dignitaries and stand for the usual pictures. Rodgers made it to the day's last stop at Spofford Junction around six in the evening, but upon landing, he hit a cactus bush hard enough to flatten one of his tires. As he came to a stop, the tilted biplane swirled to a halt. Cal looked down at his spent wheel and must have laughed at the appropriate way the day's flying had ended.[5]

By now, Rodgers had logged 2,706 miles in his continental journey. The distance was not just taking its toll on Betsy but on him as well. Still, when asked by reporters how he was doing, his confidence was unwavering. "I will not stop until I have reached the Pacific Ocean or am disabled by accident or killed," he bluntly replied. The *Vin Fiz* management team was so confident in their Iron Aviator that they sent John Rodgers ahead to California to scout possible finishing spots for Rodgers. He reported back that Tournament Park in Pasadena would be most ideal, with the expected number of spectators being in the tens of thousands.[6]

The mechanic team led by Taylor continued its nightly routine of thoroughly inspecting every inch of the *Vin Fiz*. Nothing was to be overlooked, from frayed wires to a loose bolt. The biplane was a beautiful wreck that Taylor, Shaffer, and the Kid willed into existence daily. They must have marveled at their work and at the extreme measures they took to continually rebuild and patch up the machine to somehow make the *Vin Fiz* flight worthy. Taylor was also in awe at Cal's unshakable confidence and stubbornness to continue:

> Rodgers didn't seem to mind the fact that the motor was getting worse and worse, and the plane itself was in none too good condition. I kept telling him he should lay over for several days to go over it completely, and that it was dangerous to go on without doing so. He would only laugh at my pessimistic opinions and seemed to [at this point] handle the plane really better than ever.[7]

The next morning, locals helped clear a path in the field for takeoff. Though they were in a fairly isolated area, about three hundred American and Mexican field hands watched as Rodgers climbed aboard, got the engine started, and Taylor gave him the thumbs up to take off. Apparently, a cactus had been missed when the path was cleared because the *Vin Fiz* struck it before liftoff and skidded to a stop with both propellers splintered. It was enough damage to delay Rodgers's taking off until the next morning. Texas newspapers were noting Rodgers's difficulty with the terrain because it was slowing him down, and he was having trouble daily "making his way across the cactus patches and mesquite thickets."[8]

Taylor was none too happy about the condition of the biplane now and said as much to Cal. It was becoming unsafe to fly a wreckage such as her. There was only so much he could do. He told Cal they would undoubtedly, inevitably, with such a wrecked plane, miss something that could prove fatal. Cal just smiled at Taylor, patted him on the shoulder, and said, "Fix her, I'll fly her."[9]

Cal used the rest of the day to tour ahead on his planned route and look for suitable places to put down for refueling and emergencies. The terrain was so bad that he was becoming concerned about his options to

19. "I will not stop until I have reached the Pacific"   147

land in west Texas as he continued, though he would never have shared his concerns with anyone. Rodgers couldn't tell his mother or Mabel; he wouldn't want to worry them. And he certainly wouldn't tell Taylor, who was becoming uptight as the *Vin Fiz* deteriorated before his eyes. The prospect of not making it out of the state was very real. Large areas of desert and steppe terrain choked with cactus, mesquite, and chaparral created a wicked scenario for any kind of emergency landing.[10]

Rodgers and the *Vin Fiz* reached Sanderson, Texas, around 5:30 p.m. the next day, where another large crowd, estimated at around five thousand, waited for the Iron Aviator to make his appearance. As usual, the *Vin Fiz* hung in the distant skyline like a bird before roaring into view, soaring up above, circling the field, before swooping down and landing. The landing was again a bumpy one because the plane came to a rough stop on the rocky ground and became entangled with a chaparral bush, resulting in some minor damage. One can only guess Taylor's reaction. Luckily, it was nothing that would prevent Rodgers from continuing in the morning. Taylor, Shaffer, and Wiggin again had extra work to do on account of the terrain.[11]

However, that afternoon, the mechanics' team took a major blow because Charles Taylor received a distressing telegram from Los

Rodgers and Charles Taylor moving the *Vin Fiz* into position for takeoff (Library of Congress).

Angeles that his wife was critically ill. He hastily packed and left. Shaffer and Wiggin were now in the lead spots, which had to be daunting because Taylor was a brilliant mechanic. But they had no choice, and they were determined to keep the *Vin Fiz* in top shape. Rodgers later stated that "we miss him greatly," which was an understatement; Taylor's leaving was a major problem. Even Shaffer admitted that Taylor was instrumental in keeping the engine running. The week ahead was crucial, and dangerous terrain lay ahead because they still had miles to go.[12]

The headline read "Rodgers Lands at Sanderson," but right next to it in the *Galveston Daily News* was an even bigger headline, "Most Sweeping Anti-Trust Action Ever Brought." This was the era of trust-busting, first initiated by President Teddy Roosevelt. The defendants were well known, J.P. Morgan, Andrew Carnegie, John D. Rockefeller, and Charles M. Schwab, to name a few. The elimination of unfair, monopolistic practices by unfettered megacorporations was well on its way. Through vertical and horizontal integration, these robber barons dominated their respective industries, but not anymore. Though, to be fair, also known as captains of industry and benefactors of the gospel of wealth, these tycoons were a large part of the revolution in the daily lives of Americans during the late nineteenth and early twentieth centuries. By now, the government was eliminating its laissez-faire practices and beginning the Progressive change to government regulation of big business. The robber barons were paying the price.[13]

Cal rolled for takeoff the next morning at 8:15 a.m., full of hope and optimism for making El Paso, when the wheels struck an unexpected depression, which, combined with a gust of wind that caught his rudder, tossed the plane into a barbwire fence, ruining the skids and damaging a wing. Shaffer and Wiggin rushed over and determined that the damage would, of course, cause a delay, but that they could get the *Vin Fiz* ready in a few hours. Rodgers was thoroughly upset that once again he couldn't avoid trouble. It wasn't until 11:30 a.m. that he took to the sky, making the day's new goal, Sierra Blanca, a real challenge. It would take him over the last of the really rough stretch of terrain, which was the good news. The bad news was that his reward for getting there would be crossing the Paisano Pass and its 5,074-foot summit—the highest he would pass until he crossed into California. The twelve-mile pass resides between the Twin Mountains and Paisano Peak and is surrounded by a canyon land of volcanic deposits and alluvial washes of sand and gravel and the desert mountain range.[14]

After takeoff, Rodgers had some trouble ascending to the desired height because the air was "light" from the altitude and wind currents

19. "I will not stop until I have reached the Pacific"   149

swirling about from the surrounding mountains, but with effort, he reached 2,500 feet. He stayed with the Union Pacific Railroad as it went through Marathon, heading up toward Alpine. The country landscape was now rising as it headed for the summit, and Cal had to continuously do the same, which was difficult. To make matters worse, he noticed a set of low-hanging clouds that were rushing toward him. The clouds soon enveloped him for a time, causing some concern on the *Special*. Mabel was no doubt fretting every time they lost sight of Cal. But more importantly, it caused Rodgers concern because he was now flying blind. "I could hardly see my hand," Cal reported later. "I was worried and afraid I'd lose my direction," so he had to continue pulling up hard on the elevator to make sure he didn't smash into the ground and pray he didn't wander off course toward the mountain. Eventually, he punched out of the clouds and lowered his elevation to about one thousand feet to stay under the cloud cover. He landed without incident at Alpine, a scheduled stop for fuel, and waited for the *Special* to catch up.[15]

Beyond Alpine was the Paisano Pass. The *Vin Fiz* could only clear the summit by three hundred feet, a dangerously low altitude if he had engine trouble. Fortunately, the *Vin Fiz* was running well, the winds were slight, and he had made good progress. As he passed Marfa, the going was slow because the railroad line meandered around every hill. So Cal took a chance and hopped up over the hills, cutting out all the zigzagging, hoping to pick up the railroad on the other side of the mountain range. He was successful and several times cut off significant time by doing so.[16]

Still, reaching El Paso would not happen on this day. Once out of the mountains, the terrain straightened and allowed the *Vin Fiz* to pick up the pace, once doing a mile in a reported forty-seven seconds. He made it into Sierra Blanca at 5:28 p.m. and waited for the *Special* to catch up. His day was done.

Rodgers had done some of his best flying over the rough terrain of west Texas and the Paisano Pass. Over the next two days, the plan was for him to leave Texas behind for Arizona. From El Paso, the goal was to make Arizona, leaping over the corner of New Mexico.

When Rodgers arrived at the field the next morning, a large crowd was occupying too much of the planned runway, including automobiles, and they would not move. So Rodgers, Shaffer, and Wiggin had to move the *Vin Fiz* and then quickly take off in the opposite direction. He got up in the air at nine in the morning and made a circle around the city and over the railroad station where the *Special* was heading out for El Paso. Rodgers followed suit and shot out over the Union Pacific Railroad, heading slightly northwest. The western sky was ablaze in orange from the morning sun. The train had to stop at a flag station. Rodgers, still making his way up to altitude, circled above until he achieved two thousand feet and continued.[17]

"Everything ran smoothly for a while … but before long trouble developed," Cal wrote later. The engine was starting to overheat, and the water pump was leaking. "I knew I had to find a landing place very soon." And indeed he did; the engine began steaming, and Rodgers had very little time. When an engine severely overheats, the gasoline becomes increasingly unstable and can combust erratically, causing severe damage to the pistons and even erupting in an explosion. The clock was ticking.[18]

But the terrain was broken up—ragged and mountainous; there was no place to land. Rodgers had no option but to reduce speed as much as possible and "coax" the engine along. Hair-raising minutes passed as the engine steamed and shuddered. Fort Hancock was ten miles away; he had to make it there and hope for a good place to land. Upon seeing the outskirts of the city, he dropped, "trusting there would be an available landing place." At about a mile out, he saw a good field just in time because his engine was spent, and he began to lose altitude, rapidly forcing him down. His engine off, he glided as far as he could but was forced down just before the good field and into one filled with sagebrush. The *Vin Fiz* careened through the field, smashing bush after bush and damaging a skid before jerking to a stop. It was a little after ten in the morning. The *Special* arrived twenty minutes later, and Shaffer, Wiggin, and crew fixed the skid and repaired the water pump. It wasn't until 1:45 p.m. that Rodgers got back up in the air, headed for El Paso. Once off the ground, Cal noticed how beautiful the terrain was. "I would have enjoyed more of it if it hadn't been dangerous going over the mountains."[19]

Soon El Paso came into view. Forty miles out, he identified smoke from the city, and when he was thirty miles out, he could "see the city itself." El Paso had been waiting in anticipation for the *Vin Fiz* since Saturday. The wind was head-on and "puffy," so Rodgers made poor time. He arrived over the metropolis at 3:15 p.m., and again, the welcome was massive. Washington Park, in the center of El Paso, was filled with what could only be described as a "big crowd." It was Texas big, to be sure. Rodgers circled the field several times, and on the last one, he was seen waving his leather cap toward the crowd. The crowd was enthusiastic again in its welcoming of the flying legend, the great aviator.[20]

Perhaps it was the rugged "frontier" individualism of the West and the Southwest that made Cal so appealing to these people. He

19. *"I will not stop until I have reached the Pacific"*

represented everything they believed in. This lone rider on his machine, taking on the impossible and doing so with humble confidence and determination, epitomized the spirit of the West.[21]

There were few doubters now about Cal's grit, toughness, and greatness. The *New York Times* wrote a front-page editorial that said as much:

> "There is not as much talk as there should be about the courage and persistence of C.P. Rodgers…. Rodgers has completed two thirds of the trip and has had everything happen that can happen outside of death…. The margin of safety of the aeroplane is still too small to be rated as practical, but Rodgers inspires one to wait confidently for someone to make the aeroplane good enough."

20

"Thrilled as they never were before"

> "Thrilled as they never were before and probably never will be again."
> —*Arizona Daily Star* on Rodgers's arrival

It was clear to everyone by now that Cal was succeeding and making his way despite his plane, which was now frighteningly unreliable. Still, Rodgers didn't blink or waver; he kept on. Rodgers and his team decided to stay grounded in El Paso the next day so they could thoroughly go over the engine and make sure it was running as well as possible. Shaffer and Wiggin discovered that the spring in the magneto was shot and was the cause of the engine problems. Making these repairs was necessary because the *Vin Fiz* needed to be in excellent running order with the hard flying that was surely ahead. Arizona's vast deserts, where towns were a hundred miles or more apart, were a daunting challenge. There was also a mountain range as you crossed into California. Cal and Mabel, as usual, toured the area and visited with the locals before having a quiet dinner in the dining car.[1]

Rodgers took off at 10:15 a.m. on Tuesday, October 31, heading for Deming, New Mexico. The field was shorter than he liked, but he got up in the air and circled El Paso before setting off toward New Mexico. Flying into a headwind, the *Vin Fiz* did not make great time, but Cal arrived at Deming without incident. He didn't have to wait long before the *Special* arrived, just a few minutes behind. Rodgers lifted off at one o'clock, heading for Lordsburg, making another scheduled stop before starting his final leg of the day to Wilcox, Arizona, arriving at 4:35 p.m.[2]

The next morning, Cal didn't get out of Wilcox until after eleven, and the *Special* was delayed even longer, waiting on an engine car from Southern Pacific Railroad that was getting repairs. That morning,

Rodgers and his crew discovered damaged rollers in each of the propeller chains and had to replace them, taking several hours to do so. Rodgers was heading toward Dragoon Pass with an elevation of 4,351 feet, again taking time to loop his way up high enough to make it over. To add to his difficulty, there was a strong headwind coming from the west.[3]

The *Vin Fiz* again electrified the masses, as horns and sirens blared as people emptied from virtually every building and peered up into the sky, blocking out the sun with their hands. Seemingly emerging from the orange and yellow glow of the sun, the biplane swept across the skyline, circling the University of Arizona campus. "Thrilled as they never were before," wrote the *Arizona Daily Star*, "and probably never will be again." Indeed, thousands gathered and watched as Rodgers performed dips and dives, "shooting up and dropping down wheeling, turning, and pivoting at dangerous angles." The crowd was reportedly wild as "cheers greeted every daredevil move."[4]

Rodgers was scheduled to land on the university campus, but it was overrun with people. "The grounds were too crowded," Rodgers said later. "I didn't want to swoop down there and kill anyone." He banked away and headed for a section of town that was not as occupied and put down.[5]

It didn't take long for the *Vin Fiz* and Rodgers to be found, and the masses again fell upon him. When interviewed later, Rodgers was asked if he would do the entire trip from New York over again under the same conditions. "Yes, providing that anyone interested enough would put up a certified check of $100,000." The newspaper reporter noted that Cal's "tone" left "no doubt" that he wouldn't want to replicate the struggles and recent frightening experiences again.[6]

In an observatory at the university, Robert G. Fowler watched Cal circle the city and perform his stunts. He probably felt a bit melancholy watching Rodgers as he neared the end of his historic journey and hearing the stories of his near-death incidents, crashes, and accidents so far endured. Fowler had virtually the entire country ahead of him in his attempt. As the *Vin Fiz* flew away, Fowler was taken by automobile to meet Rodgers. They reportedly exchanged well wishes and some light conversation because they had never met before. "I'm very glad to meet you," said Fowler. "You've had a lot of hard luck." And Cal had; Fowler could only hope for better.[7]

The *Special* arrived, and the biplane was refueled as Rodgers ate lunch. While the *Vin Fiz* team was off the *Special* working, the general passenger agent had the engine car taken away, and no one knew until later. So, when Cal took flight at 2:51 p.m. and circled around to see where the train was, he saw that the crew was standing around waiting for the engine to come back. Rodgers speculated: "There has been great rivalry between Tucson and Phoenix," and he suspected that they "probably wanted to keep me in Tucson another night." It wouldn't work. Cal pointed the *Vin Fiz* west and took off.[8]

Rodgers headed out while the train waited for an engine car. The headwind didn't allow him to make the progress he wanted, and by five, as the sun was melting into the horizon, he was forced to stop for the day at Maricopa, Arizona, about forty-five miles south of Phoenix. The train was still an hour behind, so Cal used the time to look over the *Vin Fiz*. During his inspection, he discovered that both propeller chains had more rollers that needed to be replaced.[9]

The repairs were made into the evening and early morning hours, not allowing Rodgers to get underway until after nine the next day. He flew over Tempe, where again people crowded streets and rooftops to see him. The *Vin Fiz* appeared over Phoenix at 10:30 a.m., and he circled town several times before finding the fairgrounds for his scheduled landing. But he discovered that spectators were "scattered all over the place," and he could not land. There was a police contingent, but they could not keep the crowd (numbering in the thousands) back. Rodgers tried to wave the crowd off the field as he passed over, but they misunderstood and only cheered and waved back. He came around again, and this time got so low—fifty feet, reportedly—that he frightened the crowd, inducing many to duck. Cal headed back to town, found an empty racetrack, and put the biplane down. It took some time for the contractor with fuel and oil to find Rodgers, and as he waited, a crowd quickly grew. Again, he had to protect the *Vin Fiz* from souvenir seekers.[10]

Cal got back into the air at 12:10 p.m. and headed back to Maricopa, where he picked back up the Southern Pacific line and headed toward Yuma. One hundred and five miles later, the *Vin Fiz* was low on gas and had to put down at Stoval, Arizona, just after two in the afternoon. Stoval was just a water tank station in the middle of the desert surrounded by sand dunes. He found a clear stretch of land right next to the tracks and landed. This time, the fuel had to come from the *Special*, but it was several hours behind Rodgers on account of having to wait for an engine train again. Refreshingly, Stoval was practically a ghost town. No crowd. No nothing. "This is the first and only time that people did not spring up from nowhere," Rodgers said later. The water house had a telegraph operator, and Cal had him send word to the train. Two hours later, the *Special* arrived. The sun was low on the horizon; reaching Yuma was not possible, so they stayed in Stoval for the night. Shaffer informed Cal that they were out of fuel, so they had to wait for a passing train and hopefully purchase some. Luckily, a "westbound express" appeared heading their way, and seeing the *Vin Fiz* and Cal Rodgers waving them down, it happily stopped. As the sun set, Rodgers had dinner on the train with Mabel and Maria, while his crew procured the fuel.[11]

Rodgers had to be feeling a combined sense of excitement and relief. He would be in California tomorrow, and if all went well, he could reach Venice. He and Mabel, together, retired early to bed with the goal of lifting off by seven.

21

"But as long as someone had to establish the long-distance record"

> "But as long as someone had to establish the long-distance record, I am glad I am an American and glad that an American did it."
>
> —Cal Rodgers

Leaving Stoval at 7:30 a.m., Rodgers gracefully lifted off into a brilliant sapphire skyline, with just over three hundred miles separating him from the coast. The excitement had to be intense; the journey had been long and weary, and he was so close to the finish line and history. He approached Yuma an hour later, making good time and traveling about sixty miles. He was scheduled to stop for breakfast, but feeling that maybe he could make Pasadena, he pushed on, much to the disappointment of Yuma, where once again thousands awaited the Birdman. He did come down, fly low over rooftops, and wave to the people as he passed. Still, the crowds were disappointed as he drifted away to the west.[1]

The terrain was rough during this stretch. "This is the worst part of the desert that I have come across so far," Rodgers later said. The sand blew across the large sand dunes baked in the Arizona sun. Cal was amazed. "There were some hills just of sand fully as large as mountains." Still, there was a strange beauty in the barrenness of the desert as the sun cast an orangish glow across the sand-spilled terrain. Cal was at four thousand feet roaring past Imperial Junction and out over the desert at a reported seventy-five miles an hour because the wind was finally at his back. His eyes fixed west, on the impending coast, the ocean, and destiny.[2]

As the Iron Aviator passed over the Salton Sea, his worn-out engine

21. "Someone had to establish the long-distance record" 157

exploded. The blast sent shrapnel slicing the air, shredding Rodgers's leather jacket, and peeling skin off parts of his arm and shoulder. The biplane lurched and almost rolled because of the explosion. Rodgers was all but sent hurtling toward the earth in an unrecoverable dive at over a hundred miles an hour. Miraculously, Cal kept his wounded hand firmly gripping the warping wire lever and elevator as the plane spun out of control. He was nearly thrown from his seat because there was no harness to hold him in. But Rodgers did not fall, and after a few perilous moments, he managed to pull his craft back from its death dive and into a circular glide as smoke poured out of the ten-inch hole in his engine block.[3]

The headlines the next day read "Rodgers Fights for Life" and "Rodgers Almost Killed in Flight." In his telegram to the *New York Times*, Cal once again downplayed the event. "As I passed over Imperial Junction I flew on a space over the Salton Sea ... [and] motor trouble developed; I was up 4,000 feet." They would later discover a screw had come loose, jamming the connecting rod to the piston, causing it to burst in two and explode through the crank shaft. "Of course I had to land immediately." The engine started to disintegrate, "tearing itself to pieces." Taylor had been right; it was inevitable that they wouldn't be able to see something that could prove deadly.[4]

The wind still turned the propellers, cranking the pistons and doing more and more damage. Rodgers had cleared the Salton Sea, which was fortunate because it was unattainable for landing. He volplaned down in large circles as the machine rattled and shook. His eyes fixed on landing, but there was nowhere clear of obstacles that he could see, and the pinkish orange landscape was rushing up toward him. "I succeeded in making a very good landing in a very bad place," he humbly said later. Somehow, again, Rodgers dodged boulders, rocks, and cacti and made a clean landing close to the railroad. Luckily, the injuries were flesh wounds, painful but not debilitating. After coming to a stop, he began working on getting his destroyed motor removed. He had some tools and wanted to start removing the motor mount bolts that connected it to the support beam. "My train was three hours behind me, and I wanted to have everything in readiness." Though injured, Cal was focused on the finish line. Two railroad men at the switching station had watched as Rodgers plummeted to the earth and then "spiraled" down and landed. They came rushing over and were surprised to see Cal so calm. After a short conversation, they helped Rodgers get the plane up on some railroad ties so he could work on it.[5]

Word reached the *Special* that the *Vin Fiz* had suffered a severe incident and that Rodgers had crashed. Mabel and Maria were no doubt in a panic, and the long ride to reach him must have been excruciating. By the time the biplane came into view, Mabel was hanging out the door, staring in "disbelief" at Cal calmly working on the plane, having removed most of the bolts securing the engine. She rushed to him, and they embraced; what was said is not known. By now, Rodgers was a battle-hardened aviator, unshakable, and his confidence unwavering.[6]

The *New York Times* correspondent aboard the *Special* noted that, as Cal's crew approached, they said, he surely "bears a charmed life." What else was there to say? He was the Ironman. Shaffer, Wiggin, and crew most likely exchanged handshakes and "good to see you" with Cal and then got to work. They had to get the lone spare motor installed on the biplane, but it also had some issues and would need an overhaul itself. By this point in the journey, not a lot remained of the original *Vin Fiz* that had left New York. They had rebuilt virtually the entire aircraft and some parts numerous times over.[7]

Shaffer had to take two cylinders out of the Wright Model B engine on hand, and he "practically built a new engine." Shaffer and Wiggin worked all night, hoping to get Rodgers back in the air Sunday morning. By five in the morning, the engine had been overhauled, installed, and tested. It ran but was far from perfect. Cal rose, had a light breakfast, and left the *Special* at daybreak. Though he had somehow landed in that field, as he walked it that morning, the terrain around the railroad line wasn't suitable for takeoff, "on account of the sage brush and mesquite trees, and the ground was also very rough." Rodgers, Shaffer, and the Kid ended up finding a spot suitable for takeoff several miles away from the railroad tracks. They walked back, unloaded the automobile, and the entire crew lifted the *Vin Fiz* over the railroad tracks and wheeled it the three miles to the spot they had found. It took hours to cut down the sagebrush and clear a path. Once complete, it was time to get the biplane in the air and complete the journey.[8]

There was again no crowd out in the middle of the desert as the crew stood quietly and watched. Ominous silence filled the massive emptiness of the desert before the engine came alive. The hum of it was all that could be heard. Rodgers was okay with silence; he had lived mostly in silence his entire adulthood. He didn't even really recognize it anyway. Mabel watched Cal ascend into the heavens and waved to him. If all went well, he would make it to Pasadena today, near the completion of his epic journey.[9]

Not long after, Mohave Indians appeared in procession.[10]

"Them's Indians at the windows," cried the train porter.

"Some of the Indians wore war bonnets, and all of their faces were daubed in color, predominantly red," recalled Mabel later. The entire

21. "Someone had to establish the long-distance record" 159

passenger car was taken aback by the sudden appearance of the Mohave Indians. "I must confess I was terrified," said Mabel. "They came I feared … in retaliation for Calbraith and his 'big bird' landing among them." As they stood in the train car dumbfounded, the backdoor of the stand porch opened, and in walked their chief. He stood there, magnificent but ominous in full native garb, "complete with war regalia" and a "painted head." Mabel recalled that everyone stood in shock, frightened. "I had no gun and there was no place to run." But the chief was not there to take "scalps," as some had immediately worried.[11]

After a few tense moments, the chief spoke, "Me come to thank White Bird." Everyone looked around, and Mabel finally replied. "What?" she gasped. "You speak English?"

"Yes, ma'am. I go to college; I speak excellent English. It's our language now." By now, the entire car was relieved, and the tension had disappeared. "We use little Indian language now, like Feathers Before Us," the chief replied, pointing outside to another Mohave Indian.

"Well thank you Chief," said Mabel. "We are happy to have you convey your thanks to our Aviator." She apologized, saying that Cal had already left. "I understand," he said. "I am giving this token of friendship to you [then] Mr. Rodgers' Squaw." He took out an elaborate and beautiful necklace. He asked her to kindly lean forward, and he gently placed the necklace around her neck. "I christen thee, squaw lady of Mr. Rodgers the human birdman, with the name of 'White Wings.'" He took her hand. "White Wings," he said, "and I leave you and White Fathers in peace."[12]

What Mabel and the others did not know was that they carried the body of a Mohave woman who was reportedly 101 years old when she danced herself to death the night after Rodgers landed in the small town. They were not upset; it was an honorable way to die—apparently taken with delirium over the arrival of a big bird that carried the white man. The members carried her to the cremation ceremony, where they performed dances in her honor. They were not dressed in war paint, but for burial purposes.

From Imperial Junction to Pasadena, Rodgers would have to fly between two mountain ranges (the San Gorgonio and San Jacinto ranges) while again traveling over barren terrain for much of the way. By this point, Cal was unfazed by the danger that surrounded him or the fact that he was on his last rebuilt engine and a completely—several times over—rebuilt biplane, one that frankly wasn't running well. He had to have started to believe in his own invincibility, because it was pure craziness to have gotten this far and to continue under such conditions.

Not long after takeoff, the engine started misfiring, and Cal had no choice but to circle back and land. Shaffer and Wiggin worked on the magneto again, got the engine restarted, and listened; it sounded all right. At least they must have hoped. Rodgers took off down the runway, got into the air, and at not one hundred feet high, the engine struggled again, and he had to come down quick and land. Everyone at this point had to be unnerved. Was there another trip left in the engine? Mabel, back on the train, watched anxiously as Cal landed the second time. It was after ten in the morning, and they had been up since five. They again adjusted the magneto, fired up the engine, and waited. After some time, it was determined to give it a go. No doubt Shaffer urged Cal to take it easy on the engine; no one knew how much it had left. Cal climbed aboard, called out as he always did, "Let 'er go," and away he went. Everyone anxiously watched as he rose, higher and higher, in large circles, gaining altitude. Eventually, he straightened out and headed northwest. They jumped into the Palmer-Singer, and Jimmy Dunn took them back to the *Special*.[13]

Cal was at four thousand feet, heading toward Los Angeles and Pasadena. Again, he wanted the altitude in case of engine trouble to allow time to volplane down to find a spot to land. "I [again] flew over the Salton Sea, as I wished to fly in as straight a line as I could," he reported later. He had to cut over the water again for a short time to get back on track. Again, it was a risk; if he had engine trouble, he might have to crash into the water. Rodgers didn't follow the railroad that wound through the terrain. He instead took a straight shot toward Beaumont over the desert to cut off the distance. Tension was high, according to reporters on the *Special*, because everyone knew the *Vin Fiz* was on its last legs. The conductor was urged to make good time to keep up. Still, the *Special* meandered through the valleys, well behind the *Vin Fiz*.[14]

As he bounced in the air currents, knowing the condition of his engine, Rodgers had an epiphany of sorts: "It was a most beautiful sight, with the lake beneath me, and the mountains on either side and the railroad winding in and out." And then he saw "a westward bound express," speeding along ahead. He was clearly at peace; the fear of the hoodoo was gone. In that moment, he did the unthinkable; he ramped up his engine and took off in pursuit. He lowered his altitude, roaring across the desert. It didn't take long before he overtook the train and pushed on, not holding back.[15]

In the desert, hamlets were few and far between. "The trip over the desert was positively weird," described one reporter who waited for Rodgers to pass over. "The great birdlike machine speeding faster than the flight of birds" beneath him. The shadow of the biplane "danced"

21. *"Someone had to establish the long-distance record"* 161

across the mountains and desert. "Occasionally residents of the desert stood straining their eyes towards the hot heavens." They were in awe, dumbstruck at what they were seeing. No one discovered where they had gotten word that an airplane was coming. Some had no idea what an airplane even was; the rest had only heard about the wonderous machines and surely had never seen one before.[16]

Rodgers reached San Gorgonio Pass and shot back up to altitude. As he did, he caught a strong headwind. As he gained altitude, he had barely crossed over the summit when his magneto started acting up again. He could tell the plugs were working themselves loose again—most likely because of threads that were worn out. At this point, he was through the pass and heading for Banning, but the engine was shaking and rattling so badly that he was worried about it "breaking loose altogether." He approached Banning and, for ten agonizing minutes, kept his eyes on the magneto, when it finally broke loose and the engine stopped. As he had countless times before, he volplaned down into a plowed field and bounced his way to a stop, again, without a disastrous crash. "I noticed my radiator [also] was leaking badly, so I got to work to take it off to repair it," Cal told reporters later. The *Vin Fiz* was a mess, and how much more it could take, no one knew. To be sure, Shaffer knew that the machine was simply unsafe to fly in its condition.[17]

Back on the *Special*, Mabel and Maria paced anxiously, waiting for word on Cal. They had seen him shoot away at great speed. Shaffer could not have been pleased that Rodgers would push his engine, knowing its condition. "Our special train sped furiously on, churning up rocks," said Mabel, "right smack into the great American desert." The *Special* learned from Southern Pacific bulletins that Rodgers was far ahead. "We figured 60 miles from the finish." One of the last bulletins read: "Rodgers passed here, very high, heading over the great San Gorgonio and San Jacinto snow-capped mountains."[18]

"We prayed as the train rushed on and on," said Mabel years later.

Back at his biplane, Rodgers was eager to fix it up and make it to Pasadena. The *Special* appeared over the ridge and came to a stop. Again, everyone greeted Cal with joy that he was okay, but soon they were back to work on the *Vin Fiz*. Once the radiator and magneto were patched back together, they cranked the engine to start and heard a horrific sound. They opened the crank case and "found that the bearing was gone"—it would be hours of work. They were there for the night.[19]

At Tournament Park in Pasadena, where Cal was scheduled to land that day, a massive crowd had formed. Perhaps as many as fifty thousand or more were expected. Again, John Rodgers had gone ahead to help prearrange Cal's arrival. They were getting progress reports and making announcements to the crowd. When word came that the *Vin Fiz* was grounded at Banning for the night, a collective moan drifted out across the stands and track. People lingered and then slowly started for home. But not everyone; a few thousand stayed, determined not to leave until they had seen the great Birdman.

That evening, Shaffer and Wiggin worked tirelessly on the engine to get it in some kind of shape to fly one last time. Rodgers's manager, DeKrafft, told John Rodgers to inform Pasadena to set Cal's arrival for three o'clock the next day. Even though they were only eighty-six miles out, they didn't really know what to expect from the airplane at this point. They even surmised that he might not make it there at all. The next morning, November 5, Rodgers rose early and had breakfast with Mabel and his mother. Shaffer and the Kid had worked all night on the engine to get it ready, but there was a problem: "all of the bearings were worn out," and they had no replacements. The engine was not going to last; it might not even make takeoff. Cal decided to "make the best of it" and take the risk.[20]

The Solar Observatory on Mount Wilson would provide early notice to Tournament Park of Cal's approach. A relay network of lookouts was in place to keep them and the anxiously waiting crowd informed of precisely when he would arrive at the park. Most newspapers simply noted, as the *New York Times* did, that an "enormous crowd" awaited. It was no longer a surprise that the turnouts for Rodgers and the *Vin Fiz* were so large. Later that morning, Rodgers started to get ready. Mabel set out his best attire: his favorite brown business suit. He then put on his usual leather vest and grabbed his heavy canvas jacket, gold-tinted goggles, and black leather gauntlets. He kissed Mabel; no doubt the moment was intense, and the two shared an embrace.[21]

As Cal and Mabel exited the estate room, the lounge car was silent. Smiling faces and warm wishes greeted him as Cal passed through and shook hands. It was just before noon when Jimmy Dunn whisked him away in the Palmer-Singer to the field where the *Vin Fiz* stood bathed in the mid-morning sun. It was a magnificent California day. Shaffer and the Kid welcomed Cal, and no doubt they told him to take it easy this time. Cal ran his hand across the wing, as he had done so many times before, and whispered, "Betsy." He admitted to the press later that day that his engine was "worn out," and he no doubt kindly asked her to get him to Pasadena.[22]

They started the engine, and it kept running. Rodgers lumbered aboard, roared down the field, and into the sky. His target was Pomona, twenty-five miles away. There the engine would rest, and they'd take on

21. "Someone had to establish the long-distance record" 163

some fuel and check the oil. He was a few miles away, up to 1,500 feet, when the engine quit. He had no time to look patiently for a place to land. He banked and looped around, trying to land as close to the railroad tracks as possible. He leveled off, dropped, and landed, lucky that the ground was decent again, and he came to a clean stop. Rodgers first checked the magneto, and it was fine. Then he noticed the fuel line connection to the tank had broken. The train came up twenty minutes later, and luckily it was one of the few things for which they had a replacement. It didn't take long, and he was back in the air around 12:25 p.m. Rodgers described the flight from there:

> It was delightful flying weather.... I flew about 4,000 feet as I had a narrow pass, called the "divide," and as I was getting nearer Los Angeles, I had to keep a lookout for my railroad tracks.... I had a headwind all day, twenty-five mile breeze, as I got to the pass it was very narrow, and I could see on either side the two mountain ranges ... as I got through the pass the country began to take on a more fertile appearance. It really was very beautiful, and I noticed immediately that I was getting into civilization again.[23]

The colors of California and the fields of orange groves struck Cal as beautiful, especially after spending days in the desert. He reached Pomona, where several thousand spectators awaited his scheduled arrival. He swept over the field, circled back around, and landed without incident. The crowd was well-behaved as he looked over the biplane and checked the engine. A short time later, the *Special* arrived with gas and oil. Shaffer and Wiggin inspected the engine while they refueled. Rodgers was not in a hurry, as he "messed around" and was in good spirits before getting ready for takeoff at 3:30 p.m. It took some time to herd the ever-growing crowd away from the strip of land for takeoff, but they did not allow for much of a runway. It was a narrow stretch of field that caused Cal concern: "There is a danger in losing control ... and the possibility of killing someone." The ground was rough, and the *Vin Fiz* hit a bounce before going airborne, with the crowd truly ignorant of the danger.[24]

Once in the air, Rodgers steadily climbed in altitude to five thousand feet. About twenty-five minutes later, he reached Pasadena, and he could most likely see in the distance the blue haze of the Pacific Ocean. He accidentally went to the wrong side of the city and had to circle back. As he descended, he could see the thousands upon thousands of people in the streets and on rooftops. Cars stopped in the streets, and people emptied out of buildings. The great Birdman was finally here.[25]

The crowd in Tournament Park watched as Rodgers headed to the wrong end of town, perplexed that he wasn't coming back toward them. When he finally swung back around and approached, a small boy in the crowd stood up, pointed, and shouted out, "There he is."[26]

The crowd let out a cheer of relief. Laughs were heard because some thought Cal had pulled a fast one on them. Ever the showman, Rodgers performed several "dives" and "revolutions" that shocked and awed the crowd, maneuvers that reminded some of the ones that Hoxsey perished from while performing at Dominguez Field earlier in the year. The *Special* was still an hour away, so Shaffer didn't have to cringe and watch in horror as Cal performed stunts that the *Vin Fiz* should not have been performing. But it didn't go unnoticed because one reporter questioned whether Rodgers was being "reckless" in his mini airshow with his worn-out biplane.[27]

Rodgers swooped down a final time, leveled, and then touched down in the "cleared center of Tournament Park." As he came to a stop, the police could not hold back the crowd as it "swept over the field," mobbing Rodgers. He stood there, a smile on his face and a cigar clenched in his teeth, as people rushed to touch the great aviator. He towered above them, completely surrounded and still grinning. "So hearty and tumultuous the greeting that Rodgers appeared overcome with emotion," wrote the *New York Times*. How could he not have been overwhelmed? The journey was reaching its climax; he was but a short hop to the ocean and the beach. His final destination was in his mind—it always was. Some in the press considered his arrival in Pasadena the conclusion of the journey.[28]

Cal Roders calling the Aero Club of America to announce he had reached Los Angeles (Library of Congress).

People stumbled and fell and were nearly

21. "Someone had to establish the long-distance record" 165

trampled as they rushed to Cal. Some women reportedly even fainted when they got close to him; a few were seen to have fallen off parked cars, while most screamed and cheered in delirium. He was swept up in a sea of humanity, with ten thousand people on the field and at least ten thousand more surrounding it. The police carried clubs and made threats, but the masses could not be quelled. M.W. Ready was the announcer and gave a detailed play-by-play for the crowd outside the stadium. It was pandemonium.[29]

Parting the sea of humanity, the police eventually got to Rodgers and cleared a small circle in the mass of people. The police chief escorted D.M. Linard, Chair of the Reception Committee, with a telephone wired to the central station, and as the crowd quieted, Cal phoned the Aero Club of America and announced he had reached Los Angeles. With that, the crowd erupted, cheering wildly. Hundreds of hats were tossed into the air, and the crowd again surged.[30]

Cal Rodgers with the American flag given to him during the welcoming ceremony draped over his shoulder, along with Mrs. R.D. Davis (middle) and Miss Irene Grosse (right) (Library of Congress).

By now, all the reception committee had reached Rodgers, and, at the sight of them, he tossed down his cigar and smiled. Mrs. R.D. Davis, wife of the president of the Pasadena Board of Trade, presented Cal with a huge bouquet of California chrysanthemums. Next was the beautiful Miss Irene Grosse, the Queen of the Carnival of Roses. She welcomed him with a kiss on the cheek. Then they, together, produced an American flag and draped it around Rodgers, who grabbed it and held on to it tightly, a smile on his face as his eyes began to tear up. The massive crowd erupted, and he was swept away by the police chief and his men and taken to a car, where Mayor Thrum of Pasadena waited and welcomed him. For the next hour, the car circled the park in what was described as a "triumphal parade." The crowd amassed around it wherever it went. Cal occasionally stood and waved but never let go of the flag. They stopped at the clubhouse, where Hoxsey's widow waited. She was overtaken with emotion and shook Rodgers's hand, congratulating him. Shortly, Cal was back in the automobile and whisked into town to the Hotel Maryland, where he had a room waiting.[31]

Once at the hotel, Cal walked right to the bar, a parade of reporters following. He stopped and looked at the bartender—and then ordered a glass of milk. After drinking it, he smiled and made a statement, again not wanting to field a lot of questions, which would have been nearly impossible as we know:

> I am glad this trip is over. I am not in this business because I like it but because of what I can make out of it.... But someone has to do this flying business, and I decided it might as well be me. The trip was a hard one, all things considered. Indeed, I believe in a short time we will see it done in thirty days and perhaps less. I was never worried at any stage of the game, not even when it looked as if it was all off. I knew I'd get through it if only to break even with the fellows who laughed at me.[32]

The *New York Times* declared Cal the "greatest aviator living," but Rodgers did not agree, saying that there were others more deserving. "But as long as someone had to establish the long-distance record, I am glad I am an American and glad that an American did it," said Cal. Then Rodgers excused himself and retired to his room to wait for Mabel and his mother to arrive from the train station. Not long after, he received word that the Palmer-Singer car had arrived.[33]

Mabel was overwhelmed with emotion, to be sure. To not have been there when he landed must have been disappointing. The car pulled up, and Mabel and Maria were escorted inside, where they had to quickly sign in at the front desk. After doing so, Mabel turned toward the elevator, and as its doors opened, there was Cal standing inside, a warm smile

21. "Someone had to establish the long-distance record" 167

on his face. She cried out, rushed into his arms, and after a kiss, she said simply, "I'm so glad."[34]

The press called it a "transcontinental flight," and rightfully so because it was the first ever journey of its kind. But for Rodgers, it was a coast-to-coast flight. He was not done, in his mind, until he dipped the wheels into the Pacific Ocean.

22

"He [Rodgers] remains outwardly unimpressed"

> "He [Rodgers] remains outwardly unimpressed; he remains the same cool imperturbable aviator as when people were joking of his efforts to cross the country."
> —*New York Times*

The next morning, Rodgers slept in, not appearing at the hotel restaurant for breakfast until late morning. When he arrived, he ordered three glasses of milk. Outside, a throng of people tried to get a look or even get inside to see the great aviator. A group of women congregated around the hotel, peering in windows, and some tried to sneak in. It was so bad that when it was time to leave, a little before noon, they had to sneak him out the back of the hotel and into the Palmer-Singer, where Jimmy Dunn whisked him away.[1]

Rodgers had not won over everyone in the press; for some, his aloofness and withdrawn nature were unbecoming. A reporter for the *New York World* wrote, "He [Rodgers] remains outwardly unimpressed," a quiet and reflective individual who never said too much, if anything at all. He was "the same cool imperturbable aviator as when people were joking of his efforts to cross the country." Cal mentioned it himself; when he started his quest, there were plenty of skeptics, and in private circles, he was most assuredly the subject of many jokes.[2]

Joining Rodgers for breakfast were, of course, Mabel and his mother, Maria, along with Shaffer, Wiggin, his cousin John, and most likely members of the *Vin Fiz* team. Everyone was in good spirits, and it was noted that Cal looked "refreshed." As he ate his meal, Rodgers playfully quizzed Mabel. "How many gallons of gas do you think Betsy used on the trip?" She just gave him a look. "One thousand, two hundred and thirty gallons," he said with a smile. "It shows it right here in

22. "He [Rodgers] remains outwardly unimpressed"   169

the newspaper," he said, laughing. Wiggin and Mabel read from a list of the parts used, "eight propellers, two radiators, six cylinders, two engines, two tails," and on and on. Wiggin had kept a record of every part replaced and how many times. By the time they were done going over the list, the table was silent. Mabel remembered something they had forgotten—what about the bottle of Vin Fiz?[3]

"That made it, didn't it?" she asked, knowing the answer. "It sure did, and the strut beside it. It must have been made of special glass," Rodgers mused. "It was indestructible, and I gave it my best to destruct it," he said as they all laughed. Wiggin had to correct Rodgers—the strut had been replaced as well.

"I want to confirm that I don't consider the trip complete," Cal told reporters later that morning, "until I have actually touched the Pacific Ocean." There were some who doubted the nation would care if Rodgers finished in the sand and tide. But for him, that was where the journey ended; he had made that very clear from the beginning. He was drawn to the ocean, and he and Mabel had already privately decided not to return to New York but to stay in California, with its vast warmth and elegant array of colors.

"What was the secret behind such a strenuous accomplishment?" asked a reporter. Cal took a slow draw from his cigar and replied, "Simple, you just keep going until you get there." Does that mean that other aviators, Fowler, for example, could and would equal his task? "I don't believe it can be done in thirty days [currently]," Rodgers said. But yes, he fully anticipated many more to make the journey, Fowler among them.[4]

Cal's mechanics, Taylor and Wiggin, were known to call Rodgers the "Iron Aviator" during his journey. He miraculously survived sixteen crashes and accidents, while his plane didn't even come close to surviving intact. Wiggin wryly noted to the press that only the rudder and drip pan remained from the original machine. In many ways, it was despite his airplane that Rodgers had made it to California. Cal arrived on the West Coast a changed man as well; not unlike that bottle of grape soda, though still all there, it was not the same. He was a more confident and assured individual, but he could also finally remove the burden he had been carrying. He had finally lived up to the name that he had simply endured for so long. He endured, and he conquered.[5]

The final leg of the *Vin Fiz* journey would, of course, be to a coastal town, and negotiations began immediately, causing the delay of the flight for a week. Mabel was fine with this development because she wanted Cal to rest a little. The hysteria that followed Rodgers's arrival in Pasadena produced a bidding war. Venice, Santa Barbara, San Diego, and Long Beach all competed for the opportunity to "host" Cal's arrival on the coast. Meeting after meeting took place between Lawrence Peters, Cal's handler, and the various Chamber of Commerce presidents, mayors, and business representatives from the respective cities. Thousands of dollars would be required to "win" the right to host the landing. In the end, Long Beach won the bidding war. It was agreed that Rodgers would finish his journey on Sunday, November 12, taking off from Tournament Park, flying the forty miles to Long Beach, and landing on the beach. Rodgers left the bargaining to his handlers and took Mabel's advice to relax.[6]

After breakfast, Cal had a full day of press stops and appearances, which was not very relaxing. But first, he insisted on seeing the ocean. So he grabbed Mabel and took the Palmer-Singer, reportedly at high speeds, through the city to the ocean at Venice, where he "dipped his hands" into the water. The vastness and emptiness of the ocean rapture many, and Cal was no doubt one of them. One cannot help but feel so small, so insignificant next to it while peering into the limitlessness of the cobalt-colored water. What was said is not known, but he and Mabel had to have shared a personal moment of triumph in the sand, gazing out at the water with their shoes in their hands. The press got word of the high-speed trip and talked up Rodgers as not just a daredevil in the air but on four wheels as well. He was, after all, a racer on land before he was one in the air.[7]

The announcement of a Sunday flight was immediately protested by the Long Beach Ministers' Association. They felt the arrival of the *Vin Fiz* would make Long Beach a "circus town" and, most importantly, lower the "moral standard" of the principality. Perhaps they got word of what Rodgers's presence had done to poor Billy Sunday and his services back in September in New York. Whatever the reason, DeKrafft tried to downplay the date, even stating that Rodgers "would rather make the flight on Saturday, so far as he is personally concerned." Things heated up; even the Women's Christian Temperance Union chimed in, criticizing the arrival of the Birdman on the Sabbath. It was sacrilegious and disrespectful to the Almighty. In the end, the mayor decided the show must go on, and Sunday was going to be the day. It allowed for the most people to travel and see the flying "circus" on a day everyone had off.[8]

As Rodgers made his rounds, he was treated every bit like the celebrity he was. Women waited outside his hotel to give him flowers and well wishes. Mabel could not have been impressed. When he visited the First Bank of America that afternoon, it suspended business to all its clients except Cal so he could conduct his business in privacy. Back at the hotel, telegrams from around the country were pouring in from admirers and

22. "He [Rodgers] remains outwardly unimpressed"   171

political figures, even from the president of the United States. Cal also visited several schools, including Wilson High School, where a flock of students and locals presented him with flowers. He was mobbed wherever he went; after all, it was hard to miss the six-four gentleman with a constant cigar in his mouth. Everyone knew who he was. Though Rodgers was every bit the celebrity, he had DeKrafft announce that he did not want to speak at any celebration in his honor. The reaction to his perceived standoffish and aloof behavior was always one of confusion and sometimes even frustration by the press and others. Why was he so shy? Few people knew of his disability. He and Mabel simply didn't talk about it, and not once does a single newspaper mention Cal's hearing issue. Most likely, no one knew. Some just thought he was slow or aloof.[9]

That night, there was a "farewell dinner" at the Maryland Hotel. The Armour Company was calling back its executives and most of the team that had accompanied Rodgers on the *Special*. The press, officials from the Wright Company, and many others were in attendance. Though always quiet, Rodgers made a statement and gave a toast to his team. "Anybody who starts across the continent in an aeroplane can make the trip I did," said Cal. "He would have to stick with it, that's all, and keep going despite misfortunes and mishaps." He told those in attendance that he didn't think it would take long before planes would make the trip in just days, but, he said, they would "never carry very many, and aerial transportation" would be very expensive. It was unfathomable to envision the future of aviation based on the crudeness of the current machines.[10]

Hearst offered Rodgers a $500 prize for making the trip, which he immediately turned down. In refusing the prize, he took a shot at Hearst and others offering prizes for near-impossible feats. "I can offer a million dollars to the first man to be shot out of a cannon from here to New York," he said, "and be pretty sure not to have my money taken away from me. That's the way with some of these folks who put up big aviation prizes." The science of aviation was still in its infancy and incredibly dangerous, and he felt that prizes such as the ones Hearst offered only encouraged extreme risk-taking. Though Rodgers was one of those risk-takers, after taking on the journey and the risk, he seemed to have had second thoughts. Did his statement reflect a true change of heart, or was it simply a case of posturing with regard, perhaps, to Hearst's frankly offensive offer? Rodgers never elaborated.[11]

The Armour Company considered the journey more or less completed, and the flight to the ocean was, in their minds, for show. Most of the *Vin Fiz* crew, including the mechanics' team, were dismissed, and the *Special* was sent back to Chicago. Taylor had been on a leave of absence due to his wife's illness, and it was still just Shaffer and Wiggin, now with no help. Lawrence Peters was Cal's manager, and he handled the final preparations and negotiations for the flight to the beach. If there was any sign of how little the Armour Company considered the final leg of the trip, it was their appointment of Jimmy Dunn, the chauffeur, as director of day-to-day operations of the *Vin Fiz*. DeKrafft did stay to help manage the press and public relations. Though Dunn was most likely happy or amused to still be hanging around, it spoke volumes. It was time to end the journey; it had cost upward of $200,000—the most expensive advertising campaign in history.[12]

On November 9, Rodgers visited Long Beach and agreed to a suitable stretch of sand near the pier to land on. The details were left with Peters, John Rodgers, Long Beach Police Chief Moyar, and the Long Beach Mayor, Windham. Meanwhile, the skeleton mechanic crew of just Shaffer and Wiggin continued working on the battered *Vin Fiz*, which was beyond "worn out." The engine was spent, but a new one was not an option because the Armour Company had gone well over its budget. They had to make do and get it in some kind of working order to go twenty-five more miles.[13]

On the morning of his final hop, Tournament Stadium was again packed with onlookers. The *Vin Fiz* stood in the center of the park in a fenced-off area being worked on for hours. It's unclear who was in charge or who was even working on the biplane. Charles Taylor was mentioned as having come back (his wife was apparently recovering), and, of course, Shaffer and Wiggin would have been there. The condition of the motor was not in dispute. Taylor supposedly urged Cal not to fly until he had a new engine, but that was not an option. They were out of parts and the bearings needed to be replaced, and, as a result, the engine could seize at any moment. Rodgers was undeterred. It "was nothing" but a hop, skip, and a jump, he said—just a twenty-five-mile-wide one, Wiggin noted.[14]

The preparations at Long Beach were immense and costly because the entire town had to be mobilized to accommodate the massive crowd that was expected. Though the Armour Company was not impressed with the continuation of the journey, the city of Long Beach was preparing for the "most important" event in its history. The landing spot near the pier was packed with people, along with a temporary grandstand. Cal's getting to the ocean seemed to mean something to more than just him. The boardwalk was lined rows deep with spectators. Police Chief Moyar had nearly his entire force on location for crowd control. He even called in reinforcement just days before in the form of Company H of the seventh California National Guard.[15]

22. *"He [Rodgers] remains outwardly unimpressed"*   173

A train brought in nine cars full of people from Pasadena alone. The traffic into Long Beach was jammed a mile long. By three in the afternoon, the crowd was electric in anticipation. Leading up to Cal's arrival, the local newspaper declared, "Long Beach will be advertised as it never has been before." And they were right; the crowd was massive. Every major newspaper was represented, and even the Selig Moving Picture Company was there to film the arrival of Rodgers and the *Vin Fiz*. The California press had become fond of the "aloof" Rodgers, describing him as a "quiet and modest man."[16]

Because the engine needed yet more attention, Rodgers didn't get into the air until three thirty in the afternoon. He circled above the packed grandstand and the surrounding crowd for miles, all with eyes fixated on the *Vin Fiz*—none more intently than Shaffer and Wiggin. He then swooped out over the Maryland Hotel, where Mabel and Maria waited outside to wave. After he passed, they jumped into the Palmer-Singer, and Jimmy Dunn sped away, promising to get them to the beach before Cal.[17]

Rodgers then turned south toward Long Beach. He didn't get far before the engine started sputtering, threatening at any moment to stop. Cal rapidly descended, spied a strip of land near the railroad at Covina Junction, and put the biplane down. By this time, Shaffer had to have instructed Cal that his plane was no good, if he hadn't before. Still, Rodgers was insistent; he had to reach the ocean. That was the completion of the journey, ocean-to-ocean; that was Cal's journey.[18]

It was around 5:30 p.m. when the engine was working enough to possibly get the *Vin Fiz* into the air and the final twenty miles or so to Long Beach. It was dusk when Cal once more folded himself into the pilot's seat. Rodgers smiled at Mabel, who stood by the train with Maria, and then he instructed Wiggin and Shaffer to let 'er go. The glow of the sun, which had already dropped to the brim of the ocean, cast just enough light to watch the silhouette of the *Vin Fiz* take off. He got up into the air, but right away Betsy was kicking and bucking, and down below they could hear her "spitting" and "sputtering" as Rodgers desperately tried to keep the biplane in the air. He managed to keep the *Vin Fiz* moving and disappeared in the distance toward the ocean. It was then that Rodgers noticed a string of bonfires dotting the landscape, leading him toward Long Beach. He locked onto them and followed their glow toward the water.[19]

As Rodgers approached Compton, about twelve miles southwest of Covina Junction, now in pitch-black darkness, he could only follow the glint of moonlight reflecting off the railroad track and the bonfires that ended at the ocean's border. He should never have been in the air, but there he was, determined to finish. Unfortunately, the *Vin Fiz* had had enough—had been through enough. She was done.

An eyewitness suggested Cal had to avoid some trolley wires as his dead plane plunged to the ground. His altitude at the time of the crash is debatable, perhaps two hundred feet or less. The trolley wires would have been visible, like "fluorescent mercury," because they were loaded with electricity. He was near the Compton train station when he came down into a field. According to the witness, his plane "tilted ... fifty degrees shearing away from the dangerous wires," and crashed down into a freshly plowed field on Orr Ranch. Rancher Orr was in his field because he had just finished working for the day when he heard the *Vin Fiz* coming in hot. The plane careened into the ground almost straight down, but on a tilt, so that the left wing struck first, then the nose. Rodgers was impaled into the ground with the wreckage, the biplane collapsing all around him. He lay there, motionless, in a tangled heap as Orr ran over. He called out to the aviator, who didn't respond.[20]

When word reached Long Beach of the crash, Mabel and Maria were notified and taken back to the scene of the crash. Then the announcement was made to the crowd, which was met with massive disappointment. The mayor and Chamber of Commerce members did their best to put on a happy front and declared that everyone should not worry.

As Orr approached, he found that the engine, ripped from its block, had "thrown itself against Rodgers' side," and the fuel tank was "on his neck." Surely, he was dead, Orr assumed. He pulled the fuel tank off Rodgers, got down on a knee, and listened for sounds of breathing. Orr would later say that the soft dirt formed a "cushion" that saved Cal, and luckily the engine narrowly missed crushing Cal, landing by his side, not on him. Slowly, people emerged and tried to get Cal out, but he was unconscious. The Palmer-Singer arrived from Long Beach a short time later. Mabel rushed over and found Cal unconscious. She was in shock, fearing he was dead. Orr had fetched a local doctor, who arrived as Rodgers finally regained consciousness. Doctor E.T. Holcombe found that Cal was seriously injured, but he was unsure how extensively.[21]

Around eight in the evening, Rodgers was driven to the hospital in Pasadena. There he was evaluated, kept overnight for observation, and released the next day, but he was injured. Both his ankles had been crushed, and he had numerous bumps and bruises. Rodgers, Mabel, and Maria were provided with a bungalow in town for him to recuperate. A few days later, members of the press were allowed into Cal's room at the bungalow. "I'm feeling mighty good," he said as he puffed on his cigar. He was indeed feeling well enough for his doctor to allow the mini press

22. "He [Rodgers] remains outwardly unimpressed" 175

The *Vin Fiz* almost completely destroyed in Compton, California (San Diego Air & Space Museum).

conference, telling everyone Rodgers had no serious internal injuries, just bruises and a couple of sprained ankles from the crash.[22]

Rodgers told the press he would be recovered by week's end and hoped to get to the beach soon, but it was mostly up to the necessary work on the *Vin Fiz*. It was yet again a complete wreck. Mabel was asked about the crash. "I was afraid of just this trick," she said. "Cal should have kept on last week until he finished. I wanted him to rest and made him change his plans. He will get well and finish, though." An interesting admission, but the delay was out of her control due to negotiations for the landing spot and the repairs required for the engine that ended up failing anyway. Rumors swirled that Rodgers's crash resulted from his mechanics' error. "No, oh, no. They were not to blame," he said emphatically. "It was the plane, the engine, it was all worn out." Mabel herself was beginning to worry. "We prayed that both Cal and his tired machine would be able to hold out."[23]

Rodgers told the *New York Times* that he thought he had fallen unconscious in the air due to "ethereal asphyxia," a condition where lack of oxygen causes a person to fall asleep. This condition could happen, but Rodgers's altitude was not significant enough, and rancher Orr was a witness and clearly saw him alert and struggling, reaching for his levels, trying to avoid the wires, and then crashing. Cal simply didn't remember how or why he crashed, most likely the result of a concussion. "I don't know how it happened. I don't know whether something went wrong with the machine or something was the matter with me," he mused. Later that week, Orr sent Peters a ten-dollar charge for damage sustained to his field from Rodgers's crash.[24]

The *Vin Fiz* was so destroyed that Shaffer didn't think it could be reconstructed. The heap of wreckage had to have befuddled him. He was so dismayed by it that he reached out to the Wright factory. They told him he would need a special machine to fix the shattered mounts, supports, and wings, or he could ship the entire biplane back to Ohio for repairs. They decided on getting the machine sent to them. It is unknown how they paid for the special equipment and spare parts because it is doubtful the Armour Company would have.[25]

Lawrence Peters, the *Vin Fiz* and Rodgers's personal manager now, was asked about the condition of the *Vin Fiz* because, by all accounts, the biplane was destroyed. "It is impossible to tell how long it will take to rebuild an aeroplane," he derided. "As soon as one is constructed and Mr. Rodgers is well he will complete his transcontinental flight." The issue was that no one had any idea how long either of those would take. Would the pilot or his machine heal more quickly?[26]

The *Vin Fiz*, or the smashed remnants of it, were taken to a warehouse (a sun parlor, as it was described) in Long Beach, where the rebuild took place. Shaffer and Wiggin were most likely joined by Charles Taylor, whose wife was recovering. A new engine was ordered and would ship out from Ohio with the parts necessary to rebuild the aircraft. Again, who paid for that is unclear. By this point, it wouldn't be surprising if the Wrights offered it or if Rodgers was privately financing his journey. Taylor estimated the work would take two weeks to complete. Though the event organizers had hoped for a Thanksgiving landing on the beach, Taylor told Peters not to plan on it; it would be early December at best.[27]

On the night of November 17, Rodgers started having chest pains. They lingered on into the morning, and his physician, Dr. F.E.C. Mattison, ordered an x-ray of his chest, which came back negative. He had not cracked his breastbone or any ribs. The muscles and cartilage were still healing and extremely tender and sore. But it could also have been stress and anxiety.[28]

Rodgers continued to recuperate while Lawrence Peters fielded offers from promoters and agents. There was interest in an aviation meet later in the year that would feature Rodgers and the *Vin Fiz*. Pasadena wanted to purchase the plane and display it for tourists. Even vaudeville came knocking, inquiring about the possibility of Cal putting on arial shows for audiences. San Francisco wanted Rodgers to come down for an exhibition flight after making the coast. When a newspaper reporter

22. "He [Rodgers] remains outwardly unimpressed"

relayed this to Shaffer, who was still mired in the rebuild and in no mood, he jabbed, "He will break his neck in Frisco in this machine if he is not careful." Enough with future plans—he just wanted to finish the job at hand.[29]

By December 5, Rodgers and the *Vin Fiz* were healing, but not very fast. The headline read that they were both "Mending Slowly," and it was true. Rodgers was hurt more seriously than they let on. He had torn ligaments and deep muscle bruises, and he had to use crutches for several weeks just to walk because of the severity of the injury. He and his doctors denied that his ankles were broken, but he still had to use the crutches for part of the time. Meanwhile, at the sun parlor on Pleasure Pier in Long Beach, Taylor and Shaffer were fast at work, with Wiggin attaching the newly arrived engine to the rebuilt frame, along with a new gasoline tank and connector. The biplane was taking shape day by day, looking more and more like it once did, though it was heavily patched together.[30]

Cal had casts on his legs, and some questioned whether he could fly. "Plaster casts won't bother me," he said. "I can fly with feet amputated if necessary, and I'm going to touch the Pacific with my skids if it kills me." Later in the week, Rodgers's physicians disputed whether he would need the casts to stay on for very long because his ankles were only sprained. "I feel mighty fine," Cal reiterated. He gave a press conference while he "puffed contently" on his trademark black cigars. California liked Cal. He was charismatic, confident, and, by appearance, fit the bill as a playboy. As of the seventeenth, Shaffer reported that they had at least five days of work left on the *Vin Fiz*, and plans could soon be made about the completion of the journey.[31]

As they prepared to finally finish the journey, there had to be some who wondered if anyone still cared. Cal's name appeared less and less in newspapers as nationally the excitement of his historic adventure seemed to have run its course. Peters and probably everyone close to Rodgers had to have worried that the *Vin Fiz* dipping its tires into the Pacific Ocean would be seen as anticlimactic. The Armour Company said as much when they withdrew their train and crew. The question on Peters's and many others' minds was would anyone really care whether Cal made it to the coast?[32]

23

"I am proud to have blazed the way to the Pacific"

> "I am proud to have blazed the way to the Pacific coast by the air route, as proud as those hardy pioneers who made the wagon trail and the men who later linked both sides of the continent by rail."
>
> —Cal Rodgers

The answer to whether people still cared came as Peters and Rodgers met with Long Beach city officials yet again. After brief negotiations, it was arranged that Rodgers would leave from near the same spot in Compton where he had crashed and fly to Long Beach, landing near Pine Pier. The mayor of Long Beach and representatives of the Chamber of Commerce, along with the police chief, still anticipated a massive crowd—one estimated to be as large as fifty thousand. Once again, all the town's resources were going to be utilized to accommodate the event. They felt it was still going to be a defining moment for the city, and the largest event ever held in Long Beach. Rodgers would take flight on Sunday, December 10, in the afternoon and land sometime around three. Again, the religious community groaned, and some noted that the only thing Rodgers ever did on Sundays was crash—indeed, most of his accidents occurred on Sundays. Maybe the Almighty was speaking to him, and he wasn't listening. If Cal had been religious, that might have been an ominous sign for him. A full-page ad was taken out in the *Los Angeles Times* announcing the event. They still expected people to come from across the state. From Los Angeles to New York, newspapers again started to pick Rodgers's story up and make note of him finishing his coast-to-coast journey.[1]

During the first gathering back in November, the crowd had been

23. "I am proud to have blazed the way to the Pacific"   179

so large that there were not enough bathrooms or drinking water. The Pacific Electric Railroad this time stepped up and offered to set up more bathrooms and water stations. Vendors prepared to provide food and beverages for the expected massive crowd of fifty thousand or more. What was missing was an overhyped Vin Fiz contingent handing out soft drink paraphernalia, something that was not noted at the time. Whether the Armour Company came out and visibly supported the completion of the trip is not known.[2]

Rodgers was seen in Long Beach on Saturday for one last press appearance, and he was still using crutches. Though it appeared he was otherwise in good physical health, it was still disconcerting that the day before the big flight he could not walk without the aid of crutches, as noted in the newspaper. He then visited the sun parlor and the rebuilt *Vin Fiz*, and reportedly, the engine "sang most beautifully" when started. Betsy was in great shape; Rodgers, on the other hand, was a whole different story. On Saturday night, Rodgers, Mabel, and Maria had a private dinner at the Virginia Hotel in Pasadena. It had been a long journey, and the completion of it was much anticipated. Though so little is known about the personal interactions between Mabel and Cal, there had to be a sense of relief for her, especially. One more day, she hoped.[3]

The next day, Taylor, Shaffer, and Wiggin stood in the morning sun in awe at what they had accomplished. The *Vin Fiz* had to have stood magnificently bathed in an array of light in the sun parlor—completely overhauled and rebuilt. Today, they were making history. They started the new engine up one last time, and it hummed like the well-oiled and non-sputtering one she was. They had to have laughed as they congratulated each other on the incredibly difficult task of rebuilding an entire biplane in just a little over a week once all the parts and machinery had arrived. They carefully loaded Betsy onto a flatbed truck to be driven to Compton for the afternoon departure.[4]

All morning, the excitement was growing in Long Beach as, again, the mass of humanity slowly accumulated and began to choke Ocean Boulevard and Pine Avenue as people descended upon the pier and the stands. The traffic again backed up for miles. Every rooftop was packed. All the tall buildings in town amassed spectators. The police of Long Beach had roped off the stretch of sand that Rodgers would land on near the pier, and people began congregating along it, rows deep, by noon. It became clear early on that the estimate of a crowd of fifty thousand was going to be fairly accurate, if not exceeded. By the end of the day, the estimate would be that over sixty thousand people had flocked to the beach to get a glimpse of history and the great Birdman. They came from all over; one man proudly told one newspaper that he brought his two daughters from a thousand miles away just to see Rodgers and the *Vin Fiz*. He wanted them to be aviators someday.[5]

Sunday afternoon was a perfectly clear, sunny California day. There was a brisk wind that ultimately would delay Cal's takeoff for about thirty minutes, but otherwise it was picturesque. He was driven from the hotel as usual in the Palmer-Singer by Jimmy Dunn, accompanied by Mabel, to Orr field in Compton, where he had crashed. Shaffer, Taylor, and Wiggin were already there, going over the biplane one last time. A police contingent roped off the field because there were several thousand people on hand waiting to watch Rodgers take off. The drive must have been emotional for Rodgers because, in some places, people lined the streets waving to him.[6]

Once at the field, Rodgers put on his vest, gloves, and gold-tinted goggles and, with some help, climbed aboard. He was still using the crutches and would have to carry them aboard the *Vin Fiz* to use after he landed. Numerous newspapers described the biplane as "patched" together. She was patched together, but the motor was new and strong, and that's what mattered. Cal lit a cigar, waved, and called out for them to let 'er go, and the *Vin Fiz* roared down the field around 3:40 p.m.[7]

Spectators and onlookers packed the streets and buildings around Compton. Cal swung back toward the hotel and circled until he gained altitude, then headed toward Long Beach. The *Vin Fiz* raced along the skyline to the delight of everyone below. Two other airplanes, Frank Champion in a Blériot monoplane and Beryl Williams in a Curtiss biplane, had been arranged to escort the *Vin Fiz* over Long Beach. He flew southward over Signal Hill and out across Devil's Gate at about 1500 feet, so everyone below could get a good view of him. Cal could stay relatively low because he knew he had a strong engine and wasn't concerned about having to find a place to land due to a dead aircraft like he had for so many weeks prior.[8]

Cal was late due to the delays before takeoff, and as four o'clock came and went, the massive crowd in Long Beach became restless; some feared another crash. Then the horn at the sun parlor sounded, alerting those who understood its significance of the approaching airplanes. Not long after four o'clock, the crowd could see the "black speck" on the northeastern horizon over the city. Then two more "specks" out of the south came into view. Within a few minutes, the specks had turned into flying machines. They grouped into formation and swung out over the ocean. Champion and Williams (who was carrying Earl Daugherty, a student of aeronautics) intercepted the *Vin Fiz* at 4:04 p.m. The crowd by now was cheering and screaming; fathers put children on their

23. "I am proud to have blazed the way to the Pacific"   181

shoulders; people pointed and waved hats. The airplanes circled for several minutes until Rodgers swept down, almost skimming the ocean just a few dozen feet from the water, resulting in wild cheering from the crowd. Cal always knew how to put on a show.[9]

Rodgers ascended one more time and banked around and back, the *Vin Fiz* motor running perfectly; he leveled off and aligned for landing. Above him, Champion and Williams circled in holding patterns. Cal made a perfect landing in the sand, coming to a stop with the wheels of the biplane rolling into the spent waves swimming up the beach. With a big grin on his face, Rodgers became emotional, chomping on his cigar. It was almost 4:30 p.m., with an orange glow on the horizon over the Pacific Ocean. The sunlight danced across the water, sweeping up to the *Vin Fiz* and Cal.[10]

In attendance somewhere along the beach was a young Tubal C. Ryan. Seeing Rodgers fly made such an impact on him that he grew up to be a pilot and started Ryan Airlines. He would design the Ryan ST that the military used to train pilots for World War II. By the time the war was over, his company had grown into a $55 million enterprise. There are countless stories told later by those in the audience about how seeing Rodgers and his airplane inspired them to fly.[11]

First Williams, then Champion, swept down over the crowd and

Cal Rodgers and "Betsy" on the beach in Long Beach, California. Note that this is most likely sometime after the event. His legs are healed, and there is no crowd (San Diego Air & Space Museum).

headed back toward Dominguez Field, where they had taken off. Then, from the stands near the pier, Cal's mother came rushing out first, followed by Mabel, who was seen crying as she approached. The police held back the surging and cheering crowd for a few moments. Cal got off the biplane with his crutches and embraced his mother and Mabel, all standing in the sand. Maria was heard to say, "Oh Cal, I'm so glad it's all over."[12]

At this moment, the rope that the police futilely held on to broke, and the mass of humanity rushed to Rodgers and the *Vin Fiz*. The police had the wherewithal to collapse back and around Rodgers, Maria, and Mabel. The crowd was well-behaved for the most part; people simply wanted to touch and shake hands with the great aviator. Cal shook hands and smiled and nodded, pretending to hear what was being said to him. Slowly, they made their way to an automobile on the pier. It took an hour to maneuver through the throngs of people. Once at the car, Cal got into the back and led a parade of sorts through the filled streets to the Virginia Hotel, where he and Mabel had a room.[13]

Once back at the hotel, Rodgers informed the media that he would not take questions just yet. He was worn out from the journey and from his constant struggle to hear and understand the questions in a room full of reporters. He instead released a final statement through Peters (DeKrafft having returned to Chicago).

> I am proud to have blazed the way to the Pacific coast by the air route, as proud as those hardy pioneers who made the wagon trail and the men who later linked both sides of the continent by rail, for this new epoch in aviation means the advancement of my chosen work, pointing out as it does what an air route of travel will mean to the next generation.[14]

With that simple and eloquent statement, Rodgers staked his claim on history, placing himself among the pioneers. Indeed, it was much deserved. The decision to go from east to west was not just an Armour decision for marketing purposes. Rodgers knew history, and from the time of Washington and Jefferson, the nation had always had its eyes on the West. That was where greatness invariably lay. Earth shakers and history makers always went west. The country's westward expansion manifested its destiny onto the plains, up the mountains, and all the way to the Pacific Ocean—the West was where history was made. By choosing to go that route, the more difficult one, to be sure, Rodgers's journey was a symbolic one as much as it was a historic one.

24

"The spirit of man and his willingness to sacrifice his life"

> "The spirit of man and his willingness to sacrifice his life if need be to show that the air can be conquered is what moved me most."
> —Robert Callier, Aero Club of America's president, on Rodgers's historic journey.

Cal and Mabel took a train back to Pasadena and the Maryland Hotel the next day. Shaffer and the Kid took the *Vin Fiz* to Dominguez Field near Long Beach along with the original Wright Model B that Rodgers had purchased from the Wrights back in July. Rodgers made it officially known that he and Mabel had no intention of returning east to live. "Pasadena is the best place in California," he stated. "The air currents are fine for flying." He even leased part of the old Empire Ranch northeast of the city, about 120 acres, on which he planned to build a hangar. His goal was to instruct future aviators, develop better airplanes, and advance the science of aviation. Rodgers most likely fell in love with California during his first West Coast trip in 1901, when his mother essentially made him go.[1]

The couple spent the holidays at the Maryland Hotel, occasionally attending dinner parties and visiting with guests. Cal was invited to be the guest of honor at the Tournament of Roses Parade during the annual football bowl season after the New Year. There was no queen of the tournament, and instead, Rodgers was proclaimed "King of the Air." He was, of course, asked to fly over the parade and throughout Pasadena, which he did, to the delight of all Pasadena. Again, he was the star attraction, as the entire city was out in force to watch the Birdman.[2]

Around this time, a report came out that Rodgers was devising a plan to cross the Atlantic Ocean—a seemingly impossible plan. The Aero Club of France was even willing to put up a $100,000 prize. There were newly designed engines that could top one hundred miles per hour, and gas tank capacities were increasing. Fixed-wing monoplanes were getting bigger and stronger. In time, it would be possible, he thought, to make it all the way across the ocean in one twenty-four-hour flight. It was a bold plan that he seriously studied, predating Charles Lindberg's successful transatlantic trip by sixteen years.[3]

Rodgers received a telegram in early January inviting him to New York from the Aero Club of America to receive a special medal in honor of his historic journey. President Taft would also be on hand. It was an incredible honor, and one that Cal would have seen as the culmination of his success in making history and following in the footsteps of his famous forebears. A few weeks later, he took a train alone because Mabel chose to stay behind. He attended the ceremony on January 27 at the famous Sherry's Restaurant in downtown New York. Dressed in a tuxedo, Rodgers sat at the head table with President Taft's secretary (Taft was still on his way to the event), along with Wilbur Wright, Rear Admiral Robert E. Peary, Captain Charles deForest Chandler of the United States Army, and other prominent dignitaries and politicians.

After the meal, there were recognitions and speeches, and then Robert Collier, the Aero Club of America's president, stood at the podium and gave a short introduction. He spoke of the state of aviation and of those who dared to fly and advance the science of aviation, citing Cal's historic accomplishment. "The spirit of man and his willingness to sacrifice his life if need be to show that the air can be conquered is what moved me most," said Collier as he introduced Rodgers. Cal, as always, was uncomfortable speaking, but in the moment, a sense of pride had to have filled him as he rose and faced that room. It was filled with adoring faces, some of whom were among his doubters months prior. He bowed and received the medal, and the room erupted with cheers and a round of applause. As the applause dissipated and everyone was seated, Cal hesitated, and then read a short speech that, by all accounts, only those at the head table could hear. His low voice from his deafness made speeches such as this difficult for him. When he finished, erratic applause broke out, and he returned to his seat, where Wilbur Wright offered a smile and a handshake. Shortly after, President Taft finally arrived, and all eyes were on him as he entered the room and shook hands. The rest of the evening belonged to the president, but at some point, he found Rodgers and congratulated him on his historic journey.[4]

Back in Pasadena, Mabel and Cal settled into daily life. Cal spent

24. "His willingness to sacrifice his life"   185

his days at Dominguez Field or on Long Beach, flying and tinkering with his planes. Those who wanted a ride paid fifty dollars to go up with the great aviator. There were plans that summer to go on a series of trips to Mexico City or even up to Winnipeg. He also never lost interest in the possibility of a transatlantic journey and continued to tell Mabel about what an epic flight it would be.

About this time, Mabel consented to an interview and was asked, "What kind of man is your husband?" She paused and smiled. "Mostly a stubborn one." After some laughter, she continued, "He has reserves of strength and a will above the ordinary man." She was asked if the transcontinental journey had changed Cal in any way. "Well, he used to sleep very soundly. Now he wakes up in the middle of the night. Sometimes he seems to have fallen into a pit in his mind and is trying to climb out." Maria, who was standing nearby, blurted out, "Non-sense, he's the same boy he always was. I should know," again showing the divide between her and Mabel, one that was never fully bridged.[5]

As spring arrived, Rodgers set up a temporary tent hangar for his Wright Model B on Long Beach, where he had finished his transcontinental journey, to entertain tourists and make some money. Daily, hundreds and sometimes thousands gathered to watch Cal fly. Rodgers, Wiggin, and Shaffer continued to work on the biplane, making constant adjustments and improvements. Ultimately, each day, a few visitors would pay the hefty price to fly with Rodgers, much to the delight of the crowd. Cal never disappointed, performing dives and loops and always wowing those in attendance on the beach.[6]

On Wednesday, April 3, 1912, Rodgers, the Kid, and Shaffer were again working on the Model B as another large crowd of five thousand or more gathered, hoping to see Rodgers fly. Cal was in good spirits as he joked with Shaffer and Wiggin all morning. He had a short business meeting with Edmund Allyn of the Aluminum Casting Company of Cleveland, whom he also offered to take up for a ride after testing his plane. Around three in the afternoon, Cal took the biplane up for a test run after some minor adjustments. The airplane roared into the air, easily rising above the massive pier and then banking out over the ocean. The brilliant, glowing sun hung in the afternoon sky as Rodgers crossed in front of it before turning back toward the beach. As the crowd watched Rodgers's approach, a flock of seagulls bathing in the sun on the beach finished their afternoon meal and lifted en masse into the sky.[7]

The gulls ascended right in front of Rodgers, causing him to crank on his elevator and bank hard, scattering the flock in every direction, including the one in which he tried to evade them. The biplane rose briefly, then dipped rapidly as Rodgers tried to avoid the pier, which was right in front of him. After a few seconds and without warning, the biplane dropped nose first from several hundred feet, slamming into the water and onto the beach just feet from where he had finished his historic journey.[8]

The crash was so violent that the biplane crumpled onto Rodgers, partially submerged in several feet of water. At first, no one moved; there was just shock. Everyone expected the Iron Aviator to rise from the wreckage, cigar in mouth, as he had so many times before. But it was not to be. Wiggin and Shaffer, along with two lifeguards, rushed to the twisted aircraft and frantically tried to pull Rodgers out. Eventually, they got Rodgers's limp body out of the biplane and gently dragged him up the beach to dry sand. But by then, they already knew. On their knees, they looked for signs of life, but there were none. The biplane had crushed Rodgers, and he died on impact.[9]

The mob plundered the Model B, most likely thinking it was the *Vin Fiz*, taking anything they could carry away. Later that evening, Shaffer and Wiggin solemnly loaded what was left onto a truck and took it back to the Dominguez Field hangar. Rodgers was the 147th aviator to be killed while flying. At least half of those who dared to fly from 1910 to 1912 perished. A doctor examined his body and listed the cause of death as a broken neck and massive internal injuries.

Mabel was alone in her room at the Maryland Hotel when word came of Cal's death. At first, she simply refused to believe it. "No, it's not true," she cried. When the news was confirmed, she was unable to make the trip to Long Beach. She was rendered prostrate and bedridden as physicians were called in to sedate her. Cal's mother, Maria, was out of the country, and news of her son's passing took over a week to reach her before she could return.[10]

The lifeguards at the biplane sometime after Rodgers crashed onto the beach (San Diego Air & Space Museum).

24. "His willingness to sacrifice his life"

The next day, the *New York Times* ran a front-page story about Rodgers's tragic death. The article noted that after his near-fatal crash at Compton a few months prior, Rodgers was quoted as saying, "I am not afraid of death in an aeroplane." When death came, he said, it would be painless—an admission that he knew he would most likely perish while flying. Cal's death saddened and shocked many in the aviation world. Death was never unexpected by these early pioneers; most aviators came to terms with the inevitability of it. But some had come to truly believe Rodgers was invincible—that he was the Iron Aviator.[11]

The night of the crash, Shaffer and Wiggin examined the wrecked

Rodgers's Wright Model B wreckage on Long Beach (San Diego Air & Space Museum).

The Wright Model B being prepared for loading and removal off Long Beach (San Diego Air & Space Museum).

The Wright Model B wreckage being loaded onto a truck for transport to Dominguez Field (San Diego Air & Space Museum).

24. "The spirit of man and his willingness to sacrifice his life" 189

biplane and found a seagull wedged between the fuselage and rudder. It was the first documented bird strike leading to an airplane crash and fatality in United States aviation history. The moment that happened, Rodgers was doomed. Eyewitness reports told of Rodgers chasing seagulls and acting erratically and even irresponsibly. Rumors of Cal acting stupidly became so bad that, days later, Mabel had to release a statement revealing Shaffer's discovery. "It was neither due to chasing seagulls nor carelessness that Cal met his death," she wrote.[12]

Shaffer said that "Cal, I am sure, knew that death was staring him in the face the last 100 feet." Rodgers's sudden death greatly affected Shaffer and Wiggin; it was they who had given Cal the Iron Aviator moniker. They had truly come to believe that Rodgers had the luck to avoid the hoodoo—that he was indestructible.[13]

Harriet Quimby became the first American woman to receive an aviator's license on August 1, 1911, just weeks after Cal received his license. She also wanted to fly in the Chicago meet, but her instructor, the renowned Andre Haupert, forbade her to do so, saying the location was too dangerous. By 1912, she was a skilled pilot and became the first woman to fly across the English Channel. Before becoming an aviator, she was a Hollywood actress and screenwriter, having written numerous movies for famed director D.W. Griffith and his Biograph Studios.[14]

After Cal's death, the Vin Fiz Company approached Quimby about becoming their spokesperson to replace Rodgers. They needed someone big, someone bold, and she fit the bill. It was a wise choice, but also one that demonstrated the Armour Company's progressive stance. Quimby was charismatic and adored by the press, who referred to her as the "Dresden China Aviatrix" or "China Doll" because of her fair complexion and petite figure. But make no mistake, she was a fierce and fearless flier.[15]

On July 1, 1912, as the new Vin Fiz soda representative, while performing at the Third Annual Boston Aviation Meet, Harriet took up William A.P. Willard, the event's organizer, to perform some simple arial maneuvers. It was late in the afternoon when she took off and ascended to about one thousand feet. While making a simple turn, though it's not exactly known what happened, her monoplane "suddenly turned over" and threw her and Willard from the craft, dropping them to the earth. The crowd watched in horror as the victims plunged into the shallow water of Dorchester Bay. It took several hours and dozens of men to dig them out. Luckily, the aircraft crashed into the bay and did not kill or injure anyone else. It was another tragic ending for an early aviation pioneer. Weeks later, Harriet's mechanic stated that the machine and the pilot were flawless, and that blame resided with the passenger, who must have panicked and lurched forward. The Armour Company never replaced Quimby. The Vin Fiz soda company lasted a few more years but was ultimately discontinued in the early 1920s.[16]

Cal's childhood friend and cousin John Rodgers, drove up from San Diego to help Mabel take Cal's body home to Pittsburgh to be buried. In full military dress, Rodgers escorted Cal the entire train ride back to Pennsylvania. Mabel draped the American flag that was presented to Rodgers in Pasadena over his casket. The train retraced much of the route that Rodgers and the *Vin Fiz* had taken, often stopping so crowds that had gathered along the tracks could pay their respects to the fallen aviator, the great Birdman.[17]

Calbraith Perry Rodgers was laid to rest in Allegheny Cemetery in Pittsburgh on July 6, 1912. A massive six-foot-four tombstone marks his grave, with the image of the *Vin Fiz* in flight encased in bronze and an inscription:

I Endure
I Conquer

"I believe Icarus was not failing as he fell,
but just coming to the end of his triumph."[18]

Afterword: "The Iron Aviator"

On October 2, 1941, California Congressman John Carl Williams Hinshaw addressed his fellow congressional representatives on the House floor and gave a rousing dedication honoring Cal Rodgers and his transcontinental flight. He asked for his peers to recognize Cal's incredible accomplishment and the "adversity conquered by Rodgers." He felt that Rodgers's name was slipping from history and that his achievement was worthy of recognition. Just as Charles Lindbergh or Amelia Earhart had been honored and recognized, Rodgers deserved to be as well. Hinshaw noted that Rodgers's transcontinental triumph helped to advance the science of aviation and was why "the United States has seen such a marvelous advance in aviation" during the last thirty years. Planes were being designed to carry "75 passengers sitting up for distances of 3,000" miles. Rodgers and his history-making journey showed the promise and possibilities of long-distance flight. He finished his speech honoring Rodgers and his achievement:

> The air commerce of the world was started by Calbraith Rodgers in 1911. One can hardly estimate 50 years of progress to this Nation when in 1961 our children view the aircraft of the future.[1]

By the end of 1911, because of Rodgers and others who flew, there were a dozen companies making airplanes; the Wrights and Curtiss no longer had a monopoly. There were another fifty companies making spare parts for airplanes. Investors were interested, and millions were being funneled into airplane manufacturing. This new, wondrous field of aviation would eventually revolutionize travel and reduce time and space like nothing else before.[2]

Years after Rodgers's death, a reporter caught up with Charles Taylor and asked him what kind of man Calbraith Perry Rodgers had been and what he thought of his transcontinental accomplishment:

Before his death Rodgers performed many other noteworthy feats, and I saw him many times. We would always talk over that memorable flight, and it was always his opinion that it had been his greatest achievement. Mere failure to win a monetary prize did not rob him of the feeling of triumph which was rightly his after weeks of the greatest strain possible. I am almost as proud of my association with him on his project as I am of the fact that I built the first airplane motor and helped Orv and Will with that first ship.[3]

Taylor stayed in California with his wife and family for a time until word came of Wilbur Wright's death from typhoid fever on May 30, 1912. Within two months, he had lost two people he dearly loved and respected. He returned to Ohio to help Orville, working on and testing new engine designs at the Dayton-Wright Company until 1920, when he returned to California to open his own machine shop. At around the same time, he put his life savings into a can't-miss real estate investment. The start of the Great Depression in 1929 wiped out both the shop and real estate venture, and sadly, his wife also passed away after a long struggle with her illness. For a time, no one knew where Taylor was or what he was doing until 1937, when auto tycoon Henry Ford hired a detective to track Taylor down. Ford was constructing a museum, and he wanted to recreate the Wrights' bicycle shop and the first airplane motor, and he had to find the man responsible. When the detective found Taylor, he was barely scraping by making thirty-seven cents an hour at the North American Aviation Company in Los Angeles.[4]

Taylor agreed to take the job and left California to work on Ford's historical restoration project until 1941, when he again returned to California, where he took a job at a defense factory, working sixty-hour weeks to support the war effort. There, the humble inventor of airplane engines worked quietly alongside mechanics who had no idea that he was an aviation pioneer. He worked all through the war until 1945, when he suffered a massive heart attack and was hospitalized. He never fully recovered and did not work again. Years before, Orville Wright had generously given him an $800 annual annuity for life, but it was not enough to make ends meet without consistent employment. He ended up in the Los Angeles hospital's charity ward nearly destitute. A proud man who never boasted about himself for financial gain, he lived in poverty until 1955, when a reporter stumbled onto his story. Taylor was then eighty-seven years old. Once the aviation community became aware of Taylor's situation, it acted. The Aircraft Industries Association raised money to get Taylor out of the charity ward and into a proper retirement home, where he died a few months later, on January 30, 1956—exactly eight years after Orville's passing. Taylor's name,

Afterword: "The Iron Aviator" 193

much like Rodgers's, has remained largely forgotten, save for the diehard aviation enthusiast.[5]

Frank Shaffer had been expecting to go up with Cal during the flight that killed him, something that most likely haunted him for a time. A little while after Rodgers's death, Jesse Brabazon purchased the wrecked Wright Model B and hired Shaffer to help rebuild it. Shaffer traveled to Cicero, Illinois, with the biplane and delivered it to Brabazon. However, Brabazon thought he was buying the original *Vin Fiz* and ultimately reneged on his purchase. So, Shaffer had it shipped back to Long Beach and returned to California, out a significant sum of money. In May 1912, Shaffer was attempting to raise money for a monument to Rodgers and hatched a plan. He was a loyal and true friend and wanted to honor Rodgers by getting a monument dedicated to him. To get money, he was going to attempt to break the American distance record over water, flying from Long Beach to Catalina Island. However, after several delays and a wrecked skid, his investors backed out. Though he was never able to attempt a record-breaking flight, Shaffer did end up selling the Wright Model B to the city of Long Beach to help raise enough money (about one hundred dollars) for a small memorial tablet to be placed in Rodgers's memory. Shaffer never married and died a bachelor in December 1955 at age sixty-nine.[6]

The *Vin Fiz* ended up in John Rodgers's possession after Cal's death. Had Cal survived just a few months longer, the biplane would have belonged to Earl Daugherty, a businessman who had already started negotiations to purchase the airplane. After some consideration, John Rodgers offered it to the Smithsonian Institution, which, in a colossal error in historical judgment, declined. They already had a Wright biplane, and they apparently didn't need the transcontinental one. Not knowing what to do with the historic machine, Mabel asked to take possession of it, and he agreed.

Mabel and Wiggin had started a relationship a year after Cal's death and organized a tour of flights with the *Vin Fiz* across the nation. As they toured the country, Wiggin performed mini airshows. On October 2, 1912, Wiggin officially became a pilot after passing his aviation test, and he was issued Pilot's Certificate #175. While they had the *Vin Fiz*, Mabel and Wiggin attended the Chicago Air Meet in 1912, where they were treated like celebrities. During their travels, Wiggin raced the airplane against a motorcycle in Tampa, Florida, losing by just a "nose." Cal's mother, Maria, got word of their travels and, in a fit of jealousy, hired an attorney and sued for possession of the aircraft. Without enough money to hire a lawyer for what would have been a long legal battle, Mabel relented and allowed Maria to acquire the aircraft. From there, Maria donated it to the Wright Company in Ohio. No one there really knew what to do with it; refurbishing it was costly, and the company was barely getting by. Less than a year later, sometime in 1916, the company was sold and dismantled. Maria got the *Vin Fiz* back and donated it to the Carnegie Institute in 1917. It remained in their possession until the Smithsonian wised up and purchased it in 1934. It remains on display to this day.[7]

Wiggin and Mabel continued to champion Cal and his historic journey, but no one cared. Eventually, they settled in Florida, opening a flying school at Jacksonville Beach. They ran it together until Wiggin's death on November 8, 1964, after a long illness. Later, Mabel moved to Miami and lived her last days alone, "broke and on welfare," in a retirement home until her death in 1972 at age 89. Her only visitor during her final years was a loyal niece.[8]

Long Beach had initiated plans to erect a large monument honoring Rodgers and the *Vin Fiz* after Cal's death, but years passed, and the plan was abandoned. Long Beach in 1911 considered Rodgers's arrival "the" event of the century and felt hosting his final landing placed the principality on the proverbial map. Ten years later, no one cared. As historian Eileen F. Lebow notes, Cal Rodgers's transcontinental flight had a historical longevity problem. The flight happened during aviation's infancy, and "an accumulation" of aviation achievements and other historical factors followed: more world records, World War I, Charles Lindbergh, and others. History, historians, and the media have thus far largely ignored the courageous and daring historic journey of Calbraith Perry Rodgers, the Iron Aviator. It is my hope that this book sheds more light on his incredible story.[9]

Chapter Notes

Preface

1. "The Flight of the Vin Fiz Flyer," *Del Rio News-Herald*, February 18, 1973; "The Story of Pilot Cal Rodgers," *Hammond Times*, September 17, 1961. "Cal Rodgers: Our First 'Lone Eagle,'" *Daily Jeffersonian*, June 13, 1977; Milicent L. Hathaway, "Trends in Heights and Weights," *Yearbook of Agriculture* (Washington, DC: US Department of Agriculture, 1959), 182; Harvey A. Schultz, "Don't Fowl Out," *Approach Magazine*, April 1984, 3; Sumner M. Blossom, "The World's Greatest Adventure, A Triumph of the Airplane," *Popular Science*, October 1927, 33; Robert van der Linden, *Milestones of Flight* (Minneapolis: Zenith Press, May 15, 2016), 19. The documented weight of the aircraft has varied, from seven hundred to nine hundred pounds.

2. "The Flight of the Vin Fiz Flyer," *Del Rio News-Herald*, June 15, 1977; "Cal Rodgers: Our First 'Lone Eagle'"; E.P. Stein, *Flight of the Vin Fiz* (New York: Arbor House, 1985), 169.

3. "Then and Now," *Middletown Times Herald Record*, September 15, 1961; "Tom Tiede Recalls Cal Rodgers: Our Forgotten First Lone Eagle," *Del Rio News-Herald*, June 15, 1977; "Cal Rodgers: Our First 'Lone Eagle.'" Rodgers has been called "the Iron Aviator" by various sources.

Chapter 1

1. Charles Wiggin, as told to Howard Eisenberg in "First Across the Continent," *Air and Space/Smithsonian Magazine*, September 2011.

2. Wiggin, "First Across the Continent;" E.P. Stein, *Flight of the Vin Fiz* (New York: Arbor House, 1985), 36–37.

3. Wiggin, "First Across the Continent;" Stein, *Flight of the Vin Fiz*, 36–37. In the early twentieth century, *aviators* was the term applied to what we today call pilots. I use the terms interchangeably. For our purposes here, planes, aeroplanes, biplanes, and monoplanes all mean the same general thing, even though they have different nuances to them. For example, biplanes have two wings and monoplanes just one.

4. Wiggin, "First Across the Continent;" Stein, *Flight of the Vin Fiz*, 36–37.

5. "Among the Invited Guests," Rodgers Family Papers, December 18, 1873; *United States Army and Navy Journal and Gazette of the Regular and Volunteer Forces* 16 (September 23, 1878): 116; Eileen F. Lebow, *Cal Rodgers and the Vin Fiz: The First Transcontinental Flight* (Washington and London: Smithsonian Institution, 1989), 12–13.

6. Stein, *Flight of the Vin Fiz*, 265.

7. Lebow, *Cal Rodgers and the Vin Fiz*, 16–17.

8. Andrew Small, "When Cities Went Electric," *Bloomberg*, March 15, 2017, https://www.bloomberg.com/news/articles/2017-03-15/the-war-of-currents-was-waged-in-cities. By 1907, only 8 percent of Americans lived in homes served by electricity nationwide.

9. Charlie Wentz, "Who Was Calbraith P. Rodgers?" *American Philatelist*, November 2011, 1014–1015; Roy

A. Tucker, Aero Club of Pittsburgh, as quoted, no. 299, *National Air and Space Museum*, undated item.

10. Stein, *Flight of the Vin Fiz*, 267.

11. "Pioneer Flight," *Branding Iron*, no. 74 (September 1965): 4–5; Frank Strother, "Flying Across the Country," *World's Work*, January 1912, 404. The extent of his hearing loss is unclear. Though his hearing loss was not complete, it was substantial enough that those around him noted significant changes in his actions and speaking.

12. Strother, "Flying Across the Country," 404.

13. Strother, 404.

14. Lebow, *Cal Rodgers and the Vin Fiz*, 19–20; Wentz, "Who Was Calbraith P. Rodgers?" 1014–1015.

15. *Times* (Philadelphia, Pennsylvania), October 17, 1898, 8. Cal attended St. Luke's, not Mercersburg, his second year, even though they list him as a freshman, something not previously noted by past historians. Whether he graduated is not known, though it is a likely assumption.

16. *Times* (Philadelphia, Pennsylvania), October 23, 1898, 8; October 29, 1898, 8; November 2, 1898, 8; November 20, 1898, 10; December 4, 1898, 8.

17. Lebow, *Cal Rodgers and the Vin Fiz*, 21.

18. Rita Goodman, "Widow of Air Pioneer Lives Destitute," *The Guide*, Coral Gables, FL, April 18, 1968; *World*, March 24, 1905; Strother, "Flying Across the Country," 404.

19. Stein, *Flight of the Vin Fiz*, 268–269.

20. Stein, 268–269.

21. Wentz, "Who Was Calbraith P. Rodgers?" 1014–1015.

22. Stein, *Flight of the Vin Fiz*, 271.

23. Wentz, "Who Was Calbraith P. Rodgers?" 1015.

Chapter 2

1. *Times-Democrat* (New Orleans), January 1, 1911; *Aeronautics*, February 1911, 61–62.

2. *Times-Democrat* (New Orleans), January 1, 1911; *Aeronautics*, February 1911, 61–62.

3. *Oakland Tribune*, January 1, 1911; *Aeronautics*, February 1911, 61–62; William M. Miller, *Eugene Ely, Daredevil Aviator* (Jefferson, NC: McFarland, 2014), 155.

4. *Aeronautics*, February 1911, 61–62.

5. "Early Fliers Flamboyant Gang Out for Fun and Money," *Moline Daily Dispatch*, November 10, 1958, 10.

6. Miller, *Eugene Ely, Daredevil Aviator*, 155.

7. *Aeronautics*, January 1911, 29; *Aeronautics*, February 1911, 61; "Fatalities Will Make Flying Safer," *Aero: America's Aviation Weekly*, January 7, 1911 (hereafter cited as *Aero*).

8. *Aeronautics*, January 1911, 15; Louis C. Hunter, *A History of Industrial Power in the United States 1780–1930*, vol. 2, *Steam Power* (Charlottesville: University Press of Virginia, 1985). From 1811 to 1851, 21 percent of river accidents were caused by explosions.

9. "My Most Thrilling Experience by Air," *San Francisco Call*, April 7, 1912; R.E. Bilstein, *Flight in America: 1900–1983: From the Wrights to the Astronauts* (Baltimore: Johns Hopkins University Press, 1984), 24–25; Waldemar Kaempffert, *The New Art of Flying* (New York: Dodd, Mead, 1911), 163–164.

10. Kaempffert, *The New Art of Flying*, 166; *Aeronautics*, January 1911, 15.

11. "Ethereal Asphyxia Causes His Fall," *San Francisco Call*, November 16, 1911; *Anaconda Standard*, November 16, 1911.

12. Volplaning was the technique of circling down to buy time to find a spot to land. Pilots also used a technique called *terracing*, whereby they lowered a hundred feet, leveled off, continued on for a distance, then dropped again a hundred feet, all while judging the air currents and keeping the plane stabilized.

13. *Aeronautics*, February 1911, 54.

14. "As of March 1911," *Aeronautics*, March 1911, 83; *Aeronautics*, March 1911, 97.

15. *Grand Forks Evening Times*, July 24, 1911; *Chicago Record-Herald*, August 19, 1911; Steven R. Hoffbeck, "Shooting Star: Aviator Jimmie Ward," *Minnesota Historical Society Magazine*, no. 54 (Winter 1995): 336. The causes of aviator deaths are hard to pinpoint; in the

September 20, 1911, article "Aviator Killed in Sight of 5,000, Ninety-Third Flier to Die," the *New York Times* lists the death toll to date as 93, broken down by year: 1908, 1; 1909, 4; 1910, 33; 1911, 55.

16. *Oakland Tribune*, January 1, 1911.

17. "Hopes Death Won't Halt Air Progress," *Chicago Examiner*, August 18, 1911; "Signs of the Time," *Aero*, August 5, 1911, 392.

18. *New York Times*, September 11, 1910.

19. "Competitive Aviation Reprehensible," *New York Times*, August 18, 1911.

20. *Chicago Examiner*, September 23, 1911.

21. *Saturday Evening Post*, January 7, 2012, http://www.saturdayeveningpost.com/2012/01/07/history/post-perspective/paying-price-learning-fly.html; Gavin Mortimer, *Chasing Icarus: The Seventeen Days that Forever Changed American Aviation* (New York: Walker, 2009), 148.

22. Frank B. Elser, "The Wings of Icarus," *Saturday Evening Post*, December 16, 1911.

23. *Chicago Daily Tribune*, September 26, 1911.

24. "Early Exhibition Aviators," US Centennial of Flight Commission, https://www.centennialofflight.net/essay/Explorers_Record_Setters_and_Daredevils/early_exhibition/EX7.htm; Augustus Post, "The Present and Future of Man Flight," *Munsey's Magazine*, June 1912, 324.

25. *Aeronautics*, February 1911, 78; "Aviators Get Small Pay for Gambling with Death," *Chicago Examiner*, August 18, 1911; Mortimer, *Chasing Icarus*, 25.

26. Post, "The Present and Future of Man Flight," 325.

27. Post, 330.

Chapter 3

1. Alexandra M. Lord, ed., *American Aviation Heritage* (Washington, DC: National Park Service, National Conference of State Historic Preservation Officers, Wright-Patterson Air Force Base, OH: US Air Force, March 2011), 42–43.

2. Arthur George Renstrom, *Wilbur & Orville Wright: A Chronology Commemorating the Hundredth Anniversary of the Birth of Orville Wright, August 19, 1871* (Washington, DC: NASA), 30, https://ntrs.nasa.gov/api/citations/20040000754/downloads/20040000754.pdf; Charlie Wentz, "Who Was Calbraith P. Rodgers," *American Philatelist*, November 2011, 1015; Eileen F. Lebow, *Cal Rodgers and the Vin Fiz: The First Transcontinental Flight* (Washington and London: Smithsonian Institution, 1989), 23–24, 26–27; E.P. Stein, *Flight of the Vin Fiz* (New York: Arbor House, 1985), 28–29.

3. *Automotive Journal*, Wright Papers, Manuscript Division, Library of Congress, Washington, DC; Marshall Weiss, "Orville's Aviators," *Dayton Jewish Observer*, June 2010, https://daytonjewishobserver.org/2011/05/anthology-expands-on-life-and-death-of-first-jewish-aviator/.

4. *The Wright Flying School* (New York: Wright Flying Field, 1916), 11–18; Renstrom, *Wilbur & Orville Wright*, 30.

5. Stein, *Flight of the Vin Fiz*, 28–29.

6. Andrew Drew, "Learning to Fly a Wright Biplane," *Aero: America's Aviation Weekly*, August 5, 1911, 385–386; Dr. Richard Stimson, "Learning to Fly the 1911 Wright Type B Airplane," WrightStories.com, https://wrightstories.com/learning-to-fly-the-1911-wright-type-b-airplane/. Much of the dialogue between Cal and Welsh has been pulled from Andrew Drew's experiences being instructed by Clifford Turpin and Welsh in 1911.

7. Stimson, "Learning to Fly the 1911 Wright Type B Airplane;" Drew, "Learning to Fly a Wright Biplane," 385–386; Stein, *Flight of the Vin Fiz*, 29–30; Lebow, *Cal Rodgers and the Vin Fiz*, 28–29.

8. Drew, "Learning to Fly a Wright Biplane," 385–386; Stein, *Flight of the Vin Fiz*, 28–29. Stein presents a standoffish and condescending view of Rodgers by the others at the factory early on.

9. Stein, 30–31; Lebow, *Cal Rodgers and the Vin Fiz*, 28–29.

10. Stein, 30–31; Lebow, 28–29; Drew, "Learning to Fly a Wright Biplane," 385–386.

11. Stein, 30–31; Lebow, 28–29; Drew, 385–386.

12. Waldemar Kaempffert, *The New Art of Flying* (New York: Dodd, Mead, 1911), 60–61. Kaempffert goes into extensive detail on flight instruction.
13. Drew, "Learning to Fly a Wright Biplane," 385–386; Stein, *Flight of the Vin Fiz*, 31–32.
14. Drew, 385–386; Stein, 31–32.
15. Drew, 385–386; Stein, 31–32.
16. Sherwood Harris, "Coast to Coast in 12 Crashes," *American Heritage Magazine* 15, no. 6 (1964), https://www.americanheritage.com/coast-coast-12-crashes.
17. Stein, *Flight of the Vin Fiz*, 31–32; Lebow, *Cal Rodgers and the Vin Fiz*, 31–32; Drew, "Learning to Fly a Wright Biplane." Lebow describes Rodgers getting to handle the levers by himself with Welsh alongside. Stein stated that Rodgers got to fly "solo."
18. Stimson, "Learning to Fly the 1911 Wright Type B Airplane;" Stein, 31–32.
19. Stimson; Stein, 31–32; Lebow, *Cal Rodgers and the Vin Fiz*, 34.
20. Stimson; Stein, 31–32; Lebow, 35.
21. Stein, 34–35.
22. "The Distance for the Circuit Tests: Instructions Governing the Conduct for Tests for Aviators' Certificates," *Flying Association at the Office of the Aero Club of America* 3 (1912): 58; Aero Club of America, *Aero Club of America Rule Book*, New York: Contest Committee, Aero Club of America, 1922, 176–177.
23. "The Distance for the Circuit Tests," 58; *Aero Club of America Rule Book*, 176–177.
24. "Letter to Organizer," McCormick Collection, August 2, 1911.
25. "Longest American Cross-Country Flights," *Aeronautics*, March 1911, 90.

Chapter 4

1. *Chicago Daily News Almanac and Yearbook for 1911*, 362; *Aeronautics*, September, 1911, 89; *Popular Mechanics* 16 (1911): 490; *Aero*, August 5, 1911, 387; *Chicago Examiner*, August 13, 1911; "The Chicago Meet," *Aero*, September, 1911, 89; "Aviators Know Risk, Why End Meet?" *Chicago Examiner*, August 17, 1911; "Receipts and Estimated Expenditures of Meet," *Chicago Examiner*, August 21, 1911. The meet took in $144,000 and had an estimated attendance rate of six hundred thousand daily. Still, by this estimate, the meet lost over $50,000.
2. "Taking Flight," *Chicago Tribune*, July 27, 2003; "Plans are Laid," *Aero*, April 15, 1911, 89.
3. "Taking Flight," *Chicago Tribune*, July 27, 2003; Eileen F. Lebow, *Cal Rodgers and the Vin Fiz: The First Transcontinental Flight* (Washington and London: Smithsonian Institution, 1989), 42–44; "Lougheed Attacks Aero Club Officers," *Chicago Examiner*, August 14, 1911.
4. "The Chicago Meet," *Aero*, September 1911, 89; "Chicago International Meet Begins Saturday," *Aero*, August 12, 1911, 405–406; Letter to E.G. Ryan, McCormick Collection, December 11, 1911.
5. "Chicago International Meet Begins Saturday," 406.
6. "Aeroplane-itis," *Chicago Examiner*, August 12, 1911; "Flying Fever," *Chicago Examiner*, August 13, 1911.
7. "Airmen Depend on Their Mascot for Good Luck," *Chicago Examiner*, August 20, 1911.
8. *Automobile Topics*, August 19, 1911, 1023; *Popular Mechanics* 16 (1911): 490.
9. "Four Accidents Only Slightly Mar Meet," *Chicago Examiner*, August 13, 1911; *Automobile Topics*, August 19, 1911, 1023; *Popular Mechanics* 16 (1911): 490; Gavin Mortimer, *Chasing Icarus: The Seventeen Days that Forever Changed American Aviation* (New York: Walker, 2009), 194.
10. "Boy Lost at Air Meet," *Chicago Examiner*, August 14, 1911.
11. "Hydroplane for the First Time in History," *Chicago Examiner*, August 15, 1911; *Automobile Topics*, August 19, 1911, 1023; "The Chicago Meet," *Aero*, August 26, 1911, 454–455; "Deaths and Accidents During Chicago Meet," *Chicago Examiner*, August 21, 1911.
12. "Hydroplane for the First Time in History;" *Automobile Topics*, 1023; "The Chicago Meet," 454–455; "Deaths and Accidents During Chicago Meet;" *Chicago Examiner*, August 16, 1911. Some reports suggest that the engine did not explode but that he simply lost control.

13. *Automobile Topics*, 1023; "The Chicago Meet," 454–455; *Cairo Bulletin*, August 16, 1911.
14. "Stop Meet," *Chicago Examiner*, August 16, 1911.
15. *Chicago Daily News Almanac and Yearbook for 1911*, 363.
16. "Aviation Women are Brave in the Face of Death Terror," *Chicago Examiner*, August 17, 1911.
17. "Edison Hunts Arial Safety Guards," *Chicago Examiner*, August 17, 1911.
18. *Aero*, August 5, 1911, 387; *Aero*, August 12, 1911, 405–406; *Chicago Daily News Almanac and Yearbook for 1911*, 363.
19. *Aero*, August 5, 1911, 387; *Aero*, August 12, 1911, 405–406; *Chicago Daily News Almanac and Yearbook for 1911*, 363; "The Chicago Meet," *Aero*, September 1911, 91.
20. *Chicago Daily Tribune*, August 16, 1911.
21. "Cal Rodgers Wins Rich Duration Prize," *Chicago Examiner*, August 21, 1911.
22. *Popular Mechanics* 16 (1911): 490.
23. *Popular Mechanics*, 490; Mabel Rodgers-Wiggin, "First Airmail Flight," *AOPA Pilot: Voice of General Aviation* 6, part 2, 38–41.

Chapter 5

1. Charles R. Morris, *The Tycoons: How Andrew Carnegie, John D. Rockefeller, Jay Gould, and J.P. Morgan Invented the American Supereconomy* (New York: Holt Paperback, 2005), 273–274; "New York Urbanized Area: Population & Density from 1800," Demographia, http://demographia.com/db-nyuza1800.htm; Devin Gannon, "NYC Water Towers: History, Use, and Infrastructure," 6 sqft New York City, August 17, 2022, https://www.6sqft.com/nyc-water-towers-history-use-and-infrastructure; "What Was the Greatest Era for Innovation? A Brief Guided Tour," *New York Times*, May 15, 2016.
2. Nathan Miller, *New World Coming: The 1920s and the Making of Modern America* (New York: Scribner, 2010), 150; Morris, *The Tycoons*, 273–274, 288–289; Ellen Terrell, "Andrew Carnegie—Man of Steel," *Library of Congress Blogs, Inside Adams: Science, Technology and Business*, December 3, 2012, https://blogs.loc.gov/inside_adams/2012/12/andrew-carnegie-man-of-steel/.
3. Kenneth Whyte, *The Uncrowned King: The Sensational Rise of William Randolph* Hearst (New York: Counterpoint, 2009), 32–36; Morris, *The Tycoons*, 288–289.
4. Morris, *The Tycoons*, 288–289; "Historically Speaking: 19th-Century Norwich Had Many Millionaires," *Norwich Bulletin*, August 2, 2014. The term "millionaire" was first coined in 1786 by Thomas Jefferson when talking about Democracy: "The poorest labourer stood on equal ground with the wealthiest Millionary."
5. "W.R. Hearst Backs Flight from New York to S.A.," *San Antonio Light*, August 6, 1972.
6. "Principal Prize Courses for Airmen this Year," *New York Times*, March 5, 1911.
7. "Richest Aviation Prize Ever Offered in America," *Chicago Examiner*, September 1, 1911.
8. "Society Women Enthusiastic Aviation Followers," *Chicago Examiner*, August 15, 1911. Mrs. Armour discussed watching the meet with her husband, stating, "I can't beguile him away from the field until the last birdman is safely out of the sky." "Society Leaders Appear ... Each Aviation Day," *Chicago Examiner*, August 18, 1911; Harper Leech and John Charles Carroll, *Armour and His Times* (New York: D. Appleton-Century, 1938), 1–3, 78–81, 349–355.
9. "New Heads for Armour Firm," *Sunday Inter-Ocean*, October 6, 1901; Michael Beggs, "'Gentlemen, I Am the Liquidator!' J. Ogden Armour, 1907," https://owlofathena.net/2019/02/21/gentlemen-i-am-the-liquidator-j-ogden-armour-1907/. A lot of my insights into Mr. Armour come from newspaper articles, interviews, and reading his two books, *The Packers, the Private Car Lines, and the People* (1906) and *Business Problems of the War* (1917). In these works, he correctly discussed the innovation of the private freight car and the meat packing industry and observed the early warning

signs of economic trouble that the farmers were facing leading up to the Great Depression.

10. "Aviators Go East," *Chicago Examiner*, August 23, 1911; "He Planned to Fly It," *Chicago Daily Tribune*, August 26, 1911.

11. "Aviators Go East;" "Society Women in Biplane," *Chicago Examiner*, August 25, 1911. The picture thus far has been lost to history.

12. "Wind Holds Atwood to 39 Miles in a Day," *Chicago Examiner*, August 22, 1911.

13. "Wind Holds Atwood to 39 Miles in a Day;" Eileen F. Lebow, *Cal Rodgers and the Vin Fiz: The First Transcontinental Flight* (Washington and London: Smithsonian Institution, 1989), 71–72.

14. "Great Transcontinental Dash," *Chicago Examiner*, September 3, 1911.

15. "Hearst Race Rouses Nation," *Chicago Examiner*, September 1, 1911; *Scientific American*, September 16, 1911, 267.

16. *Chicago Examiner*, September 2, 1911; *New York Times*, September 2, 1911.

17. "Frisbie's Body En Route East," *Chicago Examiner*, September 4, 1911.

18. *Chicago Examiner*, September 2, 1911; *New York Times*, September 2, 1911.

19. *Chicago Examiner*, September 2, 1911; *New York Times*, September 2, 1911.

20. *Chicago Examiner*, September 2, 1911; *New York Times*, September 2, 1911.

21. "Parmelee Sets Twenty-Six Days," *Chicago Examiner*, September 3, 1911.

22. *Chicago Examiner*, September 4, 1911; "Parmelee Sets Twenty-Six Days."

23. "Rodgers Will Seek Low Places," *Chicago Examiner*, September 3, 1911.

24. "Rodgers Will Seek Low Places."

25. "Rodgers Will Seek Low Places."

26. Lebow, *Cal Rodgers and the Vin Fiz*, 74.

Chapter 6

1. "Soars 2,700 Feet with Woman Passenger," *Alton Evening Telegraph*, August 28, 1911.

2. "Soars 2,700 Feet with Woman Passenger."

3. E.P. Stein, *Flight of the Vin Fiz* (New York: Arbor House, 1985), 39–40.

4. *Fox City Magazine* (Stevens Point, WI), May 2014, 18.

5. Charles E. Taylor, "The First Transcontinental Flight," *Slipstream*, June 1928, as read by California Congressman Hinshaw during the October 2, 1941, congressional session, House Congressional Record (Washington, DC: United States Congress), 7607–7608.

6. John Demeter, "First Transcontinental Flight," *FAA Aviation News*, November 1968, 12; *Stevens Point Daily Journal*, September 16, 1961; "50 Years Ago Pilot Crossed U.S. in 49 Days, 13 Crashes," *Abilene Reporter-News* (Abilene, Texas), April 28, 1961.

7. Eileen F. Lebow, *Cal Rodgers and the Vin Fiz: The First Transcontinental Flight* (Washington and London: Smithsonian Institution, 1989), 84.

8. Taylor, "The First Transcontinental Flight."

9. Demeter, "First Transcontinental Flight," 12; *Stevens Point Daily Journal*, September 16, 1961; "50 Years Ago Pilot Crossed U.S." Cal routinely made hops at or above sixty miles per hour during his journey, often aided by the wind, of course.

10. "Armour Will Finance Air Flight," *Inter-Ocean* (Chicago), September 10, 1911; "J. Ogden Armour Finances Rodgers' Flight to Coast," *Chicago Examiner*, September 11, 1911; Lebow, *Cal Rodgers and the Vin Fiz*, 80.

11. "Armour Will Finance Air Flight."

12. Mabel Rodgers-Wiggin, "First Airmail Flight," *AOPA: Voice of General Aviation* 6, part 2, 38–41.

13. "Special Car Carries Parts for Rodgers from Chicago," *Chicago Examiner*, September 13, 1911; *Lake County Times* (Hammond, Indiana), September 27, 1911; Lebow, *Cal Rodgers and the Vin Fiz*, various pages.

14. "Here and There," *Olean Times*, September 27, 1911. *The San Antonio Light* even goes as far as to say that DeKrafft was responsible for arranging Armour Company support for Rodgers, October 23, 1911.

15. *Chicago Examiner*, September 9, 1911.

16. San Francisco Chronical, September 11, 1911; Lebow, *Cal Rodgers and the Vin Fiz*, 76–77; *New York Times*,

September 12, 1911. The Nineteenth Amendment to the Constitution giving women the right to vote did not pass until August 18, 1920.

17. "Fowler Reaches Auburn on Flight East," *Fresno Morning Republican*, September 12, 1911; Sherwood Harris, "Coast to Coast in 12 Crashes," *American Heritage* 15, no. 6 (October 1964), https://www.americanheritage.com/coast-coast-12-crashes.

18. "Special Car Carries Parts for Rodgers from Chicago," *Chicago Examiner*, September 13, 1911; Lebow, *Cal Rodgers and the Vin Fiz*, 80, 95.

19. "Fowler Falls in Biplane," *Oakland Tribune*, September 12, 1911.

20. "Fowler Falls in Biplane;" Harris, "Coast to Coast in 12 Crashes."

21. "Aviator Ward Arrives After Engine Trouble," *Middleton Daily Times Press*, September 14, 1911.

22. "Ward's Biplane Wrecked at Owego," *New York Times*, September 17, 1911.

23. "Fowler Caught in Hotel Fire," *San Francisco Call*, September 18, 1911.

24. "Great Welcome Provided for the Daring Aviator," *Middleton Daily Times Press*, September 13, 1911; Harris, "Coast to Coast in 12 Crashes."

25. "Wires Condolence to Ward," *Middleton Daily Times Press*, September 20, 1911; "Ward Withdraws After a Fall," *Middleton Daily Times Press*, September 22, 1911.

26. "Fowler is Greatest Aviator," *Oakland Tribune*, September 24, 1911.

Chapter 7

1. *New York American*, June 4, 1911; *New York Times*, June 4, 1911; Eileen F. Lebow, *Cal Rodgers and the Vin Fiz: The First Transcontinental Flight* (Washington and London: Smithsonian Institution, 1989), 75.

2. "Mails by Airplane to be Tried Here," *New York Times*, September 16, 1911; Mabel Rodgers-Wiggin, "First Airmail Flight," *AOPA Pilot: Voice of General Aviation* 6, part 2, 38–41.

3. Rodgers-Wiggin, "First Airmail Flight," 38–41.

4. Rodgers-Wiggin, 38–41.

5. Rodgers-Wiggin, 38–41.

6. E.P. Stein, *Flight of the Vin Fiz* (New York: Arbor House, 1985), 46–47.

7. *Middletown Daily Press*, September 19, 1911.

Chapter 8

1. *New York Times*, September 16 and 19, 1911; "'Vin Fiz' Commemorative Flight," *Southwest Historical Quarterly*, 134; *Middletown Daily Times Press*, September 19, 1911; "Pioneer Flight," *Branding Iron*, no. 74 (September 1965), 5.

2. "'Vin Fiz' Commemorative Flight," 134; *Middletown Daily Times Press*, September 19, 1911; "Pioneer Flight," 5.

3. "Coast to Coast in 13 Crashes," *Stevens Point Daily Journal* (Wisconsin), September 16, 1961; "Pioneer Flight," 4.

4. "50 Years Ago Pilot Crossed U.S. in 49 Days, 13 Crashes," *Abilene Reporter-News* (Abilene, Texas), April 28, 1961; "The Legend Of Vin Fiz," *Airport Journals*, November 1, 2006; "'Vin Fiz' Commemorative Flight," 134; Paul Wittreich, *Forgotten First Flights* (Bloomington, IN: Xlibris, 2009), 17–18. It has been described as either a bottle of the soda or champagne that she brought forth.

5. "50 Years Ago Pilot Crossed U.S.;" "The Legend of Vin Fiz;" "'Vin Fiz' Commemorative Flight," 134; Wittreich, *Forgotten First Flights*, 17–18; "First Trans-Continental Aeroplane Flight," *Gas Power*, January 1912, 80.

6. "'Vin Fiz' Commemorative Flight," 134; French Strother, "Flying Across the Continent," *World's Work*, 341; Charles Wiggin, as told to Howard Eisenberg in "First Across the Continent," *Air and Space/Smithsonian Magazine*, September 2011, https://www.airspacemag.com/history-of-flight/the-first-across-the-continent-41006907; "First Trans-Continental Aeroplane Flight," 80.

7. "'Vin Fiz' Commemorative Flight," 134; Strother, "Flying Across the Continent," 341; Wiggin, "First Across the Continent;" "First Trans-Continental Aeroplane Flight," 80.

8. Charles E. Taylor, "The First Transcontinental Flight," *Slipstream*, June 1928, as read by California Congressman Hinshaw during the October

2, 1941, congressional session, House Congressional Record (Washington, DC: United States Congress), 7607–7608.

9. "'Vin Fiz' Commemorative Flight," 134; Strother, "Flying Across the Continent," 341; *Middletown Daily Times Press*, September 18, 1911; Charles S. Wiggin, *First Transcontinental Flight* (New York: Bookmailer, 1961).

10. *Middletown Daily Times Press*, September 18, 1911.

11. *Middletown Daily Times Press*, September 18, 1911; E.P. Stein, *Flight of the Vin Fiz* (New York: Arbor House, 1985), 45.

12. *Middletown Daily Times Press*, September 18, 1911; Stein, *Flight of the Vin Fiz*, 42–43; Sherwood Harris, "Coast to Coast in 12 Crashes," *American Heritage* 15, no. 6 (October 1964), https://www.americanheritage.com/coast-coast-12-crashes.

13. *Middletown Daily Times Press*, September 18, 1911; Stein, *Flight of the Vin Fiz*, 42–43; Harris, "Coast to Coast in 12 Crashes."

14. *Middletown Daily Times Press*, September 18, 1911.

15. *Middletown Daily Times Press*, September 18, 1911; "'Vin Fiz' Commemorative Flight," 134.

16. *Middletown Daily Times Press*, September 18, 1911; "'Vin Fiz' Commemorative Flight," 134; *Richmond Palladium and Sun-Telegram*, September 18, 1911.

17. *Middletown Daily Times Press*, September 18, 1911; Strother, "Flying Across the Continent," 342; "'Vin Fiz' Commemorative Flight," 134; *Richmond Palladium and Sun-Telegram*, September 18, 1911.

18. *Middletown Daily Times Press*, September 18, 1911; Strother, "Flying Across the Continent," 342; "'Vin Fiz' Commemorative Flight," 134; *New York Times*, September 19, 1911.

19. *Middletown Daily Times Press*, September 18, 1911; Strother, "Flying Across the Continent," 342; "'Vin Fiz' Commemorative Flight," 134; Harris, "Coast to Coast in 12 Crashes;" "Rodgers Plane Hits the Hen Coop 25 Years Ago," *Middletown Times Herald*, September 17, 1936; *Richmond Palladium and Sun-Telegram*, September 18, 1911.

20. *Middletown Daily Times Press*, September 18, 1911; Strother, "Flying Across the Continent," 342; "'Vin Fiz' Commemorative Flight," 134; Harris, "Coast to Coast in 12 Crashes;" "Rodgers Plane Hits the Hen Coop;" *Richmond Palladium and Sun-Telegram*, September 18, 1911; *Evening World* (New York), September 19, 1911.

21. *Evening World* (New York), September 19, 1911.

22. Stein, *Flight of the Vin Fiz*, 54–55.

23. *Flying: A Century of Flight*, December 2003, 25.

Chapter 9

1. Charles S. Wiggin, *First Transcontinental Flight* (New York: Bookmailer, 1961); Sherwood Harris, "Coast to Coast in 12 Crashes," *American Heritage* 15, no. 6 (October 1964), https://www.americanheritage.com/coast-coast-12-crashes; *Middletown Daily Times Press*, September 19, 1911.

2. *Middletown Daily Times Press*, September 19, 1911; Wiggin, *First Transcontinental Flight*.

3. *Middletown Daily Times Press*, September 19, 1911; Wiggin, *First Transcontinental Flight*; *Middletown Daily Times Press*, September 20, 1911.

4. E.P. Stein, *Flight of the Vin Fiz* (New York: Arbor House, 1985), 55–57.

5. *Middletown Daily Times Press*, September 19, 1911; Stein, *Flight of the Vin Fiz*, 55–57.

6. *Middletown Daily Times Press*, September 19, 1911; Stein, 60.

7. *Middletown Daily Times Press*, September 19, 1911.

8. "Flies 96 miles in 69 Minutes," *New York Times*, September 22, 1911.

9. *Mathews Journal* (Virginia), September 28, 1911.

10. Peter Rohrbach, "The First Aircraft Mechanic," *FAA Aviation News*, January/February 1989, 12–13; Charles E. Taylor, "My Story of the Wright Brothers," *Collier's Weekly*, December 25, 1948; "Charles E. Taylor: Who Is He and Why Should We Honor Him?" Aviation Pros, May 8, 2006, https://www.aviationpros.com/home/article/10383610/charles-e-taylor-who-is-he-and-why-should-we-

honor-him; Charles E. Taylor, "The First Transcontinental Flight," *Slipstream*, June 1928, as read by California Congressman Hinshaw during the October 2, 1941, congressional session, House Congressional Record (Washington, DC: United States Congress), 7607–7608.
    11. "Aviator Rodgers Departure," *Middletown Daily Times Press*, September 21, 1911.
    12. "Appreciates Middletown," *Middletown Daily Times Press*, September 20, 1911; *Middletown Daily Times Press*, September 21, 1911; "Flies 96 miles in 69 Minutes."
    13. "Flies 96 miles in 69 Minutes."
    14. *Middletown Daily Times Press; Mathews Journal* (Virginia), September 28, 1911.
    15. *Middletown Daily Times Press*, September 21, 1911.
    16. *Middletown Daily Times Press*, September 21, 1911.
    17. Letter to Mabel, as quoted in Stein, *Flight of the Vin Fiz*, 34–35; *Middletown Daily Times Press*.

Chapter 10

    1. "Rodgers Flies to Hancock," *Middletown Daily Times Press*, September 21, 1911.
    2. "Rodgers Flies to Hancock."
    3. "Aviator Rodgers Has Delayed," *Middletown Daily Times Press*, September 23, 1911.
    4. "Aviator Rodgers Has Delayed."
    5. "Aviator Rodgers Has Delayed."
    6. "Aviator Rodgers Has Delayed."
    7. "Aviator Rodgers Has Delayed."
    8. E.P. Stein, *Flight of the Vin Fiz* (New York: Arbor House, 1985), 75.
    9. *Atlanta Georgian and News*, September 23, 1911.
    10. *Atlanta Georgian and News*, September 23, 1911; Stein, *Flight of the Vin Fiz*, 76.
    11. *Chicago Examiner*, September 24, 1911.
    12. Stein, *Flight of the Vin Fiz*, 77.
    13. *New York Times*, September 24, 1911; *Lincoln Nebraska State Journal*, September 24, 1911.
    14. *Chicago Examiner*, September 24, 1911; Stein, *Flight of the Vin Fiz*, 78.
    15. *Chicago Examiner*, September 24, 1911.
    16. *Chicago Examiner*, September 24, 1911.
    17. Stein, *Flight of the Vin Fiz*, 78.
    18. Mabel Rodgers-Wiggin, "First Airmail Flight," *AOPA Pilot: Voice of General Aviation* 6, part 2, 38–41.
    19. *Chicago Examiner*, September 23, 1911; Stein, *Flight of the Vin Fiz*, 75.
    20. Stein, 87.
    21. *Chicago Examiner*, September 24, 1911.

Chapter 11

    1. *Wellsville Daily Reporter*, September 25, 1911; E.P. Stein, *Flight of the Vin Fiz* (New York: Arbor House, 1985), 88; Cal Rodgers's *Vin Fiz* Flight Log, September 24, 1911, Smithsonian National Air and Space Museum Archives.
    2. *Wellsville Daily Reporter*, September 25, 1911.
    3. *Wellsville Daily Reporter*, September 25, 1911; Stein, *Flight of the Vin Fiz*, 88–89; *Olean Evening News*, September 25, 1911.
    4. *Chicago Examiner*, September 25, 1911; *Bradford Era* (Pennsylvania), September 25, 1911; Stein, *Flight of the Vin Fiz*, 89.
    5. Stein, *Flight of the Vin Fiz*, 89; Clemente Lisi, "How Billy Sunday Traded His Bat for a Bible and Came to Love New York," *Religion Unplugged*, April 22, 2020, https://religionunplugged.com/news/2020/4/21/baseball-how-billy-sunday-traded-his-bat-for-a-bible-and-came-to-love-new-york; *Syracuse Herald*, September 28, 1911, 8, for the Sunday quote.
    6. *Olean Evening News*, September 25, 1911; *Olean Evening News*, September 28, 1911; *Wellsville Daily Reporter*, September 25, 1911; Stein, *Flight of the Vin Fiz*, 89–90.
    7. Stein, 90.
    8. *Chicago Examiner*, September 25, 1911; *Bradford Era* (Pennsylvania), September 25, 1911.
    9. *Warren Evening Mirror* (Pennsylvania), September 25, 1911; *Olean Evening News*, September 25, 1911; *Olean Evening News*, September 28, 1911;

Wellsville Daily Reporter, September 25, 1911.

Chapter 12

1. *Mansfield News*, September 29, 1911; E.P. Stein, *Flight of the Vin Fiz* (New York: Arbor House, 1985), 91; Eileen F. Lebow, *Cal Rodgers and the Vin Fiz: The First Transcontinental Flight* (Washington and London: Smithsonian Institution, 1989), 121–122.
2. Lebow, *Cal Rodgers and the Vin Fiz*, 121–122.
3. *Times Herald* (Olean, NY), September 27, 1911.
4. "Rain Holds Rodgers in Salamanca," *Buffalo Courier*, September 28, 1911.
5. "Rodgers Flies 204 Miles in a Day," *Chicago Examiner*, September 29, 1911.
6. *Chicago Examiner*, September 29, 1911; Ralph Stockman Tarr, *The Physical Geography of New York State* (New York: MacMillan, 1902), 7–10.
7. *Chicago Examiner*, September 29, 1911; *Mansfield News*, September 30, 1911.
8. *Chicago Examiner*, September 29, 1911; *Chicago Examiner*, October 1, 1911.
9. *News-Democrat* (Canton, Ohio), September 29, 1911; *Chicago Examiner*, September 29, 1911.
10. *News-Democrat* (Canton, Ohio), September 29, 1911; *Chicago Examiner*, September 29, 1911.
11. *Chicago Examiner*, September 30, 1911.
12. *New York Evening World*, 11, 1911; *New York Times*, July 12, 1911; *Richmond Palladium* (Indiana), October 7, 1911.
13. *Chicago Examiner*, September 30, 1911.
14. *Chicago Examiner*, September 30, 1911.
15. *Mansfield News*, September 30, 1911; *News-Democrat* (Canton, OH), September 30, 1911.
16. *Mansfield News*, September 30, 1911.
17. *Mansfield News*, September 30, 1911.
18. *Decatur Daily Democrat*, October 2, 1911.
19. *Decatur Daily Democrat*, October 2, 1911; *Fort Wayne Journal Gazette* (Indiana), October 1, 1911.
20. *Decatur Daily Democrat*, October 2, 1911.

Chapter 13

1. *Chicago Examiner*, October 1, 1911.
2. *Chicago Examiner*, October 1, 1911.
3. *Chicago Examiner*, October 1, 1911; *Chicago Examiner*, October 2, 1911. Cal's mother has been documented on two previous occasions begging Cal not to fly.
4. *Middleton Daily Press*, October 2, 1911.
5. *Chicago Examiner*, October 1, 1911; *Chicago Examiner*, October 2, 1911; *Middleton Daily Press*, October 2, 1911.
6. *Mansfield News*, October 2, 1911; *Chicago Examiner*, October 2, 1911; *Middleton Daily Press*, October 2, 1911.
7. *Mansfield News*, October 2, 1911; *Chicago Examiner*, October 2, 1911; *Middleton Daily Press*, October 2, 1911.
8. *Mansfield News*, October 2, 1911; *Chicago Examiner*, October 2, 1911; *Middleton Daily Press*, October 2, 1911.
9. *Chicago Examiner*, October 2, 1911; *Mansfield News*, October 2, 1911.
10. *Mansfield News*, October 2, 1911; *Chicago Examiner*, October 2, 1911; *Middleton Daily Press*, October 2, 1911.
11. *Mansfield News*, October 2, 1911; *Chicago Examiner*, October 2, 1911; *Middleton Daily Press*, October 2, 1911.
12. *Chicago Examiner*, October 2, 1911; *Mansfield News*, October 2, 1911.
13. *Chicago Examiner*, October 2, 1911; *Mansfield News*, October 2, 1911.

Chapter 14

1. *Fort Wayne Weekly Sentinel*, October 4, 1911.
2. "The Bayless Dam," *Philadelphia Inquirer*, October 3, 1911.
3. *Chicago Examiner*, October 3, 1911; *Chicago Examiner*, October 5, 1911.
4. *Chicago Examiner*, October 3, 1911; *Chicago Examiner*, October 5, 1911. Mentions of Cal's routine are regular and already cited. The crowd was three thousand, as reported, and would have all been as close to the plane as they could

get. At every stop, the spectators had to be asked to part to allow for takeoff.
   5. *Chicago Examiner,* October 3, 1911.
   6. "Boy Aviator is Killed," *Chicago Examiner,* October 3, 1911.
   7. "Rodgers Wrecks Plane," *Chicago Examiner,* October 3, 1911.
   8. "Rodgers Wrecks Plane."
   9. *Huntington Herald,* October 2, 1911.
   10. *San Francisco Call* 111, no. 126 (4 April 1912).
   11. "Rodgers Explains Wrecking of Flyer," *Chicago Examiner,* October 4, 1911.
   12. "50 Years Ago Pilot Crossed U.S. in 49 Days, 13 Crashes," *Abilene Reporter-News,* August 28, 1961.
   13. "Rodgers Explains Wrecking of Flyer."
   14. "Never Going to Give Up," *Fort Wayne Sentinel,* October 4, 1911.
   15. "Rodgers Flies to Grant Park Today," *Chicago Examiner,* October 5, 1911.
   16. *Lake County Times* (Hammond, IN), October 6, 1911; "Rodgers Flies to Grant Park Today."
   17. *Lake County Times* (Hammond, IN), October 6, 1911.
   18. *Lake County Times* (Hammond, IN), October 6, 1911.
   19. *Lake County Times* (Hammond, IN), October 6, 1911; *Fort Wayne Journal Gazette,* October 6, 1911; Cal Rodgers's *Vin Fiz* Flight Log, Smithsonian National Air and Space Museum Archives.

Chapter 15

   1. *Lake County Times* (Hammond, IN), October 6, 1911.
   2. "Rodgers Now Within 20 Miles," *Chicago Examiner,* October 6, 1911.
   3. *Lake County Times* (Hammond, IN), October 6, 1911.
   4. "Bad Winds Hold Rodgers," *Chicago Examiner,* October 7, 1911.
   5. "Police Bar Flier's Start," *Chicago Examiner,* October 7, 1911.
   6. *Chicago Examiner,* October 7, 1911.
   7. "Rodgers Still at Hammond," *New York Times,* October 7, 1911.
   8. "Rodgers in Chicago," *Chicago Examiner,* October 9, 1911; "Rodgers Still at Hammond."
   9. *Lake County Times* (Hammond, IN), October 9, 1911. According to the newspaper, the police did not interfere the day before as reported by the *Chicago Examiner.*
   10. *Lake County Times* (Hammond, IN), October 9, 1911.
   11. *Lake County Times* (Hammond, IN), October 9, 1911; *Chicago Examiner,* October 9, 1911; *New York Times,* October 9, 1911.
   12. "Rodgers Flying Fast Arrives in Chicago," *New York Times,* October 9, 1911; *Lake County Times* (Hammond, IN), October 9, 1911.
   13. "Rodgers Flying Fast Arrives in Chicago."
   14. "Rodgers Flying Fast Arrives in Chicago;" *Chicago Examiner,* October 9, 1911.
   15. "Rodgers Escorted to Capital," *Chicago Examiner,* October 10, 1911; *New York Times,* October 9, 1911.
   16. Mabel Rodgers-Wiggin, "First Airmail Flight," *AOPA Pilot: Voice of General Aviation* 6, part 2, 38–41.
   17. *Middletown Daily Times,* October 11, 1911.
   18. *Chicago Examiner,* October 11, 1911; *Middletown Daily Times,* October 11, 1911.
   19. *Chicago Examiner,* October 11, 1911; *Middletown Daily Times,* October 11, 1911; *Mexico Missouri Message,* October 12, 1911.
   20. *Chicago Examiner,* October 11, 1911; *Middletown Daily Times,* October 11, 1911.
   21. *Chicago Examiner,* October 11, 1911; *Middletown Daily Times,* October 11, 1911.
   22. *Chicago Examiner,* October 11, 1911.

Chapter 16

   1. "Electrical Show Opened by Edison," *New York Times,* October 12, 1911.
   2. *Joplin New Herald,* October 11, 1911.
   3. *Joplin New Herald,* October 11, 1911.
   4. Mabel Rodgers-Wiggin, "First

Airmail Flight," *AOPA Pilot: Voice of General Aviation* 6, part 2, 38–41.

5. "Rodgers, 1,520 Miles on Trip, Is in Kansas," *Chicago Examiner*, October 12, 1911; *Middletown Daily Times*, October 13, 1911; "Rodgers Halfway in Flight to Coast," *New York Times*, October 12, 1911; *Joplin Daily Globe*, October 12, 1911.

6. *Vin Fiz* Flight Log, Smithsonian National Air and Space Museum Archives; *Joplin Daily Globe*, October 12, 1911.

7. *Chicago Examiner*, October 12, 1911; *Middletown Daily Times*, October 13, 1911; "Rodgers Halfway in Flight to Coast;" *Joplin Daily Globe*, October 12, 1911.

8. *Chicago Examiner*, October 12, 1911; *Middletown Daily Times*, October 13, 1911; "Rodgers Halfway in Flight to Coast."

9. *Chicago Examiner*, October 12, 1911; *Middletown Daily Times*, October 13, 1911; *New York Times*, October 12, 1911; Dale Smith, "Walt Disney's Other Mouse," *Aviation International News*, January 3, 2023, https://www.ainonline.com/aviation-news/business-aviation/2023-01-03/walt-disneys-other-mouse.

10. *Middletown Daily Times*, October 13, 1911.

11. *Chicago Examiner*, October 12, 1911; *Middletown Daily Times*, October 13, 1911; *New York Times*, October 12, 1911; *Joplin Daily Globe*, October 12, 1911. Newspapers reported the crowd as anywhere from five to ten thousand.

12. *Chicago Examiner*, October 12, 1911.

13. *Joplin Daily Globe*, October 12, 1911.

14. Rodgers-Wiggin, "First Airmail Flight," 38–41.

15. *Chicago Examiner*, October 12, 1911; Charles E. Taylor, "The First Transcontinental Flight," *Slipstream*, June 1928, as read by California Congressman Hinshaw during the October 2, 1941, congressional session, House Congressional Record (Washington, DC: United States Congress), 7607–7608.

16. *Joplin News Herald*, October 12, 1911.

Chapter 17

1. *Joplin Daily Globe*, October 12, 2011.

2. *Joplin Daily Globe*, October 12, 2011.

3. *Joplin Daily Globe*, October 12, 2011.

4. *New York Times*, October 15, 1911, by telegraph from Cal Rodgers; *Chicago Examiner*, October 15, 2011.

5. *Chicago Examiner*, October 15, 2011.

6. *New York Times*, October 15, 1911; *Chicago Examiner*, October 15, 2011.

7. *New York Times*, October 15, 1911; *Chicago Examiner*, October 15, 2011; Cal Rodgers's *Vin Fiz* Flight Log, Smithsonian National Air and Space Museum Archives.

8. *New York Times*, October 17, 1911.

9. *Chicago Examiner*, October 16, 1911.

10. *New York Times*, October 17, 1911.

11. *New York Times*, October 17, 1911.

12. *New York Times*, October 17, 1911.

13. *New York Times*, October 17, 1911.

14. *New York Times*, October 17, 1911.

15. *Lincoln Nebraska State Journal*, October 19, 1911.

16. *Brownwood Daily Bulletin*, October 17, 1911; *New York Times*, October 18, 1911; *Abilene Daily Reporter*, October 19, 1911.

17. "Woman Recalls First Airplane Flight," *Kerrville Daily Times*, September 3, 1986.

18. *Abilene Daily Reporter*, October 19, 1911.

19. *New York Times*, October 18, 1911; *Waco Morning News*, October 18, 1911.

20. *Fort Wayne Sentinel*, October 19, 1911; *San Antonio Light*, October 19, 1911; *New York Times*, October 19, 1911.

21. *Fort Worth Record*, October 18, 1911; *Fort Worth Star-Telegram*, October 18 and 19, 1911.

22. *Fort Worth Record*, October 18, 1911; *Fort Worth Star-Telegram*, October 18 and 19, 1911.

23. *Abilene Daily Reporter*, October 18, 1911; *San Antonio Light*, October 19, 1911.

24. *Dallas Morning News*, October 18 and 19, 1911.

25. *Abilene Daily Reporter*, October

18, 1911; *San Antonio Light*, October 19, 1911.
  26. *Waco Morning News*, October 18 and 19, 1911; *Waxahachie Daily Light*, October 19, 1911.
  27. *Waxahachie Daily Light*, October 19, 1911.
  28. *Waco Morning News*, October 20, 1911.
  29. *Waco Morning News*, October 19, 1911; *New York Times*, October 21, 1911.
  30. *Waco Morning News*, October 19, 1911.
  31. *Waco Morning News*, October 19, 1911.
  32. *Waco Morning News*, October 19, 1911.
  33. *Waco Morning News*, October 19, 1911.
  34. *Waco Morning News*, October 19, 1911.

Chapter 18

  1. *New York Times*, October 20, 1911; *Waco Morning News*, October 20, 1911.
  2. Terence Fitzgerald, *Celebrity Culture in the United States* (New York: H.W. Wilson, 2008), 7–9; William A. Dill, *Growth of Newspapers in the United States* (University of Oregon, 1928), 12; J. Charles Sterin and Tameka Winston, *Mass Media Revolution* (London: Taylor and Francis, 2017); Susan J. Douglas and Andrea McDonnell, *Celebrity: A History of Fame*, (New York University Press, 2019), 87–88.
  3. Fitzgerald, *Celebrity Culture*, 7–9; Dill, *Growth of Newspapers* 12; Sterin and Winston, *Mass Media Revolution*.
  4. *Abilene Daily Reporter*, October 20, 1911. It has been speculated that Rodgers found the faulting wires. He did not—it was his mechanic crew—see the *Waco Morning News*, October 21, 1911.
  5. *New York Times*, October 21, 1911, as telegraphed by Cal Rodgers.
  6. "The Day the Aeroplane Came to Austin," *Austin Daily Texan*, January 21, 1976, 19.
  7. "The Day the Aeroplane Came to Austin," 19.
  8. *New York Times*, October 21, 1911, as telegraphed by Cal Rodgers.
  9. *Chicago Examiner*, October 21, 1911; *San Antonio Light*, October 21, 1911. "Rodgers nearly met his death while in the air at 3,500 feet," Cal Rodgers's *Vin Fiz* Flight Log, Oct. 20, 1911, Smithsonian National Air and Space Museum Archives.
  10. E.P. Stein, *Flight of the Vin Fiz* (New York: Arbor House, 1985), 219.
  11. Eileen F. Lebow, *Cal Rodgers and the Vin Fiz: The First Transcontinental Flight* (Washington and London: Smithsonian Institution, 1989), 170–171.
  12. Stein, *Flight of the Vin Fiz*, 219.
  13. *Waco Morning News*, October 21, 1911; Lebow, *Cal Rodgers and the Vin Fiz*, 170–171; Mabel Rodgers-Wiggin, "First Airmail Flight," *AOPA Pilot: Voice of General Aviation* 6, part 2, 38–41.
  14. *Waco Morning News*, October 22, 1911; *Waco Morning News*, October 23, 1911.
  15. Stein, *Flight of the Vin Fiz*, 220.
  16. Stein, 220.
  17. *New York Times*, October 23, 1911, as telegraphed by Cal Rodgers.
  18. *New York Times*, October 23, 1911, as telegraphed by Cal Rodgers.
  19. *New York Times*, October 23, 1911, as telegraphed by Cal Rodgers.
  20. *New York Times*, October 23, 1911, as telegraphed by Cal Rodgers; *San Antonio Light*, October 23, 1911.
  21. Dudley R. Dobie, *A Brief History of Hays County and San Marcos Texas* (San Marcos, TX, 1948), 28–31; *New York Times*, October 23, 1911, as telegraphed by Cal Rodgers; *San Antonio Light*, October 23, 1911.
  22. *New York Times*, October 23, 1911, as telegraphed by Cal Rodgers.
  23. Stein, *Flight of the Vin Fiz*, 225.
  24. *New York Times*, October 23, 1911, as telegraphed by Cal Rodgers.
  25. *San Antonio Light*, October 23, 1911.
  26. *San Antonio Light*, October 23, 1911; *San Antonio Light*, October 24, 1911.
  27. Stein, *Flight of the Vin Fiz*, 221.

Chapter 19

  1. *San Antonio Light*, October 23, 1911; *Waxahachie Daily Light*, October 24, 1911; *Chicago Examiner*, October 25, 1911.

2. *San Antonio Light*, October 23, 1911; *Waxahachie Daily Light*, October 24, 1911; *Chicago Examiner*, October 25, 1911.
3. *San Antonio Light*, October 24, 1911; *New York Times*, October 25, 1911, as told by Cal Rodgers.
4. *New York Times*, October 25, 1911, as told by Cal Rodgers.
5. *New York Times*, October 25, 1911, as told by Cal Rodgers; "Aviator Rodgers Finds New Dangers," *Abilene Daily Reporter*, October 25, 1911.
6. Eileen F. Lebow, *Cal Rodgers and the Vin Fiz: The First Transcontinental Flight* (Washington and London: Smithsonian Institution, 1989), 179.
7. Charles E. Taylor, "The First Transcontinental Flight," *Slipstream*, June 1928, as read by California Congressman Hinshaw during the October 2, 1941, congressional session, House Congressional Record (Washington, DC: United States Congress), 7607–7608; Lebow, *Cal Rodgers and the Vin Fiz*, 179.
8. *San Antonio Light*, October 26, 1911; *Brownwood Daily Bulletin*, October 25, 1911; *Waco Morning News*, October 27, 1911.
9. Lebow, *Cal Rodgers and the Vin Fiz*, 180.
10. *San Antonio Light*, October 26, 1911; *Brownwood Daily Bulletin*, October 25, 1911; *Waco Morning News*, October 27, 1911.
11. *Galveston Daily News*, October 27, 1911.
12. *San Antonio Light*, October 28, 1911; Lebow, *Cal Rodgers and the Vin Fiz*, 183.
13. *Galveston Daily News*, October 27, 1911.
14. *Nevada State Journal*, October 28, 1911; *New York Times*, October 29, 1911. Information on the pass found at https://www.tshaonline.org/handbook/entries/paisano-pass.
15. *Chicago Examiner*, October 29, 1911; *New York Times*, October 29, 1911.
16. *Chicago Examiner*, October 29, 1911; *New York Times*, October 29, 1911.
17. *New York Times*, October 30, 1911.
18. *New York Times*, October 30, 1911.
19. *New York Times*, October 30, 1911.
20. *New York Times*, October 30, 1911; *Waco Morning News*, October 30, 1911.
21. Frederick Jackson Turner, *The Frontier in American History* (New York: Henry Holt, 1953), 30.

Chapter 20

1. Cal Rodgers's *Vin Fiz* Flight Log, October 21, 1911, Smithsonian National Air and Space Museum Archives.
2. *New York Times*, November 1, 1911.
3. *Vin Fiz* Flight Log (Smithsonian), 11; *San Francisco Call*, November 1, 1911; *New York Times*, November 2, 1911, as written by Cal Rodgers.
4. *Arizona Daily Star*, November 2, 1911.
5. *Arizona Daily Star*, November 2, 1911.
6. *Arizona Daily Star*, November 2, 1911.
7. *New York Times*, November 2, 1911.
8. *New York Times*, November 2, 1911.
9. *Vin Fiz* Flight Log (Smithsonian); *Santa Cruz Sentinel*, November 3, 1911; *New York Times*, November 3, 1911.
10. *New York Times*, November 3, 1911; *Los Angeles Times*, November 3, 1911.
11. *New York Times*, November 3, 1911; *Los Angeles Times*, November 3, 1911.

Chapter 21

1. *New York Times*, November 4, 1911, as told by Cal Rodgers; *Arizona Republic*, November 4, 1911.
2. *New York Times*, November 4, 1911, as told by Cal Rodgers.
3. *New York Times*, November 4, 1911, as told by Cal Rodgers.
4. *San Francisco Call*, November 4, 1911; *Anaconda Standard*, November 4, 1911; *New York Times*, November 4, 1911, as told by Cal Rodgers; Charles E. Taylor, "The First Transcontinental Flight," *Slipstream*, June 1928, as read by California Congressman Hinshaw during the October 2, 1941, congressional session, House Congressional Record (Washington, DC: United States Congress), 7607–7608.
5. *San Francisco Call*, November 4, 1911; *Anaconda Standard*, November 4, 1911; *New York Times*, November 4, 1911,

as told by Cal Rodgers; Taylor, "The First Transcontinental Flight," 7607–7608.
  6. *New York Times*, November 4, 1911, correspondent to the *Special*.
  7. *New York Times*, November 4, 1911, correspondent to the *Special*.
  8. *New York Times*, November 5, 1911; Taylor, "The First Transcontinental Flight," 7607–7608.
  9. *New York Times*, November 5, 1911; *Oakland Tribune*, November 5, 1911.
  10. There is some uncertainty about where this remembrance took place. What Mabel describes may have been Mohave Indians, but there are inconsistencies with Mohave characteristics. When she wrote of the event, she clearly described approaching California and the desert. See, Mabel Rodgers-Wiggin, "First Airmail Flight," *AOPA Pilot: Voice of General Aviation* 6, part 2, 38–41.
  11. Rodgers-Wiggin, "First Airmail Flight," 38–41.
  12. Rodgers-Wiggin, 38–41.
  13. *New York Times*, November 5, 1911; *Oakland Tribune*, November 5, 1911.
  14. *New York Times*, November 5, 1911; *Oakland Tribune*, November 5, 1911.
  15. *New York Times*, November 5, 1911; *Oakland Tribune*, November 5, 1911. The train was the Los Angeles Limited, carrying a load of passengers.
  16. *New York Times*, November 5, 1911; *Oakland Tribune*, November 5, 1911.
  17. *New York Times*, November 5, 1911; *Oakland Tribune*, November 5, 1911.
  18. Rodgers-Wiggin, "First Airmail Flight," 38–41.
  19. *New York Times*, November 5, 1911; *Oakland Tribune*, November 5, 1911.
  20. *San Francisco Call*, November 6 and 7, 1911; *Buffalo Courier*, November 6, 1911; *New York Times*, November 6, 1911, as told by Cal Rodgers.
  21. *New York Times*, November 6, 1911; *San Francisco Call*, November 7, 1911; *Buffalo Courier*, November 6, 1911.
  22. *New York Times*, November 6, 1911.
  23. *New York Times*, November 6, 1911, as told by Cal Rodgers.

  24. *New York Times*, November 6, 1911, as told by Cal Rodgers.
  25. *New York Times*, November 6, 1911.
  26. *San Francisco Examiner*, November 6, 1911; *Buffalo Courier*, November 6, 1911; *New York Times*, November 6, 1911; *San Francisco Call*, November 6, 1911.
  27. *Buffalo Courier*, November 6, 1911; *New York Times*, November 6, 1911; *San Francisco Call*, November 6, 1911.
  28. *New York Times*, November 6, 1911.
  29. *Buffalo Courier*, November 6, 1911; *New York Times*, November 6, 1911; *San Francisco Call*, November 6, 1911.
  30. *New York Times*, November 6, 1911; *San Francisco Call*, November 6, 1911.
  31. *New York Times*, November 6, 1911; *San Francisco Call*, November 6, 1911; *San Francisco Examiner*, November 6, 1911.
  32. This is a combination of two quotes from Rodgers, one in the *New York Times*, November 6, 1911, and the other in the *Buffalo Courier*, November 6, 1911.
  33. *New York Times*, November 6, 1911; *Buffalo Courier*, November 6, 1911; *San Francisco Call*, November 6, 1911.
  34. *New York Times*, November 6, 1911; *Buffalo Courier*, November 6, 1911; *San Francisco Call*, November 6, 1911.

Chapter 22

  1. *Los Angeles Record*, November 6, 1911.
  2. *New York World*, November 6, 1911; Eileen F. Lebow, *Cal Rodgers and the Vin Fiz: The First Transcontinental Flight* (Washington and London: Smithsonian Institution, 1989), 213.
  3. *Los Angeles Record*, November 6, 1911; *New York American*, November 6, 1911; Charlie Wiggin, *Aviation*, November 29, 1926; Lebow, *Cal Rodgers and the Vin Fiz*, 212–213; Frank Strother, "Flying Across the Continent," *World's Work*, January 1912, 405.
  4. E.P. Stein, *Flight of the Vin Fiz* (New York: Arbor House, 1985), 307.
  5. Charlie Wiggin, *Aviation*, November 29, 1926; Lebow, *Cal Rodgers and the Vin Fiz*, 212–213.

6. *Long Beach Daily Telegram,* November 7, 1911.

7. *Los Angeles Record,* November 7, 1911; "The City of Pasadena Had Expressed Interest," *Pasadena Star,* November 6, 1911; Lebow, *Cal Rodgers and the Vin Fiz,* 214.

8. *Long Beach Daily Telegram,* November 10, 1911; Lebow, *Cal Rodgers and the Vin Fiz,* 219–220.

9. Lebow, *Cal Rodgers and the Vin Fiz,* 215, 220. Searching newspaperarchive.com and other online sources, not a single newspaper mentioned Rodgers's hearing disability.

10. *Los Angeles Record,* November 8, 1911.

11. *Los Angeles Record,* November 8, 1911.

12. C.L. Edholm, "Oddities in Advertising," *Business: A Magazine for Office, Store and Factory* August 1913, 76; *National Druggist* April 1912, 215.

13. *Daily Telegram* (Long Beach), November 8, 1911; Lebow, *Cal Rodgers and the Vin Fiz,* 219–220; Stein, *Flight of the Vin Fiz,* 309–310.

14. *New York Times,* November 13, 1911; *San Francisco Call,* November 13, 1911; *Washington Herald,* November 13, 1911; *Daily Telegram* (Long Beach), November 11, 1911.

15. *Daily Telegram* (Long Beach), November 8, 1911.

16. *Daily Telegram* (Long Beach), November 8, 1911.

17. *San Francisco Call,* November 13, 1911.

18. *New York Times,* November 13, 1911; *San Francisco Call,* November 13, 1911; *Washington Herald,* November 13, 1911.

19. *New York Times,* November 13, 1911; *San Francisco Call,* November 13, 1911; *Washington Herald,* November 13, 1911; *Oakland Tribune,* November 13, 1911.

20. *Oakland Tribune,* November 13, 1911.

21. *Oakland Tribune,* November 13, 1911; *New York Times,* November 13, 1911; *San Francisco Call,* November 13, 1911; *Washington Herald,* November 13, 1911.

22. *Oakland Tribune,* November 14, 1911.

23. *Oakland Tribune,* November 14, 1911; *New York Times,* November 16, 1911; *Oakland Tribune,* November 13, 1911; *New York Times,* November 13, 1911; *San Francisco Call,* November 13, 1911; *Long Beach Daily Telegram,* November 14, 1911; Mabel Rodgers-Wiggin, "First Airmail Flight," *AOPA Pilot: Voice of General Aviation* 6, part 2, 38–41.

24. *Oakland Tribune,* November 14, 1911; *New York Times,* November 16, 1911; *Oakland Tribune,* November 13, 1911; *New York Times,* November 13, 1911; *San Francisco Call,* November 13, 1911; *Washington Herald,* November 13, 1911; *Daily Telegram* (Long Beach), November 14, 1911.

25. *Santa Ana Daily News,* November 15, 1911; *Daily Telegram* (Long Beach), November 14, 1911.

26. *Santa Ana Daily News,* November 15, 1911; *Daily Telegram* (Long Beach), November 14, 1911.

27. Lebow, *Cal Rodgers and the Vin Fiz,* 224.

28. *Santa Ana Daily News,* November 18, 1911.

29. *Californian,* December 5, 1911; Lebow, *Cal Rodgers and the Vin Fiz,* 226.

30. *Long Beach Press,* December 5, 1911.

31. "Rodgers to Fly in Casts," *New York Times,* November 16, 1911.

32. *Long Beach Press,* December 11, 1911; *Daily Telegram* (Long Beach), December 11, 1911.

Chapter 23

1. *Long Beach Press-Telegram,* December 7, 1911.

2. *Pasadena Star,* December 8, 1911; *Daily Telegram* (Long Beach), November 22, 1911.

3. *Los Angeles Times,* December 10, 1911.

4. *Long Beach Press-Telegram,* December 11, 1911.

5. *Long Beach Press-Telegram,* December 11, 1911; *Oakland Tribune,* December 11, 1911; *Los Angeles Times,* December 11, 1911; *Daily Telegram* (Long Beach), December 11, 1911; *Los Angeles Record,* December 11, 1911.

6. E.P. Stein, *Flight of the Vin Fiz* (New York: Arbor House, 1985), 315.
7. *Long Beach Press-Telegram*, December 11, 1911; *Los Angeles Times*, December 11, 1911; *Daily Telegram* (Long Beach), December 11, 1911; Stein, *Flight of the Vin Fiz*, 315–316.
8. *Long Beach Press-Telegram*, December 11, 1911; *Los Angeles Times*, December 11, 1911; *Daily Telegram* (Long Beach), December 11, 1911; Stein, *Flight of the Vin Fiz*, 315–316.
9. "The First Trans-Continental Aeroplane Flight," *Gas Power*, January 1912, 80; *Long Beach Press-Telegram*, December 11, 1911; *Daily Telegram* (Long Beach), December 11, 1911.
10. *Long Beach Press-Telegram*, December 11, 1911; *Daily Telegram* (Long Beach), December 11, 1911.
11. "U.S. Industry Profiles," *Flying Aviation: Past, Present, and Future*, September 1977, 248; "A Historic Transcontinental Flight," *Popular Aviation*, March 1932, 148.
12. *Long Beach Press-Telegram*, December 11, 1911; *Daily Telegram* (Long Beach), December 11, 1911.
13. *Long Beach Press-Telegram*, December 11, 1911; *Daily Telegram* (Long Beach), December 11, 1911.
14. *Long Beach Press-Telegram*, December 11, 1911; *Daily Telegram* (Long Beach), December 11, 1911.

Chapter 24

1. *Pasadena Daily News*, December 11, 1911; "The First Tran-Continental Aeroplane Flight," *Scientific American*, November 18, 1911, 449.
2. "Aviator Rodgers Heads Parade," *San Francisco Call*, January 2, 1912.
3. *Pasadena Daily News*, December 11, 1911; *Pasadena Daily News*, December 13, 1911; *Pasadena Daily News*, December 26, 1911.
4. *New York Sun*, January 28, 1912; Eileen F. Lebow, *Cal Rodgers and the Vin Fiz: The First Transcontinental Flight* (Washington and London: Smithsonian Institution, 1989), 239–240.
5. E.P. Stein, *Flight of the Vin Fiz* (New York: Arbor House, 1985), 298.
6. *New York Times*, April 4, 1912.

Figures vary, but the *New York Times* reported that as many as four thousand people showed up daily to watch Rodgers.
7. *San Francisco Call*, April 4, 1912; *Oakland Tribune*, April 4, 1912; *Long Beach Press*, March 8, 1912; *Long Beach Daily Telegram*, April 4, 1912.
8. *San Francisco Call*, April 4, 1912; *Oakland Tribune*, April 4, 1912.
9. *San Francisco Call*, April 4, 1912; *New York Times*, April 4, 1912.
10. Lebow, *Cal Rodgers and the Vin Fiz*, 252.
11. *New York Times*, April 4, 1912.
12. *Armco Advertising News*, June 1912; Ed Brotak, "When Birds Strike," HistoryNet.com, March 23, 2018, https://www.historynet.com/when-birds-strike/.
13. Stein, *Flight of the Vin Fiz*, 324–325.
14. "Miss Quimby Wins Air Pilot License," *New York Times*, August 2, 1911; "Miss Quimby's Flight," *New York Times*, September 28, 1911; "When Aviation Becomes not only Dangerous but Foolhardy," *New York Times*, July 7, 1911.
15. "Miss Quimby Wins Air Pilot License;" "Miss Quimby's Flight."
16. "Harriet Quimby," *Chicago Examiner*, July 2, 1912; "When Aviation Becomes not only Dangerous but Foolhardy."
17. Stein, *Flight of the Vin Fiz*, 325–326.
18. Not on the tombstone, from Icarus in the poem *Failing and Flying* by Jack Gilbert.

Afterword

1. "The First Aviation Mechanic," *Famous Flyers*, FAA News, January/February 12–13; Charles E. Taylor, "The First Transcontinental Flight," *Slipstream*, June 1928, as read by California Congressman Hinshaw during the October 2, 1941, congressional session, House Congressional Record (Washington, DC: United States Congress), 7607–7608.
2. R.E. Bilstein, *Flight in America from 1900–1983: From the Wrights to the Astronauts* (Baltimore: Johns Hopkins University Press, 1984), 28–29.
3. Taylor, "The First Transcontinental Flight," 7607–7608.

4. "The First Aviation Mechanic," 12–13.

5. "The First Aviation Mechanic," 12–13; Maria Papageorgiou, "Charles E. Taylor: The Unsung Hero of Kitty Hawk Gets His Day," *Federal Aviation Administration*, May 24, 2020, https://medium.com/faa/charles-e-taylor-the-unsung-hero-of-kitty-hawk-finally-gets-his-day-f55b124b41df.

6. Gerrie Schipske, *Early Aviation in Long Beach* (Chicago, IL: Arcadia, 2009), 41; Claudine Burnett, *Soaring Skyward: A History of Aviation in and Around Long Beach, California* (Bloomington, IN: Author House, 2011), 66–68.

7. Robert van der Linden, *Milestones of Flight: The Epic of Aviation with the National Air and Space Museum* (McGregor, MN: Voyageur Press, May 15, 2016), 21; Burnett, *Soaring Skyward*, 68; Charles D. Wiggin Obituary, *Middletown Daily News*, November 10, 1964. Most of the *Vin Fiz* in the museum is a complete rebuild, which took place during the journey with some refurbishing later. The Smithsonian (National Air and Space Museum) might have always been interested in acquiring the biplane, but for whatever reason waited until 1934.

8. "Cross Country," *Southland Sunday, Independent Press Telegram* (Long Beach, CA), June 24, 1973, 24.

9. Eileen F. Lebow, *Cal Rodgers and the Vin Fiz: The First Transcontinental Flight* (Washington and London: Smithsonian Institution, 1989), 253.

Bibliography

Documents and Manuscripts

Harold E. Morehouse Flying Pioneers Biographies collection, Smithsonian Institute
House Congressional Record, United States Congress, Washington, D.C.
International Aviation Meet Grant Park Chicago August 12–20, 1911, Postcard McCormick Collection
National Air and Space Museum
Rodgers Family Papers
San Diego Air and Space Museum
US Naval Academy Museum, Special Collections, Annapolis, Maryland
Wright Papers, Manuscript Division, Library of Congress

Newspapers

Abilene Reporter-News
Alton Evening Telegraph
Arizona Daily Star
Atlanta Georgian and News
Austin Daily Texan
Bradford Era (Pennsylvania)
Branding Iron: Los Angeles Corral
Brownwood Daily Bulletin
Buffalo Courier
Californian
Canton News Democrat
Chicago Examiner
Chicago Record-Herald
Chicago Tribune
Daily Jeffersonian
Daily Telegram (Long Beach)
Dallas Morning News
Decatur Daily Democrat
Del Rio News-Herald
Fort Wayne Journal Gazette (Indiana)
Fort Wayne Weekly Sentinel
Fort Worth Record
Fort Worth Star-Telegram
Fresno Morning Republican
Galveston Daily News
Grand Forks Evening Times
Hammond Times
Huntington Herald
Independent Press Telegram
Inter-Ocean (Chicago)
Joplin Daily Globe
Joplin News Herald
Kerrville Daily Times
Lake County Times (Hammond, Indiana)
Lincoln Nebraska State Journal
Long Beach Daily Telegram
Long Beach Press-Telegram
Los Angeles Record
Los Angeles Times
Mansfield News
Mathews Journal (Virginia)
Mexico Missouri Message
Middleton Daily Times Press
Middletown Times Herald Record
Moline Daily Dispatch
Nevada State Journal
New York American
New York Times
Norwich Bulletin
Oakland Tribune
Olean Evening News
Pasadena Daily News

Philadelphia Inquirer
Richmond Palladium and Sun-Telegram
San Antonio Light
San Francisco Call
Santa Ana Daily News
Southland Sunday
Stevens Point Daily Journal
Syracuse Herald
Times (Philadelphia, Pennsylvania)
Times-Democrat (New Orleans)
Waco Morning News
Warren Evening Mirror (Pennsylvania)
Washington Herald
Waxahachie Daily Light
Wellsville Daily Reporter

Journals and Magazines

Aero: America's Aviation Weekly
Aeronautics
American Aviation Heritage
American Philatelist
Anaconda Standard
Approach Magazine
Automobile Topics
Bloomberg
Business: A Magazine for Office, Store and Factory
Chicago Daily News Almanac and Yearbook for 1911
FAA Aviation News
Famous Flyers
Flying: A Century of Flight
Flying Association at the Office of the Aero Club of America
Flying Aviation: Past, Present, and Future
Fox City Magazine
Gas Power
Minnesota Historical Society Magazine
Popular Mechanics
Saturday Evening Post
Scientific American
Slipstream
Smithsonian Institution
Southwest Historical Quarterly
United States Army and Navy Journal and Gazette of the Regular and Volunteer Forces
World
World's Work

Books, Articles and Pamphlets

Aero Club of America. *Aero Club of America Rule Book*. New York: Contest Committee, Aero Club of America, 1922.

Bilstein, R.E. *Flight in America: 1900–1983: From the Wrights to the Astronauts*. Baltimore: Johns Hopkins University Press, 1984.

Blossom, Sumner M. "The World's Greatest Adventure, A Triumph of the Airplane." *Popular Science*, October 1927.

Burnett, Claudine. *Soaring Skyward: A History of Aviation in and Around Long Beach, California*. Bloomington, IN: Author House, 2011.

Dobie, Dudley R. *A Brief History of Hays County and San Marcos Texas*. San Marcos, TX, 1948.

Drew, Andrew. "Learning to Fly a Wright Biplane." *Aero: America's Aviation Weekly*, August 5, 1911.

Edholm, C.L. "Oddities in Advertising." *Business: A Magazine for Office, Store and Factory*. August 1913.

Fitzgerald, Terence. *Celebrity Culture in the United States*. New York: H.W. Wilson, 2008.

Goodman, Rita. "Widow of Air Pioneer Lives Destitute." *The Guide*, Coral Gables, FL, April 18, 1968.

Harris, Sherwood. "Coast to Coast in 12 Crashes." *American Heritage* 15, no. 6, (October 1964). https://www.americanheritage.com/coast-coast-12-crashes.

Hathaway, Milicent L. "Trends in Heights and Weights." *Yearbook of Agriculture*. Washington, DC: US Department of Agriculture, 1959.

Hunter, Louis C. *A History of Industrial Power in the United States 1780–1930*. Vol. 2, *Steam Power*. Charlottesville: University Press of Virginia, 1985.

Jackson Turner, Frederick. *The Frontier*

in American History. New York: Henry Holt, 1953.

Kaempffert, Waldemar. *The New Art of Flying*. New York: Dodd, Mead, 1911.

Lebow, Eileen F. *Cal Rodgers and the Vin Fiz: The First Transcontinental Flight*. Washington and London: Smithsonian Institution, 1989.

Leech, Harper, and John Charles Carroll. *Armour and His Times*. New York: D. Appleton-Century, 1938.

Lisi, Clemente. "How Billy Sunday Traded His Bat for a Bible and Came to Love New York." *Religion Unplugged*. April 22, 2020. https://religionunplugged.com/news/2020/4/21/baseball-how-billy-sunday-traded-his-bat-for-a-bible-and-came-to-love-new-york.

Miller, Nathan. *New World Coming: The 1920s and the Making of Modern America*. New York: Scribner, 2010.

Miller, William M. *Eugene Ely, Daredevil Aviator*. Jefferson, NC: McFarland, 2014.

Morris, Charles R. *The Tycoons: How Andrew Carnegie, John D. Rockefeller, Jay Gould, and J.P. Morgan Invented the American Supereconomy*. New York: Holt Paperback, 2005.

Mortimer, Gavin. *Chasing Icarus: The Seventeen Days that Forever Changed American Aviation*. New York: Walker, 2009.

Pauley, Kenneth, and the Dominguez Rancho Adobe Museum. *Images of the 1910 Los Angeles International Air Meet*. Chicago: Arcadia, 2009.

Post, Augustus. "The Present and Future of Man Flight." *Munsey's Magazine*. June 1912.

Renstrom, Arthur George. *Wilbur & Orville Wright: A Chronology Commemorating the Hundredth Anniversary of the Birth of Orville Wright, August 19, 1871*. Washington, DC: NASA. https://ntrs.nasa.gov/api/citations/20040000754/downloads/20040000754.pdf.

Rodgers-Wiggin, Mabel. "First Airmail Flight." *AOPA Pilot: Voice of General Aviation*, vol. 6, part 2.

Rohrbach, Peter. "The First Aircraft Mechanic." *FAA Aviation News*. January/February 1989.

Schipske, Gerrie. *Early Aviation in Long Beach*. Chicago, IL: Arcadia, 2009.

Schultz, Harvey A. "Don't Fowl Out." *Approach Magazine*. April 1984.

Small, Andrew. "When Cities Went Electric." *Bloomberg*. March 15, 2017. https://www.bloomberg.com/news/articles/2017-03-15/the-war-of-currents-was-waged-in-cities.

Smith, Dale. "Walt Disney's Other Mouse." *Aviation International News*. January 3, 2023. https://www.ainonline.com/aviation-news/business-aviation/2023-01-03/walt-disneys-other-mouse.

Stein, E.P. *Flight of the Vin Fiz*. New York: Arbor House, 1985.

Stoff, Joshua. *Picture History of Early Aviation, 1903–1913*. New York: Dover, 1996.

Strother, Frank. "Flying Across the Country." *World's Work*. January 1912.

Tarr, Ralph Stockman. *The Physical Geography of New York State*. New York: Macmillan, 1902.

Van Der Linden, Robert. *Milestones of Flight: The Epic of Aviation with the National Air and Space Museum*. McGregor, MN: Voyageur, May 15, 2016.

Wentz, Charlie. "Who Was Calbraith P. Rodgers." *American Philatelist*, November 2011.

Whyte, Kenneth. *The Uncrowned King: The Sensational Rise of William Randolph Hearst*. New York: Counterpoint, 2009.

Wiggin, Charles. "First Across the Continent." *Air and Space/Smithsonian Magazine*, September 2011.

Wiggin, Charles S. *First Transcontinental Flight*. New York: Bookmailer, 1961.

Wittreich, Paul. *Forgotten First Flights*. Bloomington, IN: Xlibris, 2009.

The Wright Flying School. New York: Wright Flying Field, 1916.

Index

academy 9–11, 77
accident 41, 64, 76, 90, 98, 99, 109, 136, 140, 144, 146
admiral 11, 61, 184
Adrian 89
advertising 54, 59, 60, 62, 69, 113, 114, 117, 172
aeronautics 17, 44, 180
aeroplane 14, 50, 57, 67, 93, 117, 151, 171, 176, 187
airborne 39, 44, 52, 86, 88, 94, 101, 105, 111, 113, 163
aircraft 1, 3, 14, 17, 18, 22, 30–32, 39, 40, 49, 54, 57–59, 65, 70–72, 75, 80, 88, 90, 91, 99, 103, 106, 135, 138, 158, 176, 180, 186, 189, 191–93
airplane 1, 5, 7, 11, 17, 23, 24, 27, 30, 33, 37, 39, 41, 42, 45, 46, 49–53, 56, 57, 61, 70, 75, 76, 78, 79, 81, 94, 101, 103, 105–7, 112, 117, 118, 122, 138, 139, 141, 145, 161, 162, 169, 181, 185, 189, 191–93
airplane hangar 5, 6, 13, 27, 28, 38, 64, 69, 112, 117, 140, 183, 185, 186
airshow 14, 164
Akron, Ohio 99, 101, 102
Alabama 5
Alamo, Texas 142
Alarm 93
Alfred 5, 9, 91
Allegheny Mountains 99, 190
Almer-Singer 64
Alton, Illinois 117
Arlington, Texas 131
Armour Company 11, 50, 54, 59, 61, 71, 74, 80, 92, 97, 117, 122, 171, 172, 176, 177, 179
Army 6–8, 25, 184
Austin, Texas 108, 138
aviation 1, 2, 5, 6, 11, 14–19, 21–25, 27, 30–33, 35, 37–39, 40–41, 43–45, 48–56, 58, 59, 63, 65, 66, 72, 74, 77, 81, 83, 90–92, 97, 98, 109, 111, 115, 117–19, 124, 125, 127, 131–33, 139, 146, 147, 150, 156, 158, 159, 164, 166, 168, 169, 171, 174, 176, 182–87, 189–94; deaths 21–23, 41, 44, 45, 65

Badger, William C. 21, 41, 42, 44, 45
balancing machine 27
Baldwin train engine 69
baseball 9, 94, 136
Beachy, Lincoln 42
Beaufort, Count De 109–11
Bennington 13
Bermuda 12
Bessemer Process 47
"Betsy" see *Vin Fiz*
billboard 62, 71, 114
Binghamton 86
Biograph Studios 189
biplane 2, 13, 15, 16, 19, 20, 22, 24, 25, 27–33, 36, 37, 40, 41, 51, 52, 54, 56–58, 60–66, 69, 70, 74, 82, 85, 87, 89–91, 93, 94, 96, 98, 101–3, 107, 109–11, 118, 119, 124, 126, 127, 130, 139, 140, 142, 145, 146, 153, 154, 157–61, 163, 164, 172–74, 176, 177, 179–82, 185, 186, 189, 193
Birdman 78, 89, 93–95, 111, 116–19, 121, 125, 139, 145, 156, 159, 162, 163, 170, 179, 183, 190
Blériot, Moisant 14
Blériot Monoplane 180
Blériot School 14
Blue Springs, Missouri 122, 123
Bordentown Military Institute 10
boxing 136
bridges 93, 101
British 9

218 INDEX

Brookings, Walter 15
Buffalo, N.Y. 10, 11, 65
Buffington 128
Buick (automobile) 90
buildings 16, 35, 93, 122, 163, 179, 180
business 11, 46, 49, 67, 70, 124, 133, 134, 136, 148, 162, 166, 170, 185
Bustleton, Pennsylvania 9

California 2, 11, 53, 59, 63–65, 68, 70, 73, 74, 103, 126, 136, 146, 148, 152, 155, 162, 163, 166, 169, 172, 173, 175, 177, 180, 181, 183, 191–93
Canisteo, Texas 89–91, 93
captain 184
car 58, 61, 63–66, 69, 74, 79, 90, 95, 98, 112, 117, 126, 140, 145, 152–54, 159, 162, 166, 182
Carnegie, Andrew 47, 136, 148, 194
carnival 57, 166
Chambers, Martha 7, 110
Cherokee Indians 128
Chicago, Illinois 1, 11, 14, 21, 33, 35, 37–39, 43, 45, 49–57, 59, 60, 64, 67, 72, 73, 76, 83, 87, 90, 92, 94, 97, 98, 100–105, 108, 109, 111–17, 121, 135, 138, 171, 182, 189, 193
Chicago Aero Club 115
Chicago Air Show 135
Chicago Athletic Club 38
Chicago Aviation Meet 23, 44
Chicago Examiner 35, 36, 43, 51, 90, 100, 104, 109, 111, 121
Chicago Tribune 36, 38, 40, 42
China 189
chrysanthemums 166
Cicero, Illinois 50, 193
Citizen Kane 47
Cleveland 185
Colorado 15, 126
Compton, California 173–75, 178–80, 187
Covina Junction, California 173
cowboys 124
crashes (airplanes) 14–16, 22, 25, 42, 43, 76, 90, 91, 109, 135, 157, 174, 175, 178, 180, 186, 189

Dallas 131, 132
Davies, Marion 47
Davis, Mrs. R.D. 165, 166
Decatur, Indiana 103, 105
DeKrafft, Stewart I. 59–62, 77, 80, 97, 113, 114, 122, 139, 140, 162, 170–72, 182
Denison, Texas 129, 130
Dickenson, Charles H. 59, 60

Disney, Walt 123
Dixon, Cromwell 109
Dominguez Field, CA 48, 164, 182, 183, 185, 186, 188
Dorchester Bay 189

Earhart, Amelia 191
electricity 7, 46, 47, 106, 121, 174
English Channel 14, 48, 189
Europe 48, 52, 58

Farmer 6, 85, 107, 108, 115, 145
Federal Aviation Administration 81
fighter (boxer) 6, 10
football 9, 10, 56, 65, 136, 183
Fort Hancock, Texas 150
Fort Wayne, Indiana 111
Fort Sam Houston 142
Fort Worth, Texas 127, 129, 130
Fowler, Robert G. 51, 53, 62–66, 77, 143, 153, 169
Frisbie, J.J. 51, 52

Gainesville, Texas 130
Galveston Daily News 148
gasoline 68, 76, 77, 103, 118, 127, 129, 150, 177
Gorman, Patrick 108
government (United States) 67, 148
Governors Island, New York 65
Grahame-White Biplane 41
Granger, Texas 138
Grosse, Miss Irene 165, 166
Grundy, Fred C. 53
Gurley Park, Texas 132, 133, 137

Harlandale, Texas 142
Harley-Davidson 11
Higginsville 122
Hills, Cameron 89
Hinshaw, John Carl Williams 191
Holcombe, E.T. 174
Hoodoo, "of Flying" 18, 66, 87, 106, 110, 136, 160, 189
Houston, Texas 142
Howard, Fred 61, 64, 76, 97
Hoxsey, Archibald 14, 15, 33, 34, 164
Hudson River 72
hydroaeroplane 42

Icarus 190
Illinois 35, 37, 50, 64, 81, 118, 193
Indiana 68, 101, 103, 107, 108, 110–12
Indians 6, 94, 95, 99, 128, 158, 159
industrialization 7, 10, 35, 46, 47, 49
Iron Aviator (Cal Rodgers) 2, 117, 131,

Index

139, 146, 147, 156, 169, 186, 187, 189, 191, 194
Iron Compass 16, 53, 90, 118, 142

Jackson, Stonewall 80
Jackson Turner, Frederick 128
Jacksonville, Florida 194
Japan 6, 11, 129
Jefferson, Thomas 182
John, Perry 7–11, 24, 25, 33, 37, 58
Johnstone, Ralph 15, 16, 21, 41–45

Kansas 52, 112, 119–24, 126, 127
kiwi bird 27

laissez-faire 148
Lake Erie 6
Lake Michigan 35, 39, 41, 42, 44, 112, 116
Library of Congress 25, 26, 58, 60, 62, 68, 71, 100, 147, 164, 165
Lindbergh, Charles 134, 191, 194
Long Beach, California 170, 172–74, 176–81, 183, 185–87, 193, 194
Long Island, New York 70
Lordsburg, New Mexico 152

Macon, Georgia 135
Madison Square Garden 10
Magneto 88, 91, 94, 95, 106, 119, 121, 122, 125, 145, 152, 160, 161, 163
Manhattan 46, 72
marathon 149
Maryland 166, 171, 173, 183, 186
Maryland Hotel 171, 173, 183, 186
McAlester 129
McBriar, Dr. Henry 76
McCoach, Police Chief John 72
McCormick, Harold 33, 35, 37, 38
McCormick-Romme Company 37
McCurdy, J.A.D. 33, 34, 41
McKinley, Pres. William 10
Meadville, PA 98, 99
Mechanics 6, 8, 30, 53, 59, 63, 70, 72, 79, 81, 82, 91, 127, 145, 169, 171, 175, 192
Mercersburg Academy 9
Merritt, E.B. 59, 117
Methodism 141
Mexico, Missouri 119, 149, 152, 185
Miami, FL 194
Michigan 35, 37, 39, 41, 42, 44, 112, 116
Michigan Boulevard 35, 37, 39
Middleton 65
Middletown 72, 74, 75, 79–83, 85
Miller, Frank H. 21, 22, 90, 91
Millionaires 47

Mills, T.D. 76
Milwaukee 49
Mississippi 71, 118, 119
Missouri 117–19, 122–24, 126
Mohave Indians 158, 159
Moisant, John B. 14
monoplane 180, 189
monopoly 148
Montgomery, Alabama 5
Morgan, J.P. 148
mountains 53, 54, 64, 66, 72, 85, 99, 103, 126, 148–50, 156, 160, 161, 182
movies 135, 136, 189
Moyar, Long Beach Police Chief 172
Murphy, Warden 118
Muskogee, Oklahoma 129

Nassau 12
naval 10, 11, 24, 58, 70, 77
newspaper 7, 9, 22, 38, 41, 47, 48, 50–52, 69, 80, 93, 101, 103, 110, 113, 119, 124, 132, 133, 136, 138, 153, 169, 171, 173, 176, 179, 180
New York 10–12, 19, 21, 32, 37, 43, 45–49, 51, 53, 55, 56, 60, 63–68, 71, 73, 75, 77, 83, 93, 94, 99, 101, 115, 117, 119, 121, 133, 136, 138, 151, 153, 157, 158, 162, 164, 166, 168–71, 175, 178, 184, 187
New York Times 19, 21, 43, 83, 115, 117, 138, 151, 157, 158, 162, 164, 166, 168, 175, 187
New Yorkers 46
Niño 101
Norman, William 115
Norton, Kansas 52

observatory 153, 162
Oklahoma 126–28

Palmer-Singer Automobile 60, 62, 69, 74, 76, 77, 79, 80, 90, 95, 98, 99, 108, 136, 139, 160, 162, 166, 168, 170, 173, 174, 180
Paris, France 48
Parmelee, Philip 18
Partitillo, Zito 41
Pasadena, California 146, 156, 158–64, 166, 169, 173, 174, 176, 179, 183, 184, 190
Paterson, New Jersey 65
Payne, John Barton 37
Pennsylvania 6, 85, 86, 99, 108, 190
Peoria, Illinois 117, 118
Peoria State Prison 118
Perry, Oliver Hazard "Commodore" 1, 5, 6, 11, 45, 126

220 INDEX

Peters, Lawrence 61, 62, 97, 170, 172, 176–78, 182
Philadelphia 9
Philip Danforth Armour 49, 108
Pioneers of Aviation 14, 17, 178, 182, 187
Pittsburgh 6, 7, 41, 136, 190
Port Jervis, New York 83
Pottsboro, Texas 129, 130
Presbyterianism 141
Progressive Era 7, 11, 148
Pulitzer, Joseph 47, 48

Robber Barons 47, 136, 148
Rockefeller, John D. 35, 136, 148
Rocky Mountains 53, 54, 126
Rodgers, Calbraith Perry 1–3, 5–7, 9–13, 17, 18, 21–25, 27, 28, 30–33, 44–46, 49, 51, 52, 54, 56–62, 64, 66–74, 76, 77, 79–81, 83, 85–91, 93–95, 97–106, 108–87, 189–94
Rodgers, Capt. Calbraith Perry (Cal's father) 6, 7
Rodgers, John 7, 10, 24, 25, 33, 70, 79, 80, 90, 139, 146, 161, 162, 172, 190, 193
Rodgers, Mabel 12, 13, 33, 45, 50, 61, 64, 67–70, 73, 74, 76, 77, 80, 87, 88, 90, 91, 95, 97, 98, 108, 109, 111, 114, 118, 122, 125, 126, 134, 136, 139, 144, 147, 149, 152, 155, 157–62, 166, 168–71, 173–75, 179, 180, 182–86, 189, 190, 193, 194
Rodgers, Maria 7, 9, 10, 12, 56, 57, 70, 74, 76, 80, 95, 97, 103, 136, 139, 155, 157, 161, 166, 168, 173, 174, 179, 182, 185, 186, 193, 194

Sabina, Texas 145
sagebrush 150, 158
Salamanca, New York 94–99
Salton Sea, California 2, 156, 157, 160
San Antonio, Texas 126, 137, 138, 142, 144, 145
San Diego, California 2, 12, 63, 73, 75, 77, 89, 116, 123, 125, 137, 169, 175, 181, 186–88, 190
San Francisco, California 11, 49, 51, 62, 63, 125, 136, 176
San Gorgonio Mountain, California 159, 161
San Jacinto, California 159, 161
San Marcos, Texas 138, 141
Santa Fe, Texas 130
Santa Fe Railroad 130
Schwab, Charles M. 148
science 15, 17, 19, 21, 43, 44, 48, 50, 52, 55, 109, 171, 183, 184, 191
scientific suicide 14, 15, 18, 91, 101

screenwriter 189
Sears Roebuck and Company 47
Seneca Indians 94, 95, 99
Shaffer, Frank 57, 61, 70, 74, 77, 79, 85, 87, 88, 95, 96, 99, 101, 103, 109, 111, 112, 115, 116, 118, 119, 121, 125, 127, 129, 134, 136, 139, 140, 142, 145–50, 152, 154, 158, 160–64, 168, 172, 173, 176, 177, 179, 180, 183, 185–87, 189, 193
Sheepshead, New York 70, 71, 128
Sheepshead Bay Racetrack 70, 71
Sherry's Restaurant 184
Sherwood Hotel 91
Sierra Blanca, Texas 148, 149
Sierra Mountains 66
Sierra Nevada Mountains 63
skyscrapers 46, 133
Smithsonian Institution 193
Space Museum (San Diego) 2, 12, 63, 73, 75, 77, 89, 116, 123, 125, 137, 175, 181, 186–88
Spanish-American War 47
The Special (train) 23, 37, 54, 58, 60, 61, 63–65, 69, 72, 85, 87, 88, 90, 94, 95, 99, 101–4, 106–8, 113, 114, 118, 119, 124, 127, 129, 131, 132, 134, 137, 139, 141, 142, 145, 149, 150, 152–54, 157, 158, 160, 161, 163, 164, 169, 171, 176, 184
Spokane, Washington 109
Springfield, Illinois 115, 118
squaw (Indian) 159
Star-Telegram 130
steamships 16
streets 72, 101–3, 114, 116, 117, 121, 124, 131–33, 154, 163, 180, 182
suburbs 7
Sunday, Billy 94, 170
Sweitzer, Maria 10, 56, 70, 80; *see also* Rodgers, Maria

Taft, Pres. William H. 184
Tampa, Florida 193
Taylor, Charles E. 27, 28, 31, 56, 58–61, 64, 70, 72, 74, 75, 77, 79, 81, 82, 85, 88, 90–92, 95, 96, 99, 101, 103, 109–12, 115, 118, 119, 121, 122, 125, 127, 129, 134, 136, 139, 140, 142, 144–48, 157, 169, 171, 172, 176, 177, 179, 180, 191, 192
technology 16
telegram 66, 112, 147, 157, 184
telegraph 37, 41, 75, 88, 102, 154
Tennyson, Alfred 5, 9
Texas 53, 103, 126, 127, 130, 141, 142, 144, 146, 147, 149, 150
Tournament Park 146, 161–64, 170

Transatlantic 184, 185
Transcontinental 1, 2, 7, 11, 22, 33, 45, 46, 48, 50–55, 57, 59, 67, 76, 83, 93, 97, 100, 115, 123, 129, 140, 167, 176, 185, 191, 193, 194
Triangle Shirtwaist Factory 65
trolley 107, 174
Troy, Ohio 21, 90
trust-busting 11, 148
Turpin, Clifford 25, 27, 32, 118
typhoid fever 192

United States 1, 6, 7, 14, 18, 23, 33, 35, 44, 46–48, 50, 51, 55, 56, 67, 72, 73, 94, 113, 121, 122, 125, 128, 133, 135, 146, 156, 161, 165, 170, 184, 166, 189, 190, 192, 193
University of Arizona 153
Uvalde, Texas 145

Vin Fiz, "Betsy" 68, 70, 72, 76, 80, 83, 94, 99, 104, 106, 108, 109, 127, 136, 139, 140, 145, 162, 168, 173, 179, 181

Ward, Jimmy 36, 39, 51, 53, 54, 59, 65, 66, 77, 81, 87, 89, 111, 117, 124, 139, 159, 168, 190, 192
Warren, Pennsylvania 99, 100
wreckage (airplane) 40, 66, 75, 76, 95, 96, 146, 174, 176, 186–88
Wright, Orville 2, 11, 26, 27
Wright, Wilbur 11, 16, 24, 26, 28, 192
Wright Brothers 1, 5, 6, 18, 22, 24, 25, 50, 51, 58, 61, 76, 80, 91
Wright Company 24, 51, 171, 194
Wright Model Biplane 20, 21, 29, 31, 33, 158, 183, 185, 187, 188, 193
Wrightman, Maria 7

yacht 10–12
Yakima, Washington 18
Yuma, Arizona 154, 156

Zito 41

www.ingramcontent.com/pod-product-compliance
Lightning Source LLC
Chambersburg PA
CBHW032041300426
44117CB00009B/1144